Hands On Heritage

BY NANCY LEE AND LINDA OLDHAM

EDITED BY DR. MARY BERRY BRENNAN

HANDS ON PUBLICATIONS

Hands on Heritage offers over two hundred ways for a child to learn about neighboring cultures by actually experiencing the activities of that culture. Physically participating in a learning activity is a "hands on" experience. The term, "hands on" is a recently coined educational term which suggests learning, by doing and experiencing, on a first hand basis.

Throughout this text the authors have used the pronoun "he" in the sense of mankind to represent either a man or a woman. This has been for ease of expression and has been done with no desire to show preference to one group or another. Someday there may be a non-sexist combination word that will denote both. Perhaps "hesh" will become an acceptable term.

ISBN: 0-931178-01-0
Library of Congress Catalog Card Number: 78-52312

Illustrations by Carol Angelo
Chinese translation and calligraphy by Grace and Tommy Wang
Spanish translation by John Palumbo
Typeset by Century Composing
Printed by Delta Lithograph

FOREWORD

Multicultural education is multi-faceted. *Hands on Heritage* deals with some of these important phases in an effort to illuminate similarities and differences and to promote the development of positive cultural attitudes.

The cultures included in this text were chosen primarily because they somewhat reflect the ethnic composition of the area where our original multicultural program was established.

Folklore and folkways often vary from village to village within the same general area. We apologize if some of the material included in this book differs from the way that you were taught the game or heard the particular story.

Many of the following activities have been suggested by people who have lived in each of these countries. We have assumed the authenticity of their suggestions because we were able to find reference to such an item or activity in the available literature. We have discovered that since so many folk traditions have been passed by word of mouth, their details often vary from individual to individual. We hope that each of you will enjoy using these materials and ideas that we have gathered. We believe that the children who join in these experiences will gain, as we have, a greater feeling of warmth toward each of these peoples.

The Authors.

PREFACE
TOGETHER WE WILL

Together we will be born at the same hospital, at the same time, in the same room, only with different mothers and different colors.

Together we will live on the same block, play together and together watch our parents dispute over great arguments of racial factors.

Together we will be separated by our parents from being playmates. Could it be because of our parents' silly racial attitudes?

Together we will join Kindergarten, learn our ABC's, drink our milk, eat our cookies, and take a nap. Yet, when we go home we are no longer playmates, we are now prejudiced enemies. Is it because of our parents' silly racial arguments?

Together we will sit next to each other in 1st grade, learn our addition, tease the teacher, play on the monkey bars at recess, and eat lunch.

Together we will be called from the same roll book in 2nd grade, learn dances from our teacher, learn to read together, and together play educational games.

Together we will join the bilingual program in the 3rd grade and learn all kinds of different ethnic backgrounds. We will learn more about our American History and meet different teachers from other bilingual programs, so that they can see how we work together. Yet when we go home we are no longer playmates, because we are now prejudiced enemies. Is it because my parents told me not to play with you?

Together we will enter 4th grade and learn multiplication. We will be on the same team playing kickball, and together pull on the girls' ponytails in class.

Together we will be happy that we are in the same class in the 5th grade, learn how to do division problems. We will learn our nouns and verbs, and we will try to bring the same thing for lunch each day. Yet when we go home we are no longer playmates, we are now prejudiced enemies, could it be because your parents don't want me to visit you?

Together we will enter junior high and be in the 7th grade. We will both be elected to student government. We will have science class together and both make the relay team in track.

Together we will both be starting pitchers on the 8th grade baseball team, have P.E. together and be the most understanding and best actors in drama. Yet when we go home we are no longer playmates, we are now prejudiced enemies. Is it because of what our parents say?

Together we will get our butch haircut for the 9th grade football team. You the first string quarterback, me the first string running back. We will both be co-editors in the journalism class and both be in the same biology class. Yet when we go home we are no longer playmates, we are now prejudiced enemies, sometimes we wonder is it all because of our parents' silly racial attitudes.

Together we will enter high school and be in the tenth grade. We will both learn to use our money in dollars and sense class, both get the same class for drivers education, and learn about each other's culture.

Together we will be juniors in high school, both of us will get our drivers license, and you being editor and me being assistant editor on the yearbook, we both will have more privileges. Yet when we go home we are no longer playmates, could it be because of our parents' silly racial arguments?

Together we will finally be seniors in high school. We will both get our own cars, our varsity jackets, be in the same class for pre-calculus and be looking toward graduation day. Yet when we go home, we are still no longer playmates, we are still prejudiced enemies, could it be, I ask you one last time, could it be because of our parents' silly racial attitudes?

Together we will finally graduate, get our diplomas and become young men.

Together we will overcome all racial factors and put together our ideas and lessons that we have learned from the past so that we both will be known as great concerned men.

Together we will work for unity — unity in ourselves, unity in our families and unity in all people.

Together we will.

by: Eddie Chavez
      Mary Meller Junior High School
      El Rancho USD
      Written as a speech to the American Legion

HANDS ON HERITAGE

TABLE OF CONTENTS

The authors dedicate this book to the principal Dennis Keizer, the teachers, the volunteers, and the children of Kettering Elementary School, who inspired us to develop our Multicultural program. To our children Sean, Kirk, Lara, Karin and Chris, who allowed us to work long hours. To our husbands Michael and Olaf, who gave us continued support and critical review in our endeavor.

CHAPTER I
AN INTRODUCTION

Our society in the United States has been viewed, by many individuals, as being basically mono-cultural. The educational focus has been to create an English speaking urban society. Ethnic groups have often faced unnecessary problems because of their unique cultural backgrounds. With the growing focus on pride of heritage, it becomes increasingly more difficult to find one's position in the alleged melting pot of America. Leon Hymovitz, in his article entitled, "Multicultural Education in the Bicentennial," emphasized that the "ME in multicultural education is a sacred entity, one to be hallowed above all other resources. The greatest gift we can share with the other person is not our own wealth but rather to reveal to him his own treasures."[1]

In their Educational Leadership article entitled "Encouraging Multicultural Education", The Association for Supervision and Curriculum Development stated that "The growing impact of the complexity of life in our highly technological and industrialized society necessitates recognition of cultural pluralism and should foster active efforts for its positive perpetuation...Cultural pluralism emerges not only as a social fact, but also as a positive ideal to preserve the integrity of all individuals. It is necessary for the development of a more humane society through democratic processes...It (multicultural education) views a culturally pluralistic society as a positive force that welcomes differences as vehicles for understanding.[2]

As people and nations become more secure, they are better able to appreciate and accept the diversity of their heritage. We are no longer an American melting pot, nor do we want to be. With increased exposure to differences, we also learn about our similiarities; our cultural differences are the highlights. In his article entitled, "Multicultural Education in the Bicentennial," Leon Hymovitz further states that "our cities are a potpourri of many cultures and ethnic groups...To provide an educational program on bases that ignore this fact, is to turn aside from reality."[3]

The development of ethnic studies departments at various colleges has occurred out of a need to re-tell history and to respect and acknowledge individual cultures. This has been an important step in the right direction. However, since basic outlooks are formed during the early stages in one's life, the exposure to ethnic attitudes needs to begin during the initial phase of formal education. Fruehling, in his study entitled, "Multicultural Education as Social Exchange; A Study By E. Aronson and Colleagues," emphasized that, "Multicultural education can be more than an opportunity to learn about others. It can be an opportunity for every student to exchange something of value from his cultural heritage in a setting of mutual cooperation and respect."[4]

In a section of the *Administrators' Checklist for Enhancing Multicultural Curriculum (Social Education,* October, 1976), James Shaver, President of the National Council for the Social Studies empha-

1. Hymovitz, Leon. "Multicultural Education in the Bicentennial: Melting Pot, Atonement, or At-one-ment," *Journal of Ethnic Studies*, V3N4: 49-57, Winter, 1976.
2. Association for Supervision and Curriculum Development, "Encouraging Multicultural Education," *Educational Leadership*, 34:288-91, January, 1977.
3. Hymovitz, op. cit., p. 52.
4. Fruehling, Royal. "Multicultural Education as Social Exchange: A Study by E. Aronson and Colleagues," *Phi Delta Kappan*: 58, 398-400, January, 1977.

sized that, "The school, as the formal educational institution of the society, has an important role to play in reducing the tensions and the injustices, including the misgivings about self, that result from unexamined ethnic beliefs and attitudes. To fulfill that role, more is needed than a course or two on ethnic groups. The entire school must be infused with concern and action — to build awareness of ethnicity as one source of the diversity within our national society: of the contribution of that diversity, as well as why it is a source of tension and dissension, and of the sense of identity and personal pride that many can and do derive from their sense of ethnic identity."[5]

The best way to understand others is to step into their shoes. Learning is most effective when you live it, feel it, do it. This may be successfully accomplished in the classroom through "hands on" activities. A multicultural program utilizes both the cognitive and affective domains to help internalize the similarities and differences of the cultures of the world that make us, as Americans, a unique people. A multicultural curriculum which focuses on the various cultural groups within our society allows us to develop respect for their historical significance. James Bank, a noted educationalist in multiethnic studies, stated in his article "Evaluating the Multiethnic Components of the Social Studies", *(Social Education,* November, 1976) that, "The multiethnic components of the social studies can be classified into two broad categories: cognitive and affective. The cognitive component is designed to increase the students' ability to conceptualize and generalize about ethnically-related events and to collect and evaluate data related to race and ethnicity...The affective component is designed to help students to analyze and clarify their attitudes and feelings related to racial and ethnic groups and to reduce racial and ethnic prejudices."[6]

The affective components of a culture are best understood by young children through "hands on" experiences. Art, cooking, and recreational activities provide some elements of a culture that are indigenous to the natural resources, the land, and the geographic area. They reflect also the mood and feelings of the people. This philosophy serves as a foundation for a learning center-based multicultural program at Charles F. Kettering Elementary School in Long Beach, California. This project utilizes the time and talents of paraprofessionals in a multi-graded, small group approach to the study of America's cultural heritage. The paraprofessionals receive the in-service training necessary to present three unique experiences for each culture. These experiences encompass the art, cooking, and recreation of a culture.

In the *Administrator's Checklist for Enhancing Multicultural Curriculum,* James B. Boyer, Professor and Multicultural Curriculum Specialist for the College of Education, Kansas State University, says that, "The multiethnic curriculum should be comprehensive in scope and sequence, should present holistic views of ethnic groups, and should be an *integral part of the total school curriculum."*[7] Further, Boyer suggests that, "Students learn best from well-planned, comprehensive, continuous, and interrelated experiences. In an effective multiethnic curriculum, the study of ethnicity should be integrated into all courses and subject matter areas from pre-school through twelfth grade and beyond."[8]

Although the lesson plans included in this text may be adapted for regular classroom use, they are best suited for a multicultural center. The multicultural center differs from the regular classroom in its approach. Social Studies in the classroom generally focuses upon factual information and the social peer group experiences. A non-graded multicultural program expands upon these principles. This approach allows the child to escape from the niche in which he is often placed when traditionally grouped in a self-contained classroom. Multi-age, or "family" grouping, that is when children of varying

5. Shaver, James. "Administrator's Checklist for Enhancing Multicultural Education," *Social Education*: (insert p. 14), October, 1976.

6. Bank, James. "Evaluating the Multi-ethnic Components of the Social Studies," *Social Education* : 538-547, November, 1976.

7. Boyer, James. "Administrator's Checklist for Enhancing Multicultural Curriculum," *Social Education*: October, 1976.

8. *Ibid.*

grade levels work together, provides the child with additional opportunities to enhance his self-concept within a different peer hierarchy. In this atmosphere, every child is encouraged to formulate and express his personal feelings and ideas regarding the building of our cultural heritage.

A distinct area for cultural studies allows a school to explore numerous cultures in one school year. In our program we have been able to cover effectively as many as five cultures each year. The successive study of numerous cultures combined with "hands on" activities promotes the development of analogies. The child begins to distinguish similarities in various cultures and, after further consideration of the differences realizes that both enrich his heritage.

CHAPTER II
ORGANIZATION OF A
MULTI CULTURAL PROGRAM

Once you have established the desirability of a multicultural program in your school, your work has just begun. One of the first steps should be an informal needs assessment. During casual lunchroom discussions, decisions may be made regarding basic directions and goals. At this time, a teacher should be chosen to represent the staff and to act as liaison to your group of paraprofessionals. These paraprofessionals need a coordinator who is directly responsible for the multicultural program. This coordinator meets regularly with the teacher representative, who in turn communicates the needs for the program as decided by the staff.

CHOOSING
A
COORDINATOR

Organizational details can be a menace during the establishment and first year of your program. It is imperative that your coordinator and teacher representative work well together. Whenever possible the teacher representative should make the final decision as to whom he will work with most effectively.

Once the teachers have made some basic decisions regarding the routine and cultures to be studied, their representative meets with the paraprofessional coordinator. Together these two representatives determine the implementation of the program. They decide together such things as the location of the multicultural center, the basic equipment and supplies, funding, staffing and scheduling. After these school policies have been clarified and the basic organization outlined, the paraprofessional coordinator can begin to implement the program. The main role for teachers is to plan. The responsibility of the paraprofessional is to execute their plan.

Casual communication between teachers and paraprofessionals should be the general rule. An occasional letter may be used effectively for some specific feedback. For example, we used the following letter at the end of our first cultural experience.

SETTING
UP THE
CENTER

Before you actually begin setting up your center, send a letter to parents stating the purposes of the new center. Inform parents that their children will be involved in several experiences that will give them an opportunity to learn about diverse cultures. Advise the parents that some of these experiences will include the preparation and tasting of foods. The parent should inform you if any child is allergic to certain foods. This is a precaution for you and the child.

In some cases you will need to avoid a particular food or make a reasonable substitution. With so many children from various classrooms, it should be the teacher's responsibility to collect these forms and alert the paraprofessionals to any allergies or dietary restrictions. Included in this introductory letter you should submit a list of necessary supplies which could easily be donated. This letter also provides an excellent opportunity to recruit additional volunteers to help staff the center.

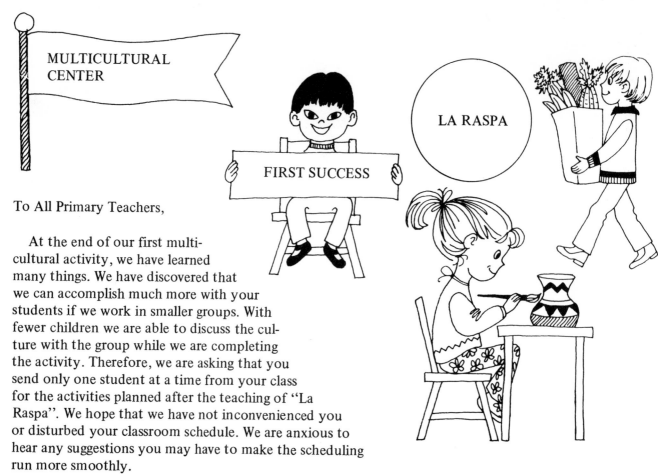

MULTICULTURAL CENTER

FIRST SUCCESS

LA RASPA

To All Primary Teachers,

At the end of our first multicultural activity, we have learned many things. We have discovered that we can accomplish much more with your students if we work in smaller groups. With fewer children we are able to discuss the culture with the group while we are completing the activity. Therefore, we are asking that you send only one student at a time from your class for the activities planned after the teaching of "La Raspa". We hope that we have not inconvenienced you or disturbed your classroom schedule. We are anxious to hear any suggestions you may have to make the scheduling run more smoothly.

The Learning Center's paraprofessionals have been very pleased with the response of the students this past week. We need to maintain this level of activity in order to keep the volunteer's interest while they are donating their time. Thank you for your co-operation and support in the inauguration of the multicultural phase of our Learning Center.

Signed by the Multicultural Coordinator and Teacher Representative

PLEASE TEAR-OFF AND RETURN TO OFFICE BY_____ (date)

HOW MIGHT WE BEST CHANGE OUR METHOD OF SCHEDULING CHILDREN

INTO THE LEARNING CENTER? _____

PLEASE LIST YOUR SUGGESTIONS FOR FURTHER MULTICULTURAL EXPERIENCES.

WHAT RECOMMENDATIONS DO YOU HAVE REGARDING PARAPROFESSIONALS?

CENTRO MULTICULTURAL

PRIMER EXITO

LA RASPA

A Todos Los Maestros Primarios:

Al cabo de nuestra primera actividad multicultural, hemos apprendido muchas cosas. Hemos descubierto que podemos realizar mucho más con sus alumnos si trabajamos con grupos más pequeños. Con menos alumnos podemos discutir la cultura con el grupo mientras que cumplimos con la actividad. Por eso pedimos que usted mande a solamente un niño cada vez de su clase para las actividades planeadas después de la enseñanza de "La Raspa". Esperamos no haberle incomodado o haber molestado su horario de la aula. Somos ansiosos de oír unas sugestiones que ustedes puedan tener para mejor fijar la hora de las visitas de los niños.

Los paraprofesionales del Centro de Aprender han estado muy contentos con la cooperación de los alumnos esta semana pasada. Tenemos que mantener este nivel de actividad para guardar el interes del voluntario mientras el voluntario ofrece su tiempo libre. Gracias por su cooperación y su apoyo en la inauguracion de la fase multicultural de nuestro Centro de Aprender.

Firmados por el Director y el
Maestro Representante del Centro
Multicultural

- -

Por favor desgarre y devuelva a la oficina por _____ (fecha) _____
¿Como pudieramos mejorar nuestro metado de fijar la hora de las visitas de los ninos a nuestro centro de aprender? _____
_____
Por favor haga una lista de sus sugestiones para mas experiencias multiculturales. _____
_____
¿Cuales recommendaciones tienen ustedes en cuanto a los paraprofesionales? _____
_____

給全體小學教師們：

　　在初次的綜合文化教育活動結束後，我們學習到許多東西。我們發覺，假如我們能夠小組活動的話，我們就能夠得到更多的效果。與較少數的小孩們，我們更能夠與小組討論文化問題並完成我們的活動。因此，我們請求你們每次在 "La Raspa" 教學後，祇從你們的玻上送一位學生來活動中心。我們希望這樣不至於給你們不方便或者防礙你們的課堂程序計劃。我們渴望著聽到你們的任何建議，你們也許能使這個程序計劃進行得更順利。

　　這個學習中心的共同教職員們對於上週末學生們的表現感到非常的欣慰。我們需要去維持這種活動的程度，而獲得這些捐獻出寶貴時間的志願教師的興趣。謝謝你們的合作與支持我們的學習中心在綜合文化教育方面的創辦下。

　　　　　　綜合文化活動中心 協商人 及
　　　　　　教師代表們簽字

- -

請撕下並繳回辦公室於下列日期 ＿＿＿＿＿＿＿＿＿＿

怎樣才能改variance我們的學習中心，對孩子們的安排方法？
＿＿＿＿＿＿＿＿＿＿＿＿＿＿＿＿＿＿＿＿＿＿＿＿
＿＿＿＿＿＿＿＿＿＿＿＿＿＿＿＿＿＿＿＿＿＿＿＿

請例出對促進 綜合文化教育經驗之意見。
＿＿＿＿＿＿＿＿＿＿＿＿＿＿＿＿＿＿＿＿＿＿＿＿
＿＿＿＿＿＿＿＿＿＿＿＿＿＿＿＿＿＿＿＿＿＿＿＿

你們對共同教職方面有何推薦？
＿＿＿＿＿＿＿＿＿＿＿＿＿＿＿＿＿＿＿＿＿＿＿＿
＿＿＿＿＿＿＿＿＿＿＿＿＿＿＿＿＿＿＿＿＿＿＿＿

MULTICULTURAL CENTER

DONATIONS

VOLUNTEERS

Dear Parents:

In Room No. 7, our Learning Center, we are continuing to offer remediation and enrichment in basic skills. We are also establishing a multicultural center. This will be a non-graded enrichment program for the primary grades. The children will participate in art, cooking and recreational experiences representative of each culture. This center is based on the philosophy that the best way to understand others is to "step into their shoes".

Our initial cultural experience will be on Monday, September 14. Ms. Jane Gothold, the curator of the Pacific Coast Archeological Society, will be talking to our students about the early Native Californians.

Our first cultural unit of study is Mexico. This unit has been planned by the teachers and utilizes the talents of paraprofessionals who are being especially trained to provide these enrichment experiences.

We need your support to make this worthwhile project immediately effective. Donations of the following items will be appreciated. Send them to school in a sack labeled LEARNING CENTER or call the multicultural coordinator___(phone number)___.

Margarine tubs
Large cannister (for storage of 20 lbs. flour)
3 lb. coffee cans
Plastic wash basins (like the hospital type)
Measuring spoons — metric & standard
Measuring cups — metric & standard
Water container or pitcher
Spatulas
Dish draining rack
Colorful yarn (leftover portions are great)
Any Mexican items, i.e. dolls, serapes, hats, posters, kitchen utensils...These items need to be labeled clearly so they can be returned to you.
Anyone interested in helping us with this study.

We cannot emphasize strongly enough how much we need these items to make our multicultural center a success. *We need additional volunteers to help with this center.* Our training program will be on September 21 at 10:00 o'clock in room number 7.

Signed by the Multicultural Coordinator and Teacher Representative

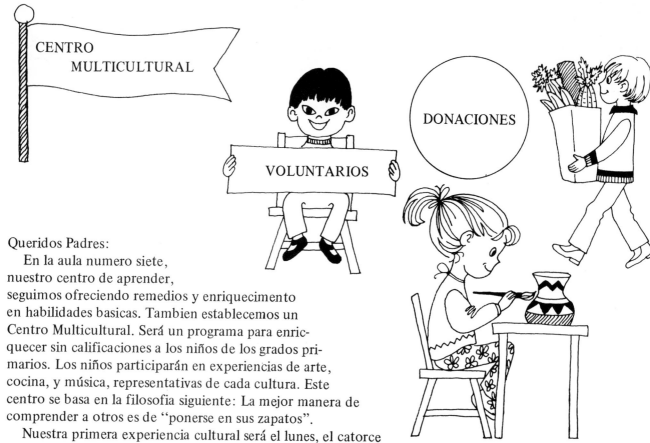

CENTRO MULTICULTURAL

VOLUNTARIOS

DONACIONES

Queridos Padres:

En la aula numero siete, nuestro centro de aprender, seguimos ofreciendo remedios y enriquecimento en habilidades basicas. Tambien establecemos un Centro Multicultural. Será un programa para enriquecer sin calificaciones a los niños de los grados primarios. Los niños participarán en experiencias de arte, cocina, y música, representativas de cada cultura. Este centro se basa en la filosofia siguiente: La mejor manera de comprender a otros es de "ponerse en sus zapatos".

Nuestra primera experiencia cultural será el lunes, el catorce de septiembre. Ms. Gothold, la conservadora de la Sociedad Arqueológica de la Costa Pacífica hablará a nuestros alumnos sobre los primeros nativos de California.

Nuestra primera unidad de estudio cultural es México. Esta unidad se ha planeada por los maestros y utiliza los talentos de los paraprofesionales que reciben instrucción especial para ofrecer estas experiencias de enriquecimiento.

Necesitamos su apoyo para hacer efectivo este proyecto en sequida. Donaciones de estas cosas siguientes serán recibidas con agradecimiento. Mándenlas a la escuela en un saco dirigido por etiqueta CENTRO DE APRENDER o llamen el supervisor multicultural _____ (numero del teléfono) _____ .

Cubas de margarina
Lata grande (para contener viente libras de harina)
Latas de café de tres libras
Palanganas de lavar plásticas (como las del hospital)
Cucharas de medir-métricas y normales
Tazas de medir-métricas y normales
Jarro o recipiente de agua
Espátulas
Un estante para secar platos
Hilado de todos colores (remanentes son buenos)
Articulos mexicanas como: muñecas, sarapes, sombreros, carteles, utensilios de la cocina. . .
Estos artículos deben tener su nombre en etiqueta claramente para que podamos devolvérselos a ustedes. Gente interesada en ayudarnos en este estudio.

No podemos acentuar bastante cuanto necesitamos estas cosas para poder hacer un éxito del Centro Multicultural. *Nos faltan mas voluntarios que pueden ayudar con este centro.* Nuestro programa de entrenamiento será el 21 de septiembre a las diez en la aula numero siete.

Firmados por el Supervisor y El
Maestro Representante Multiculturales

親愛的父母們：

在我們學習中心的第7號教室，我們繼續在提供修正與補充基本上的技能。我們並且建立了綜合文化中心，這將是對於初級學童的一個無學分的促進教育課程。這些小孩們將參加在他們所代表的文化上的音樂，烹調與藝術經驗中。這個中心的基本哲學論即：了解他人最好之方法就是"腳踏實地"。

我們的啟發文化經驗將在九月十四日星期六。——————————夫人，太平洋岸社會考古學的館長將告訴我們的學生關於早期加尼福尼亞的土著。

我們第一個學習單位是墨西哥，這個單位是被這些教師和資歷豐富而俱有特殊天才的共同教職員所籌備計劃的。

我們需要你們的支持予使這個有價值的計劃能獲得效果。我們將非常感激捐贈下列的項目。請送到學校有標明"學習中心"的袋子裡或者請電話通知綜合文化中心的協商人——————————。

奶油盛器數個
大型筒子（大約可裝20磅的麵粉）
3磅裝的咖啡罐
整膠製洗臉盆（像醫院用的）
量匙與量杯
水壺或水桶
抹刀，放乾酪，碟等的樣子
各種顏色的毛線（用剩下的是最好）
任何墨西哥項目，如洋娃娃，圍巾，帽子，繪圖廣告，廚房用俱等，———這些必需標明清楚，以他們能夠歸還你們。
任何一個有興趣幫忙我們學習者。

我們再三的強調我們是多麼的需要這些東西來使我們的綜合文化中心有個成就。我們需要更多的志願者來幫忙這個中心。我們的訓練過程將在九月廿一日早上十點_在第七教室。

綜合文化中心協商人與教師代表人簽字

MULTICULTURAL CENTER

TORTILLAS

COOKING

Dear Parent,

In our multicultural center the children will participate in many cooking experiences. Cooking provides an additional avenue for learning about similarities and differences between cultures. It also gives each child a practical extension of math, reading, language arts, and science activities.

As each child will be eating what he has prepared, it is essential that we know about any allergies or dietary restrictions. Please complete and return the tear-off by __(date)_____

Signed by the Multicultural Coordinator and Teacher Representative

- -

PLEASE TEAR-OFF AND RETURN TO SCHOOL OFFICE.

MY CHILD MAY EAT ANY FOODS PREPARED AT SCHOOL:

( ) TRUE   ( ) NOT TRUE

MY CHILD IS ALLERGIC TO THE FOLLOWING FOODS:

_____

_____

MY CHILD MUST NOT EAT OR DRINK THE FOLLOWING:

_____

_____

Child's Name _____ Date _____ Parent Signature _____

Grade _____ Room No. _____ Phone No. _____

CENTRO MULTICULTURAL

TORTILLAS

COCINA

Queridos Padres:

En nuestro centro multicultural los niños participarán en muchas experiencias de cocinar. La cocina nos presenta una manera adicional para aprender algo acerca de lo que es semejante y lo que es distinto entre las culturas. Además ofrece al niño una extensión de matemáticas, lectura, el arte de la lengua, y actividades de ciencia.

Como cada alumno comerá lo que ha preparado es esencial que sepamos si hay alergias que tiene el niño o si hay algo de dieta que el doctor prohibe. Por favor cumpla lo de abajo y devuélvanos el (fecha). _____

Firmados por El Supervisor y El
Maestro Representante Multiculturales

Por favor Desgarren y Devuelvan a La Oficina de la Escuela.
Mi niño (niña) puede comer cualquier comida preparada en la escuela.

( ) VERDAD   ( ) NO ES VERDAD

Mi niño (niña) tiene alergia con estos alimentos: _____

_____

No permito que mi niño (niña) coma o beba lo siguiente: _____

_____

Nombre Del Niño_____Fecha _____

Grado_____Aula No. _____Teléfono _____

Firma del padre o de la madre _____

親愛的父母們：

在我們的綜合文化中心裡，小孩們將參加在許多的烹調經驗中。烹調是一個學習文化間之相同與不同的途徑。它也給每位小孩從實習中延伸到學習數學、閱讀、語言的藝術和科學的活動。

每一位小孩都將吃到他們自己所做出的食品，故我們必須知道他們是否對某種食物有過敏性或禁食的食品。請將下面表格填好，並撕下繳回於＿＿＿＿＿。

綜合文化中心負責人
與教師代表們上

- -

請撕下並繳回學校辦公室

我的小孩可以吃任何學校裡所準備的食品。

（　）是　　　　　（　）非

我的小孩不可吃或喝下列食品。

_____

_____

我的小孩對下列食品有過敏性。

_____

_____

小孩的姓名 ＿＿＿＿＿＿＿＿＿＿　日期＿＿＿＿＿　父母簽字＿＿＿＿＿＿

年級 ＿＿＿＿＿＿　教室号碼 ＿＿＿＿＿　電話号碼 ＿＿＿＿＿＿＿＿

FINDING A LOCATION

A multicultural center may be located in a quiet corner of any classroom. However, the "family-grouping" approach proves far more beneficial. We were fortunate to have an existing Learning Center which had been developed in an unused classroom. The multicultural center was established in a portion of the Learning Center. If you do not have this kind of an existing set-up available, you may need to be more creative in your search for a location. In the long run, what you find will probably be more ideal for your situation.

Some obvious possibilities for your multicultural center might be the unused classroom, trailer, portable classroom, or bungalow. Do not overlook the spaces in your school that are only used on a part-time basis: i.e., nurses' office, counselors' office, cafeteria, entrance to the auditorium, teachers' lounge, office hallway or storage room. Although we have not utilized these particular locations, the use of the cafeteria and office hallways appeal to us because the entire student body frequents these areas. The learning experiences of the primary children then become an interest center for all the students of the school.

BASIC EQUIPMENT AND SUPPLIES

After determining your location, which can be any enclosure that has room for a table, chairs, and a small display area, you will need to begin organizing your supplies and equipment. Supplies for the center should be stored conveniently. This way the children can reach them and put them away after cleaning up. Supplies and their storage positions should also be clearly labeled with masking tape or gummed labels. This encourages the children to learn to read and to use the correct names for their tools. If money is available, there are many convenient storage units which may be purchased or, workable storage can be made from crates, cardboard boxes, large ice cream containers, three pound coffee cans, or other free materials. These units may be made more attractive by covering them with butcher paper, colored paper, contact paper, or oil cloth. When covering these storage units, we suggest a method of color coding for convenience: i.e., yellow — cooking supplies, blue — art materials, and green — recreational supplies. A gummed red dot may be used to denote any utensils that are sharp or that need special instructions or care.

The amount of funds available, or not available, will determine how inventive you need to be in equipping your center. We will suggest a minimum basic list of supplies for starting a multicultural center. These supplies may be purchased or acquired through donations from parents, family, friends, Parent-Teacher Associations, merchants, cultural groups. You may acquire the basic equipment and later, when funds permit, you will want to expand. These are your beginning supplies; additional materials will be needed as you cover each cultural unit.

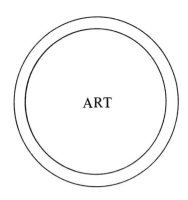

ART

Scissors
Crayons
Tape
Felt-tip pens
Glue
Straight pins
Pencils
Hole puncher
Stapler and staples
Rulers
5"x8" index cards (We use these to give
  information to the children
  and the paraprofessionals)

COOKING

Paper towels
Wax paper
Plastic or wax bags
Detergent (effective in cold water)
Cleanser
Bleach
Colored sponges (one color to clean floor and another for counters and table tops)
Dust pan and whisk broom
Can opener
Plastic serrated knives
One sharp knife (used by adults)
Popsicle sticks or coffee stirrers (for leveling off dry ingredients and stirring)
Spray bottle (for adding small amounts of water to correct a too-dry mixture)
Set of measuring spoons — standard and metric
Measuring cups — liquid and dry, standard and metric (use graduated size, nesting
  cups for dry ingredients because they may be more easily leveled)

Grater
Potato peeler
Egg beater
Pancake turner
Dish drainer
Electric frying pan
Deep fat fryer
Portable or toaster oven
Hot plate
Small sauce pan

Later, when funds permit, you may want to expand the cooking center by purchasing a sifter, strainer, cookie sheets to fit oven, oven mitts, cutting board, and an ice chest or insulated bag.

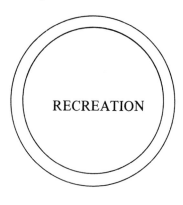

RECREATION

Tape recorder
Phonograph
Records & Tapes

DONATIONS

You may be fortunate enough to find parents or merchants who will donate many of the basic supplies which have been listed. The following items should definitely be requested as donations:

Material scraps
Yarn
Popsicle sticks (for crafts)
Margarine tubs (to be used as individual mixing bowls)
Coffee cans of all sizes (for storage containers, handwashing, and dishwashing)
Meat trays
Plastic containers (to hold a week's supply of ingredients — these are available from a bakery or delicatessen)
Large ice cream cartons (for storage of any supplies)

Representational exhibits and artifacts of the culture being studied may be borrowed from families who have traveled to that country. Other sources for exhibits might be your school district's audio-visual department, public libraries, lending art museums, and surrounding colleges. Experts in the field, foreign students, cultural groups such as Hadassah, Sons of Norway, Portuguese Study Center, UNICEF, Consulates and Embassies, and travel agencies may provide additional expertise.

FINANCING
A CENTER

There are numerous funding techniques for implementing a multicultural program. If your coordinator is willing to search for donations, this will help in defraying the costs. Your funds may be part of the school budget or special monies may be allotted through Early Childhood Education, Adult Education, or Parent-Teacher Associations. Some school districts may allow the use of money or food donations from the children's families. When a new cooking experience begins, a note may be sent home with each child to ask for contributions. Parents will expect letters throughout the year when they know that cooking is an integral part of your multicultural curriculum.

If your multicultural center includes several primary classrooms, you should send this letter on a rotation basis so that you are not overburdening any one donor. You must request specific amounts of packaged items.

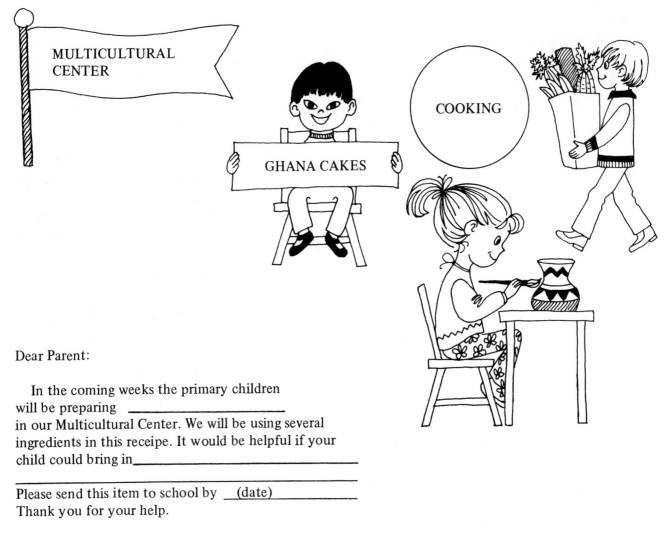

MULTICULTURAL CENTER

GHANA CAKES

COOKING

Dear Parent:

In the coming weeks the primary children will be preparing _____ in our Multicultural Center. We will be using several ingredients in this receipe. It would be helpful if your child could bring in_____

_____

Please send this item to school by __(date)_____
Thank you for your help.

Signed by the Multicultural Coordinator
and Teacher Representative

- -

PLEASE TEAR-OFF AND RETURN TO OFFICE BY_____(date)_____

Parent's Name_____

Child's Name _____

Phone Number_____

Grade_____

( ) I WILL BE ABLE TO SEND THE INGREDIENT.
( ) I WILL NOT BE ABLE TO SEND THE INGREDIENT.

CENTRO MULTICULTURAL

COCINA

PASTELES DE GHANA

Queridos Padres:

Durante las semanas que vienen los niños estarán preparando _____en nuestro centro multicultural. Estaremos usando varios ingredientes en esta receta. Nos aydaría mucho si su niño (o niña) pudiera traernos _____. Por favor manden esto a la escuela para_____(fecha)_____. Muchas gracias por su ayuda.

_____ Firmados Por El Supervisor y El

_____Maestro Representante Multiculturales

- -

Por Favor Desgarren y Devuelvan a La Oficina Para _____(fecha)_____

Nombre del padre o de la madre_____

Nombre del niño o de la niña _____

Número del Teléfono _____

Grado _____

( ) Yo podré mandar el ingrediente

( ) Yo no podré mandar el ingrediente

親愛的父母們:

　　在下幾個星期中，小孩們將在綜合文化中心烹調課裡準備＿＿＿＿＿＿＿＿＿＿＿＿。我們將用數種材料來這食譜裡。這將是個很大的幫助，假如你的小孩能帶來＿＿＿＿＿＿＿＿＿＿＿＿＿＿＿＿＿＿＿＿＿＿＿＿＿＿＿＿＿＿＿＿＿＿＿＿＿。

請送這項材料到學校於下列日期＿＿＿＿＿＿＿＿＿。
謝謝你們的幫助。

　　　　　　　　綜合文化中心員責人
　　　　　　　　與教師代表們上

- -

請撕下並繳回辦公室於下列日期＿＿＿＿＿＿＿＿＿＿

父母的姓名 ＿＿＿＿＿＿＿＿＿＿＿＿＿＿＿＿＿＿

小孩的姓名 ＿＿＿＿＿＿＿＿＿＿＿＿＿＿＿＿＿＿

電話號碼 ＿＿＿＿＿＿＿＿＿＿＿＿＿＿＿＿＿＿＿

年級 ＿＿＿＿＿＿＿＿＿＿＿＿＿＿＿＿＿＿＿＿＿

（　）我將能送來此項材料
（　）我將不能送來此項材料

Materials may also be purchased using monies from special projects, such as bake sales, paper drives, breakfasts or dinners. A year-end culminating activity and fund raiser might be a school-wide multicultural fair. The food and game booths could be designed to represent various cultures. Using the experiences from their year in the center, students might also prepare crafts and food items to be purchased.

CHOOSING THE CULTURES

In some school districts, the goal in multicultural and multi-ethnic studies has been to choose equally from the four major skin color groups: black, brown, yellow, and white. In planning your program, it is beneficial to select cultures which are representative of your school population. This helps not only to promote understanding but also to encourage parental involvement. Parents comprise a community resource for representative clothing, recipes, artifacts, etc. The cultures that you choose will be diverse and your goal should be to highlight their similarities and differences through art, cooking, and recreational activities.

INTRODUCING
THE CULTURES

Since the multicultural program utilizes paraprofessionals, it is impractical to introduce the first "Hands On" activities until the third week of school. The first two weeks should be used for collecting supplies and equipment, organizing the program, and training volunteers. Also, this time period provides opportunities to motivate children while introducing the study of our cultural heritage.

One way to begin the study of the heritages of others is to promote personal cultural awareness within the individual child. This can be done by placing a large world map outside your multicultural center. Send a letter home encouraging the parents to discuss their child's heritage.

MULTICULTURAL CENTER

HERITAGE

SURVEY

Dear Parents:

As an introductory activity to the multicultural center, we will be discussing what constitutes each child's heritage.

The outline of a world map will be placed in the hallway outside the multicultural center. We are asking that you discuss your child's heritage with him so that he may place a marker on the map indicating the one or two major countries which make up his family background. The children will have an opportunity to see the diverse heritage of their fellow students.

We invite you to visit our multicultural center and view the heritage survey map.

Signed by the Multicultural Coordinator and Teacher Representative

- -

PLEASE RETURN TEAR-OFF TO CLASSROOM TEACHER BY __(date)_____

CHILD'S NAME _____ ROOM NUMBER _____

COUNTRY OF HERITAGE NO. 1 _____

COUNTRY OF HERITAGE NO. 2 _____

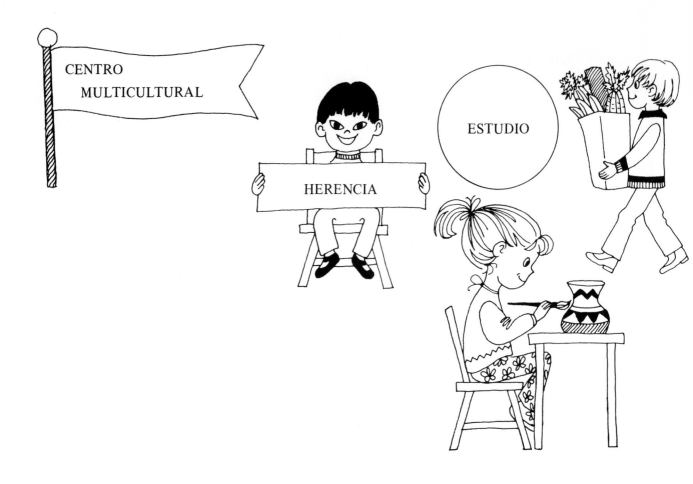

Queridos Padres:

Como actividad preliminar al centro multicultural, la clase du su niño o niña estará discutiendo lo que comprende la herencia de cada niño.

El trazado de un mapa del mundo será puesto en el corredor fuera del centro multicultural. Pedimos que ustedes, los padres, discutan la herencia de sus niños con los niños y así el hijo o la hija pueda poner una marca en el mapa indicando uno o dos sitios de uno o dos países mayores que comprenden la herencia de su familia. Los alumnos tendrán la oportunidad de ver las varias herencias de sus alumnos amigos en sus clases.

Les invitamos a ustedes a visitar nuestro centro multicultural y a mirar el mapa del estudio de herencia.

Firmados por el Supervisor y el
Maestro Representante
Multicultural

Por Favor Desgarren Y Devuelvan Al Maestro De La Aula Para ___(fecha)___ _____

Nombre del Niño o de la Nina _____ Número de la aula _____

Pais de la Herencia No. Uno _____

País de la Herencia No. Dos _____

親愛的父母們：

在綜合文化中心的介紹活動裡，你們小孩的班上將被討論到什麼是構成每位小孩的世襲因素。

綜合文化中心的走廊上，將被掛出一個世界地圖的網領。我們請求你與你的小孩先討論他的世襲因素。因此他也許能把記號放在地圖上，指出一個或二個構成他家庭背景的國家。這些小孩將有機會在他同學中看到各種世襲因素。

我們邀請你們來參觀我們的綜合文化中心和參閱民族世襲測繪圖。

綜合文化中心負責人
與教師代表們上

請撕下並繳給班上教師於下列日期 _____

小孩的姓名 _____ 教室號碼 _____

世襲國家 #1 _____

世襲國家 #2 _____

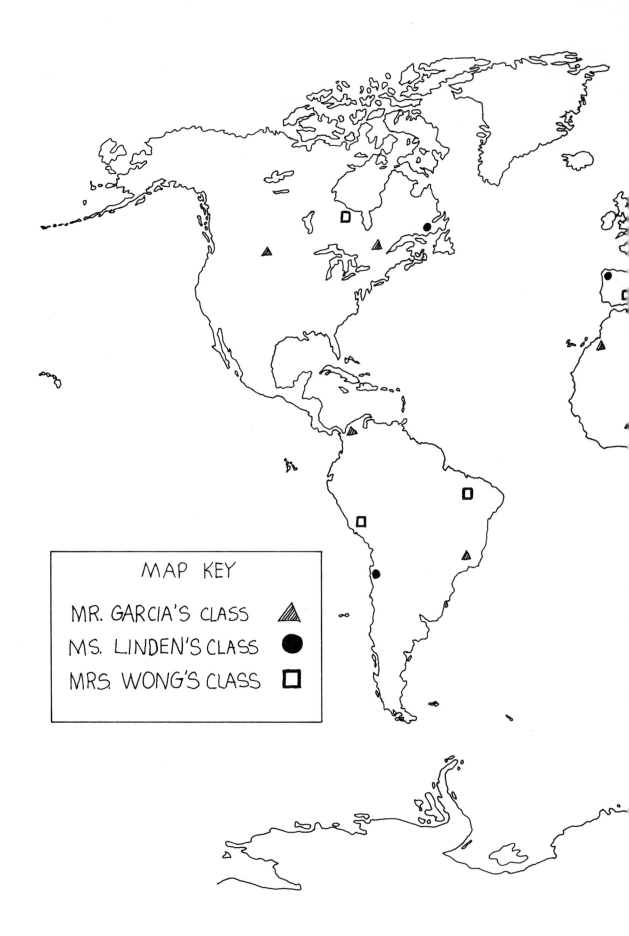

MAP KEY

MR. GARCIA'S CLASS ▲

MS. LINDEN'S CLASS ●

MRS. WONG'S CLASS □

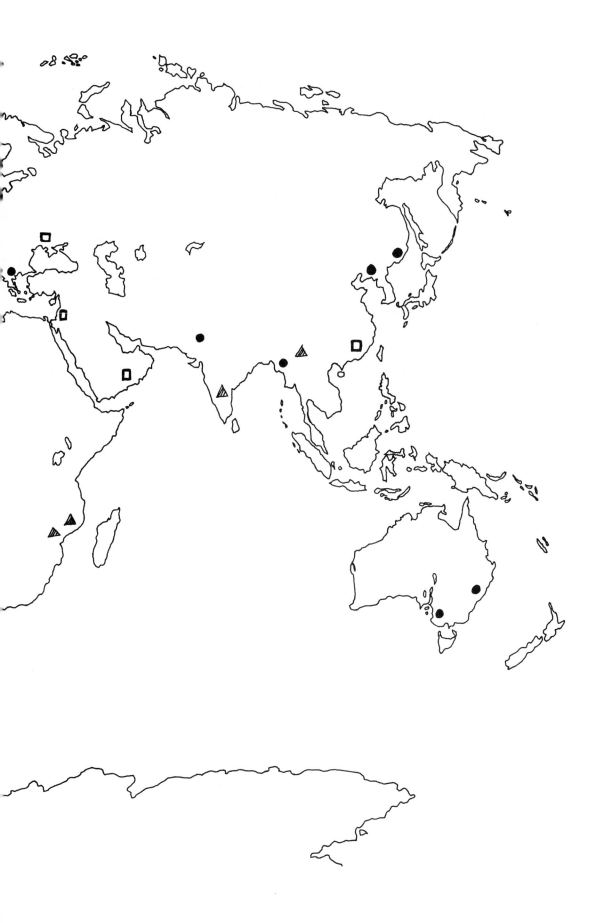

PLANNING
THE YEAR

The following is a typical example of a school year continuum. It may be helpful as a guideline in planning your total program.

SCHOOL YEAR CONTINUUM
FOR MULTICULTURAL PROGRAMS

Week No. 1
Send letter (p. 9) Donations — Volunteers
Send volunteer recruitment letters. See Ch. III
Collect equipment and supplies
Organize center

Week No. 2
Train paraprofessionals
Exhibit world map
Send letter (p. 25) Heritage Survey

Week No. 3
Indicate cultural origins of children on map
Complete center environment

Week No. 4
Lecture on Native Americans
Send letter (p. 12) Cooking — Tortillas

Week No. 5
Center opens on regular schedule

Wks. 5-7
Mexico — art experience. Send letter (p. 6) La Raspa — First Success

Week No. 8
Mexico — recreation. Send letter (p. 20) Cooking Ghana Cakes

Wks. 9-11
Mexico — cooking

Wks. 12-13
Africa — art. Send letter (p. 20) Cooking Ghana Cakes

Wks. 14-16
Africa — cooking.

Week No. 17
Africa — recreation

Wks. 18-19
Israel — art. Send letter (p. 20) Cooking Ghana Cakes

Wks. 20-22
Israel — cooking

Week No. 23
Israel — recreation

Wks. 24-25
Greece — art. Send letter (p. 20) Cooking Ghana Cakes

Wks. 26-28
Greece — cooking

Week No. 29
Greece — recreation

Wks. 30-31
Japan — art. Send letter (p. 20) Cooking Ghana Cakes

Wks. 32-34
Japan — cooking

Week No. 35
Japan — recreation

In most school districts there are 40 weeks of school with 3 weeks of vacation. Allow at least 2 unplanned weeks each year for flexibility.

Record keeping can be a problem for the classroom teacher and the multicultural coordinator. Here are some ways the teacher and coordinator can alleviate two of these problems.

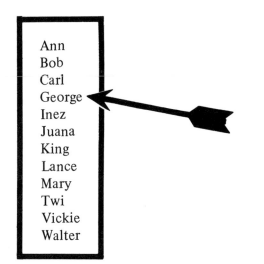

Ann
Bob
Carl
George
Inez
Juana
King
Lance
Mary
Twi
Vickie
Walter

How to know who gets a turn to go to the Multicultural Room?

Attach an arrow using stick dough.

When George returns from the Multi-cultural Center, he will move the arrow so that it will point to the next name: Inez

One way that the staff of the Multicultural Center can easily keep a record of how many children remain from each room to use the Center is to utilize a chart in this way: list each teacher's name followed by the number of students in his class. If there are 27 students in Ms. Smith's class, then her name should be listed and followed by the cardinal numbers one through twenty-seven. As each group enters the Multicultural Center, the volunteer marks off a number for each classroom represented. In this way, both the teachers and the Center are able to estimate the amount of time required to complete a particular cultural activity.

ROOM #5 MR. SMITH	1 2 3 4 5 6 7 8 9 10 11 12 13 14 15 16 17
	18 19 20 21 22 23 24 25 26 27
ROOM #2 MS DOVER	1 2 3 4 5 6 7 8 9 10 11 12 13 14 15 16 17
	18 19 20 21 22 23 24 25 26 27 28 29 30
ROOM #7 MRS. WHITE	1 2 3 4 5 6 7 8 9 10 11 12 13 14 15 16 17
	18 19 20 21 22 23 24 25 26 27 28 29

CHAPTER III
UTILIZING PARAPROFESSIONALS

Paraprofessionals have been such an integral part of our multicultural program that we feel a need to outline some suggestions on how to best utilize this tremendous resource.

RECRUITING

Our volunteers are parents, grandparents, and neighbors. Many friends from a neighboring retirement community help two to ten hours per week. Other sources for volunteers are fraternal organizations, service groups, and retirement organizations. Junior High School, High School, and college students may be successfully recruited in some areas. The key here is flexibility. If someone sounds interested and has only a half hour per week free we try to involve them for that half hour. Other valuable sources of volunteers are found by the office staff during registration, at parent-teacher meetings, by word of mouth, through flyers and telephone calls. The greatest percentage of positive responses, however, may be obtained by personal face-to-face requests made to an individual by a teacher or volunteer coordinator. All requests for volunteers should be specific. This is usually possible because most teachers request assistance during an exact time block.

During recruiting, we interview each volunteer to determine his or her best placement. A good placement is twofold. Not only must the volunteer suit the needs of the classroom but the school must also meet the needs of the volunteer. For success, the volunteer must find that niche particularly enjoyable and personally self-enhancing. Careful placement is the foundation for success.

TRAINING

The most important single characteristic a volunteer teacher's aide needs is a real liking for children. Liking a child presupposes acceptance of him and the continued interest in his activities. When training volunteers, it is important to emphasize that praise and acceptance must be genuine. Children are quick to differentiate between the adult who pretends friendliness and the one who is truly accepting. Often the semantics involved, in accepting a child as he is become a problem for the volunteers. The aide-training person can be especially helpful in this area by helping the volunteer to develop a vocabulary for positive reinforcement.

Brief discussions of ages and stages are useful to acquaint volunteers, who are not always around children, with what is the typical behavior of a certain age group. Also, Madeline Hunter and Sally Breit have written a helpful book entitled *Aide-ing in Education*. They suggest some "Do's and Don'ts" in phrasing of questions and statements which may be helpful to the aide-training person. They offer specific dialogue as examples of how to give a variety of reinforcement, ways to be more specific with praise, and how to use extrinsic motivation effectively.

Reassuring responses come easiest to the volunteer who has developed good listening skills. These responses may take the form of word or action. Listening with one's whole self rapidly builds rapport between student and volunteer. Effective listening presupposes empathy. The volunteer must possess some information on the child's background, values, and needs in order to accept him as he is and in order to begin instruction at his readiness level.

When a volunteer accepts this new role he becomes a member of the professional staff of the school. Because of this position, he becomes a recipient of privileged information. This information must, of course, be kept confidential at all times. Even a positive comment made aloud about some child, who has been tutored, could be misconstrued by some as a breach of confidence.

All jobs require that the employee exhibit a certain degree of dependability. Being a volunteer worker for children increases this necessity. Children begin to accept their tutor as a friend and are extremely disappointed when that friend does not arrive when expected. A volunteer is asked to notify the school if he is planning to be absent or arrive late.

The volunteer should present a pleasing personal appearance. Good grooming and dress appropriate for the classroom and playground contribute to the success of the volunteer and provide a positive example for the children.

Our schools encourage children to learn how to observe and to think, rather than to respond with simple yes-no answers. A skillful volunteer will spend most of the lesson time asking questions, listening, and helping the student to think for himself, rather than lecturing to him. If the volunteer supplies an answer, the student should be told how to arrive at the answer. It is of little permanent help to the student to have work done for him. However, it is equally inadvisable to allow a student to struggle unnecessarily for more than a few moments. Particularly when he is reading, the child should not struggle too long. The volunteer should tactfully step in and help by providing the child with immediate feedback as to whether his work is done in error or correctly. Also, he should not disapprove to a point of discouragement but be quick to offer praise for a task well done. Positive reinforcement can be a volunteer's most valuable tool.

The volunteer should be aware of the possibility of special problems that a child may have. These problems may include emotional, psychological, or learning difficulties. Awareness increases the volunteer's ability to deal with specific incidences; it is not the volunteer's role to handle long-range problems; the teacher is the trained professional who will make the final decision in all problem areas.

WAYS TO
KEEP AND TO
APPRECIATE
VOLUNTEERS

The motivations of a paid-versus-an-unpaid position are, of course, very different. Most volunteers are interested in working directly with children. They must feel that they are sufficiently busy and contributing. The teacher who makes specific positive statements to a volunteer can help to keep that volunteer interested and positively involved. Many teachers may benefit from in-service training on ways to best deal with volunteers and make them feel appreciated. Some thoughtful techniques include providing a specific place for the volunteer's possessions, arranging for rest periods with an invitation to the lounge, and a personal recognition by the staff of those volunteers who bear the special volunteers' nametags.

An especially creative school in our community motivates their parents to participate by awarding a point as payment for every hour volunteered. These points may be accumulated and exchanged for items from a special "store" within the school. Items in the storehouse are donated by local merchants and are given a point value by the volunteer coordinator who converts the monetary value of the item into points.

The volunteer coordinator can become a friend to many volunteers by helping to solve some of the personal problems involved in such an effort; such as, arranging for carpools, babysitting, and special tasks for working parents who would like to help.

We have employed various formal "Thank You" techniques, which we have found to work effectively. Thank you notes or letters (especially those which are handwritten) are always appreciated.

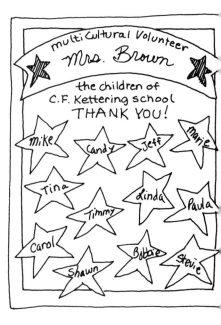

We have had special recognition certificates printed for distribution. These certificates can be personally presented at a bruch or tea so that the warmness of a personal "Thank You" may be included.

If your funds are limited, plan a pot luck brunch or luncheon and you will find that the "Thank You" still means as much. Our volunteers seem to better enjoy any gathering if we involve the children in some musical or dramatic presentation. Our three biggest successes have been: 1) a teacher wrote an original "Thank You" song for the children to sing as a surprise, 2) the children made valentines for the volunteers and the kindergarten children delivered them, and 3) our children had learned the La Raspa in the Multicultural Center and they came to a luncheon and danced as a "Thank You" to the volunteers.

HANDLING DIFFICULTIES

No matter how perfectly you have planned for, and with, all paid and volunteer staff members, there will still be special problems which occur and will need to be alleviated.

Many difficulties may be successfully avoided through adequate pre-training of your volunteer staff. Each volunteer is encouraged to avoid patronizing attitudes and to resist the urge to do a child's work for him. Specific examples are given and the volunteer is asked to pre-discuss the various coping techniques in handling possible problem situations. Role playing is often employed in order to help provide the actual vocabulary needed to meet special challenges.

Often just the physical presence of the coordinator can solve a problem. For example, sometimes a problem with a volunteer's late arrivals will correct itself if the volunteer coordinator will make himself available to greet the latecomer for several times in succession.

Any modification employed to improve volunteer services must be appropriate for the personality of that volunteer. Often a skillful teacher will aid her own volunteers toward a better understanding of learning. Sometimes a simple rewording of directions will greatly change the approach made by the volunteer. The volunteer coordinator should be available to model a behavior while working with children. If possible, this modeling should be discussed soon after it has occurred.

An in-service training period may be offered to volunteers who need to improve particular skills. Here, they have an opportunity to discuss why certain tasks are presented and why their own patient understanding is extremely important.

A last resort in dealing with volunteer problems may be to transfer a volunteer to a new area of responsibility where he might work with a different age group. Generally, you will find this extreme reaction unnecessary if other techniques have been attempted at an early enough date.

VOLUNTEER'S
HANDBOOK

We have organized a multilingual (Chinese, English and Spanish) volunteers' handbook for distribution to our staff. A partial copy has been enclosed in this text in order to stimulate adaptations for your school.

Multilingual (Chinese, English and Spanish) copies of a typical child's behavior at different ages is also helpful in preparing a volunteer to best meet the needs of the children with whom he works.

VOLUNTEER'S HANDBOOK

VOLUNTEER HANDBOOK
AN INTRODUCTION

In addition to this handbook, each volunteer should receive a district volunteer's handbook. The district handbook gives a brief history of the school district's volunteer program and includes some general suggestions for volunteer success. At our school, the volunteers expressed a need for more specific suggestions and information about the school. We hope this booklet will provide new insights.

Our volunteers work with individuals and small groups of children. Each volunteer teams with the teacher and other school staff members in helping to give children a good feeling about school and about themselves. As volunteers, you may insure that each child learns success, not failure. That's part of YOUR job.

TABLE OF CONTENTS

STEP-BY-STEP, DAY-BY-DAY:

1. Always wear your identification badge.

2. Be on time — your teacher and children depend on you.

3. Upon arrival to your work location, sign your time sheet.

4. Dress appropriately for the duties you will be performing in the classroom. You are setting an important example for the children.

5. Come to school with a positive attitude, ready to be a productive member of the classroom — as a learner yourself, and as an educational aide.

6. Be careful not to carry on private conversations with your teacher, other aides or the children during classroom time. We are concerned, as you are, with not disrupting the instructional atmosphere of the classroom.

7. Any accident, no matter how minor, should be reported to the teacher.

8. Feel free to discuss any problem you may have with your teacher, the Volunteer Coordinator or the ECE Facilitator.

9. Come to the lounge -- you are welcome to enjoy its relaxing atmosphere.

10. If you should be at school during the lunch hour, you're welcome to have lunch in the cafeteria (teachers' dining room). The cost of an adult lunch is _____. Menus are posted in the classroom and are published every Sunday in the newspaper.

11. When you are unable to come, due to illness or other personal necessity, call the office in time for your teacher to be notified so he can adjust plans for the day. The school's phone number is
_____

12. Review the other important parts of this manual and become familiar with them. Their purpose is to help you become the best classroom assistant possible.

THE ETHICAL TUTOR:

1. Classroom assistants become a part of the teaching staff and are expected to observe the same professional ethics as do certificated personnel.

2. Suggestions or criticisms of school practices or programs should be made to the appropriate leadership.

3. Should a parent ask about their own child, or someone else's, refer them to the child's teacher. Never make any *positive or negative* statements about a child to his or other parents.

4. Be as professionally discreet as possible. Never publicly discuss parents or professionals.

5. Any information found on emergency cards, or papers which you might see, should not be discussed outside school.

6. The staff may discuss children's accomplishments and needs for improving the instructional program. There may be times when you will be involved in or overhear these discussions. All of these discussions should be considered confidential.

CLASSROOM CONTROL MADE EASY:

1. Do not carry on private conversations in the classroom with other aides, children, or the teacher.

2. Check with the teacher if you feel you need to discipline a child. Be sure the teacher wants you to do the disciplining and approves of the method you want to use.

3. If there is a discipline problem, discontinue the lesson. End each lesson on a positive note, if possible, and work with the child again at a later time.

4. Be ready to admit an error, even apologize. Set a good example for children to follow.

5. Here are some ways you may be especially helpful in the classroom:

    a. Stand or sit near a developing trouble spot.

    b. Supervise independent activity and learning centers.

    c. Supervise the group while the teacher removes a child from the room to talk with him.

    d. Supervise children working at their seats and help them when they need it.

    e. Work with small groups of children so that the teacher has a smaller group with which to work.

TUTOR AND CHILD TOGETHER:

1. As tutor, your main job is to guide the child to experience success. Prevent, whenever possible, his failing at any task. With success, he is more likely to pay attention and be willing to try new learning experiences.

2. The teacher is responsible for choosing the methods and techniques used in teaching the children. You can help the teacher — be an extension of his influence. The teacher makes the ultimate decisions; you may, however, plan supplemental activities with his approval.

3. Be accepting of your students. Avoid being overly critical or using judgmental terms such as: lazy, stupid, dumb, slow.

4. Please never gossip about your students. By accepting the role of an assistant working closely with some students who have difficulty in school, you become a privileged insider. Don't abuse the right of your students to privacy.

5. Keep a sense of humor. Be enthusiastic.

6. Be positive with children. Your praise can help build their self-confidence and willingness to try.

7. Spend much of your time with children asking questions, listening, and helping them do their own thinking. Keep them from becoming "mental dropouts" who daydream through lessons.

8. Be patient. Review is an integral part of learning.

9. Avoid public humiliation or shaming which can be harmful to the student's feeling of self-worth.

10. Always check with the teacher before disciplining to be sure of procedures and techniques.

THEY MAY LEARN MORE BECAUSE OF YOU:

1. Work out a brief plan with your teacher for the things he would like you to do. Also, become aware of the objectives and philosophy of the classroom where you are assisting.

2. Learn the names of your students as soon as possible.

3. Be enthusiastic when working with children. Excite them about learning!

4. Be friendly with students, yet maintain the proper degree of dignity.

5. Be positive with children. Concentrate on the things they do well, no matter how small they may seem, and be free with specific praise when it is deserved.

6. Follow directions, but don't be afraid to ask your teacher to repeat or clarify your task.

7. Use your own initiative in the classroom. Don't wait for orders from the teacher. Begin to become aware, on your own, of tasks that need doing or of children who need help.

8. Remember that your supervising teacher is human and will have both good and bad days. Be as helpful as you can to make the classroom run smoothly.

9. Hold children's interest by changing pace, being enthusiastic, varying your approach, keeping study periods brief.

10. Assist your teacher in enforcing classroom rules. The authority for classroom procedures rests with your supervising teacher. Your job is to help carry out those procedures. Be patient.

11. Try to anticipate problem situations in the classroom and be there to "head them off".

12. When doing any written work, use the correct manuscript or cursive form (see examples in manual on next two pages).

MANUSCRIPT WRITING GUIDE

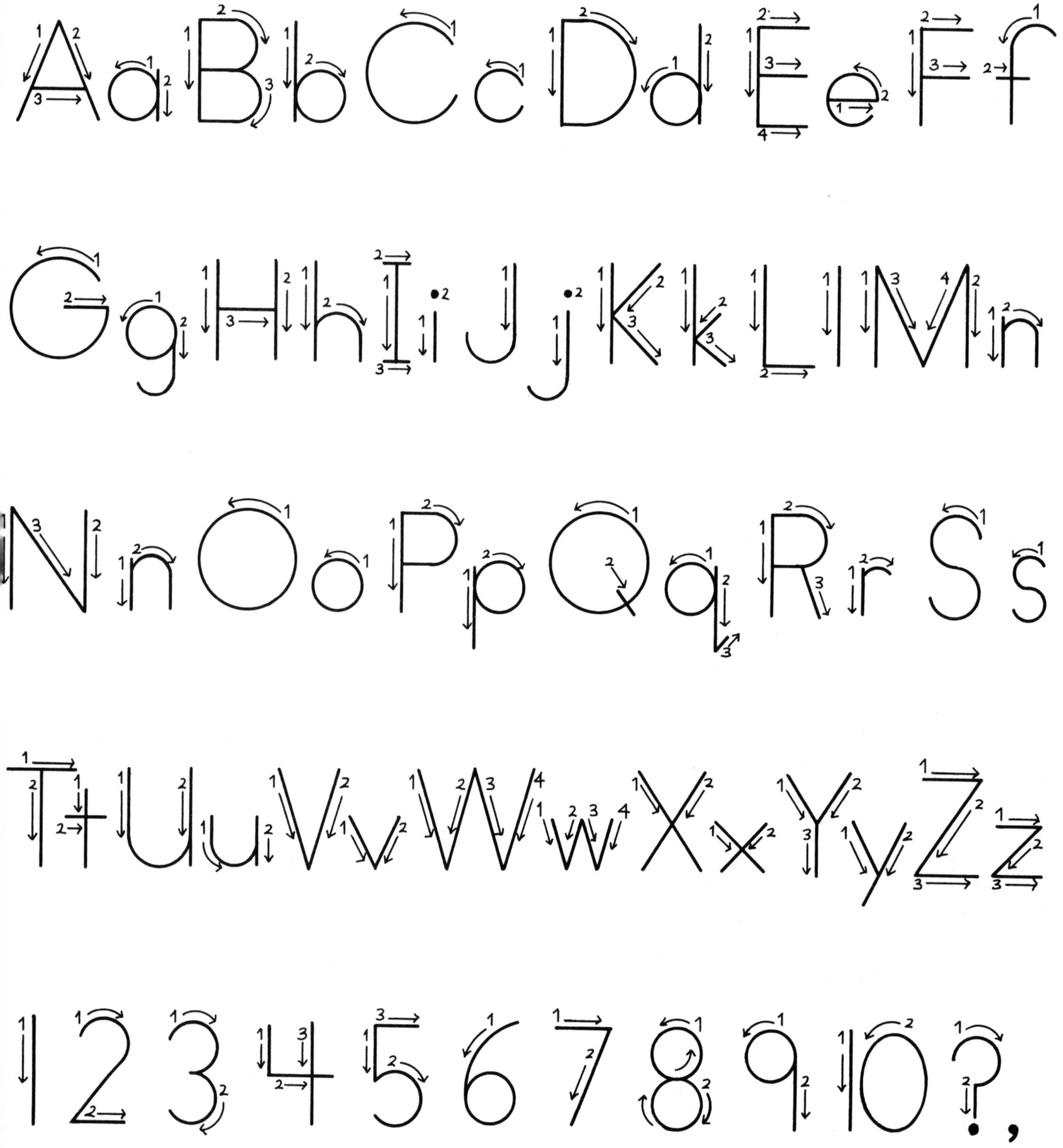

Aa Bb Cc Dd Ee

Ff Gg Hh Ii

Jj Kk Ll Mm

Nn Oo Pp Qq

Rr Ss Tt Uu Vv

Ww Xx Yy Zz

AGES AND STAGES OF DEVELOPMENT

Knowing what to expect of a child may often be helpful to the volunteer who deals with him. We have compiled our experiences with those of others (Dodson, Gesell, Ilg, and Ames) in order to briefly describe how the "average" child behaves between ages five and eight.

A child will not, of course, magically change his behavior on his birthday. The following ages and descriptions need to be viewed as flexible. They are useful if seen within the framework of individual differences.

The Five Year Old:
- enjoys learning.
- is in a happy state of equilibrium.
- does not like to be teased.
- depends strongly on his parents.
- prefers conformity and is eager to please.

The Six Year Old:
- is very active and energetic.
- exhibits extremes in his personality; in one moment, love and joy can turn to hate and tears.
- wants to be the center of attention.
- enjoys showing-off, exaggerates and tells jokes.
- has his first experiences with teasing and name calling.

- may have some fears, especially at night.
- tends to blame others for his behavior.
- breaks from his dependency on his parents by acting rebellious (he may respond in anger to even pleasant suggestions).
- finds his peers to be very important.
- may experience emotional pressures from competition.
- likes to start new projects and rarely completes them.
- finds rigid game rules difficult to accept.

The Seven Year Old:
- has days of high performance as well as days with gigantic learning gaps.
- appreciates limits on his behavior and accepts them well.
- experiences a dramatic increase in his intellectual ability — this often leads to his demanding too much of himself.
- likes adult approval and is pleasant in adult and family situations.
- likes to be alone but sometimes feels excluded or sorry for himself.
- withdraws and becomes more pensive while still enjoying periods of loud, active play.
- may feel that others cheat, while he alone is honest.

- feels that others "pick on him" — he is becoming sensitive to the feelings of others.
- prefers the neatness of a pencil to other art materials.
- enjoys finishing a task.

The Eight Year Old:
- is enthusiastic.
- is dramatic and tends to exaggerate.
- may overestimate his own ability; tackle tasks that are too difficult, and become frustrated.
- does not follow a project through to completion.
- may feel he is a failure and be critical of himself.
- may need encouragement to reschedule frustrating attempts.
- is concerned about what others think and do.
- often develops a close relationship with another child.
- likes to form clubs and to keep secrets.
- enjoys building collections and trading them with friends.

MANUAL DE VOLUNTARIO
LISTA DEL CONTENIDO

PASO POR PASO – DÍA POR DÍA:

1. Siempre lleve su insignia de identificación.
2. Venga a tiempo — su maestro y los niños dependen de usted.
3. Al llegar a su lugar de trabajo, firma su hoja de trabajo.
4. Vístase apropiadamente para las faenas que usted hará en la clase; usted servirá como un buen ejemplo para los niños.
5. Venga a la escuela con actitud positiva, listo para ser un miemro productivo de la clase — como el que aprende usted mismo, y también como el que ayuda en todo.
6. Tenga cuidado de no entrar en conversaciones privadas con su maestro, otros ayudantes, o los niños durante las horas de clase. Queremos bien, como usted, no desbaratar el ambiente de enseñar en la clase.
7. Cualquier accidente, no importa la gravedad, tiene que ser anunciado al maestro.
8. Usted puede a su gusto discutir cualquier problema con su maestro, el director de los voluntarios, o el supervisor del programa.
9. Venga al salón social — usted está bienvenido a disfrutar del ambiente relajador.
10. Si por acaso usted está en la escuela durante la hora de almuerzo se puede almorzar en la cafeteria (en el comedor de los maestros). El precio del almuerzo de los adultos es_____.
    Las listas de comida están fijadas en las salas de clase y aparecen todos los domingos en el periodico.
11. Cuando no se puede venir, o por estar enfermo, o por otra necisidad personal, llame a la oficina a tiempo para que su maestro sepa y pueda arreglar los planes del día. El teléfono de la escuela es_____.
12. Repase las otras partes importantes de este manual y familiarícese con ellas. Su objeto es de ayudarle a hacerse el mejor ayudante de clase posible.

EL MAESTRO PARTICULAR ÉTICO:

1. Los Ayudantes de las aulas llegan a ser una parte de los maestros de esta escuela y tienen que guardar la misma etica profesional como observan los maestros certificados.
2. Sugestiones o críticas de costumbres o programas de la escuela deben presentarse a la jefatura apropiada.
3. Si un padre o una madre pregunte algo sobre su hija o el hijo de otros padres, dígales que hablen con el maestro de su hijo. Nunca diga nada positivo o negative acerca de un niño a sus padres ni a los padres de otro niño.
4. Sea discreto en una manera tan profesional como posible.
5. Todos los informes que se encuentran en las tarjetas de emergencia o en los papeles que usted ve son informes que no se deben discutir fuera de la escuela.
6. Los maestros pueden discutir los éxitos de los niños y las necesidades para mejorar el programa de enseñanza. Algunas veces usted mismo tomará parte en estas discusiones o usted oirá tales discusiones que deben ser consideradas confidenciales.

GOBIERNO EN LA AULA HECHO FÁCIL:

1. No siga en conversaciones particulares en la aula con otros ayudantes, niños, o el maestro.
2. Hable primero con el maestro si usted cree que es necesario castigar a un niño. Sea seguro que el maestro quiere que usted lo castigue y que el maestro apruebe el método que usted quiere usar.
3. Si hay un problema de disciplina, no siga con la lección. Termine cada lección con una idea positiva si es posible y trabaje con el niño otra vez más tarde.
4. Cuando haga un error, admítalo, y pida perdón. Así los niños pueden seguirle como modelo.
5. Aquí tiene usted unas sugestiones que pueden servir como gran ayuda en la aula.
   a. Siéntese o esté de pie cerca de un sitio en donde se pueda iniciar un problema.
   b. Supervise la actividad independiente y los centros de aprender.
   c. Supervise al grupo mientras que el maestro salga de la aula con un niño para hablar con el niño.
   d. Supervise a los niños trabajando en sus asientos y ayúdelos cuando lo necesiten.
   e. Trabaje con pequeños grupos de niños para que el maestro tenga un grupo más pequeño con que trabajar.

MAESTRO PARTICULAR Y NIÑO JUNTOS:

1. Como maestro particular, su primera tarea es de tratar de guiar al niño hasta que éste salga con éxito. Prohiba, cuando posible, que el nino fracase en su trabajo. Con éxito, es más probable que el niño prestará atención y será más dispuesto para probar experiencias nuevas.
2. El maestro es responsable de escoger los métodos y las técnicas para enseñar a los niños. Usted puede ayudar al maestro – siendo una extensión de su influencia. El maestro hace la decisión final, pero usted puede, con su aprobación, ofrecer y planear otras actividades.
3. Acepte a sus alumnos; evite que usted sea criticón; no use palabras como: perezoso, atrasado, estúpido, torpe.
4. Por favor nunca chismee acerca de sus alumnos, al aceptar el papel de ayudante trabajando muy cerca con unos alumnos que tiene problemas en la escuela, usted se hace uno que trabaja muy íntimamente con los problemas y por eso un ayudante con privilegio.
5. Guarde una actitud de buen humor. Sea entusiástico.
6. Sea positivo con los alumnos. Su elogio puede ayudar a aumentar la confianza del alumno y así el alumno tendrá buena gana de tratar.

7. Pase mucho tiempo con los niños preguntando, eschuchando, y ayudándolos a pensar por sí mismos. Evite que sean los que se retiren del programa que sueñen despiertos durante las lecciones.
8. Tenga paciencia. El repaso es una parte tan importante en el proceso de aprender.
9. Evite poner al niño en un estado humillante o vergonzoso porque esto puede hacer daño a la idea que tiene el niño de su propio valor.
10. Antes de disciplinar al niño, consulte con el maestro para estar seguro de los procedimientos y la técnica.

LOS NIÑOS PUEDEN APRENDER MÁS CON SU AYUDA:

1. Haga un programa breve con su maestro sobre las cosas que el maestro quiere que usted haga. También sepa bien los objetivos y la filosofía de la aula en donde usted está ayudando.
2. Aprenda los nombres de sus alumnos tan pronto como posible.
3. Sea, entusiástico cuando trabaja con los alumnos! Excítelos con la idea de aprender!
4. Sea amigable con los alumnos, pero mantenga el propio grado de dignidad.
5. Sea positivo con los niños. Reconcéntrese en lo que los niños hagan bien, tan pequeño que sea y deles de buena gana el elogio específico cuando lo merezcan.
6. Siga instrucciones; pero no tenga miedo de preguntar a su maestro de repetir o clarificar su tarea.
7. Use su propia iniciativa en la aula. No espere los órdenes de su maestro. Empiece a saber usted mismo las tareas que se deben hacer o cuales son los alumnus que necesitan ayuda.
8. Dése cuenta que su maestro dirigiente es humano y tendrá sus buenos días como los malos días. Ayude tanto como pueda para que el programa funcione con menos problemas.
9. Mantenga el interés de los ninos con cambios, con ser entusiástico, variando sus ideas, teniendo cortos los períodos de estudio.
10. Ayude a su maestro a imponer las reglas de la aula. La autoridad por el procedimiento del la aula queda con su maestro de supervisor. Su tarea es de ayudar a llevar a cabo aquellas reglas. Tenga paceincia.
11. Trate de anticipar las situaciones de problemas en la aula y trate de evitarlos sin comenzar.
12. Al hacer cualquier trabajo escrito use el manuscrito apropiado o forma cursiva (observe los ejemplos en el manual en las dos páginas próximas).

EDADES Y ETAPAS DE DESARROLLO

Saber lo que se puede esperar de uno niño puede ayudar muchas veces al voluntario que trata con el niño. Hemos compilado nuestras experiencias con las de otros: Dodson, Gesell, Ilg, and Ames... para describirles brevemente como el "mediano" niño se comporta entre la edad de cinco años hasta ocho años.

Por supuesto, un niño no va a cambriar su conducta mágicamente el día de su cumpleaños. Las siguientes edades y descripciones necesitan ser consideradas flexibles y son útiles, vistas dentro del esqueleto de las diferencias de los individuous.

EL NIÑO DE CINCO ĀNOS
- se goza en apprender
- está en un feliz estado de equilibrio
- al niño no le gusta ser embromado
- depende mucho de sus padres
- prefiere la conformidad y está muy deseoso de dar placer a la gente

EL NIÑO DE SEIS ĀNOS
- es muy activo y enérgico
- exhibe extremos en su personalidad — el amor y la felicidad
pueden cambiarse y hacerse el
odio y las lágrimas
- quire ser el centro de la atención
- se goza en fachendear, exagera, y cuenta chistes
- tiene sus primeras experiencias con embromar y maltratar a uno de palabra
- puede tener unos miedos sobre todo de noche
- prefiere dar a otros la culpa por su conducta; se escapa de su dependencia de sus padres por conducirse rebeldemente (puede contestar con cólera a unas sugestiones agradables) considera a sus amigos de su edad muy importantes puede experimentar las presiones emocionales de la competencia le gusta comenzar nuevos proyectos y rara vez los lleva a cabo halla las reglas rígidas de juego difíciles a aceptar.

EL NIÑO DE SIETE ĀNOS:
- tiene dias de mucho éxito tanto como tiene días de gran falta de aprender
- comprende los limites a su conducta y los acepta de buena gana
- experimenta un aumento dramático en su capacidad intelectual — esto lo lleva a exigir demasiado de sus esfuerzas
- le gusta la aprobación de los adultos y él es agradable en situaciones de familia y de adultos
- le gusta estar solo pero a veces se siente excluido o se compadece a él mismo
- se retira y se pone más pensativo mientras que todavia se goza en periodos de juego activo y ruidoso
- puede pensar que otros defraudan; pero él solo es honesto
- piensa que los otros lo molestan, lo regañan — se pone muy sensible a las opiniones de otros
- previere la usanza de un lápiz a los materiales de arte se goza en cumplir con una tarea

EL NINO DE OCHO ĀNOS

- es entusiástico
- es dramático y se tiende a exagerar
- puede estimar más grande su capacidad, tratar tareas que sean demasiado difíciles, y puede ser frustrado
- no sigue un proyecto hasta terminarlo
- puede pensar que él es un fracaso un perdicón
- puede ser muy crítico de sí mismo
- puede necesitar ánimo para volver a proyectar sus tentativas tan difíciles
- se interesa en lo que los otros hacen y piensan
- muchas veces se crece una amistad con otro niño
- le gusta formar un club de socios y guardar secretos
- se goza en establecer colecciones y cambiarlas con amigos

50

志願者之手冊

目錄

一步接一步,一日復一日:

1. 時刻掛着你的身份名牌.
2. 準時 —— 你的教師與小孩們依賴着你.
3. 一但到達你的工作地點,請簽到.
4. 衣着適合於你在教室裡的工作,你是以身作則.
5. 抱着積極的態度來學校,準備做個有作為者----不管是學習者本身或者是教育者的助手.
6. 當在教室裡,小心不要與你的老師,其他助手或小孩們閒談私事.我們如同你一樣的關心課堂上的干擾而影响到教學的氣氛.
7. 任何意外發生,不管都做小的事,都應該報告給教師.
8. 有任何困難時,請不必介意的與你的教師,志願者的負責人或學校經辦人商討.
9. 請來休息室 —— 歡迎你來享受這愉快輕鬆的氣氛.
10. 當午餐時間,假如你應該在學校的話,歡迎你在自助餐廳用午餐(老師的餐廳).成人的餐費是#_____.菜單貼在教室,並且公告在每週星期日的報紙上.
11. 當你在生病或因私人事故而不能來學校時,請早一點打電話通知你的老師,因此他們能調整那天的計劃.學校的電話號碼是 _____.
12. 復習這本手冊的其他重要部份與充份的了解它.他們的目的是去幫忙你成為一個最優秀的教室助理者.

私人導師的倫理德性：

1. 課堂上的助理者成為教職員的一部份,是被期望着像拿執照的教師一樣的去遵守職業上的倫理道德.

2. 建議或評論學校的實施政策或課程節目,應該被通當的呈上上級.

3. 當家長問到有關他們自己的小孩或他人小孩時,請轉告他們去找小孩的老師.絕對不可正面或反面的去告訴小孩的父母或他人的父母.

4. 盡可能小心言行,絕不可在公共場合評論家長或教職員.

5. 不可在外談論任何你所在急救卡上或報告上所見的事情.

6. 教職員也許討論到小孩們的成就問題,或需要在教學課程上改進的地方,這些你也許是當事人之一,或是測面聽到的討論.都應該保持秘密.

課堂管制門徑：

1. 不要在課堂上與其他的助手，小孩或老師談論私事。

2. 假如你感覺需要去教訓一位小孩時，請與教師商談。必須確定這位教師要你去教訓或讚成你所要用的方法。

3. 假如因管訓問題而中止上課時，在中止的課業上做個記號，可能的話，在下堂課繼續教下去。

4. 隨時準備承認自己的錯誤，甚至道歉，做個好的榜樣給小孩跟從。

5. 下列方法，將對你在課堂上有特別幫助：
   a. 站近或坐近將有糾紛發生的地點。
   b. 監督獨立活動與學習中心。
   c. 當教師把一位小孩單獨叫出去與他談話時，監督這些小孩。
   d. 監督小孩在自己的尖位上工作，並在他需要時幫忙。
   e. 與小組的小孩一起工作，這樣教師才能和另外更小組的小孩一起工作。

師生之相處:

1. 做一個個別教師,你的主要工作是引導小孩獲取成功的經驗,可能的話,防止他(她)們避免任何的失敗。一但成功,他(她)們更會專心而願意嘗試新的學習經驗。

2. 老師要負責去選擇教學的方法與技巧。你可以幫助老師──延伸他(她)的影响力。老師有決定一切之權,但你可以經過他/她的同意後計劃補充一些活動。

3. 接受你的學生們,避免過份的批評或裁判性的名詞,如懶惰,笨瓜,愚笨,怠慢等字。

4. 請不要講學生們的閒話,做為一個助理工作的角色,而與那些在學校中有困難的學生們接近,則你成為一個有特權的圈內人,不要對你的學生濫用職權。

5. 保持幽默感,並須熱誠。

6. 對小孩要積極,你的嘉獎能幫助他們建立信心,而志願去嘗試。

7. 多化些時間在小孩們上,詢問或傾聽問題,幫助他們作自己的思想。避免成為"心理上的退學者"在上課中做白日夢。

8. 要有耐心,復習仍是學習中必要的部份之一

9. 避免在公眾中侮辱或耻笑學生,這樣會損傷他們的自尊心。

10. 經常與老師商談訓導之方法與技巧是否恰當。

因你的關係,他們也許能學習得更多:

1. 關於那些他們所希望你去做的事,你要與你的老師策劃出一個簡明的計劃,同時你要瞭解幫助課堂的目的與哲理。

2. 盡快的去記住你的學生的姓名。

3. 當與學生共同工作時,必需抱着熱誠,刺激他們學習的精神。

4. 對學生們要友善,但仍需保持適當的單嚴。

5. 對小孩們要積極,集中在那些他們所能做得好的事情上,不論是多小的事,值得嘉獎則嘉獎。

6. 跟從指示,但不要怕詢問你的老師重複一遍或指明你的工作。

7. 要有自文自發的精神,不要等待老師的命令。開始去了解你自己的工作或是那些需要你去幫忙的學生。

8. 切記你的監督老師也是人,他也有好與壞的日子。盡可能作一個好幫手,使課堂上進展得順利。

9. 改變步驟,抱着熱誠,變換方針,保持學習期的簡潔,等,來保持學生們的興趣。

10. 幫助你的老師來實施教室規則。課堂程序之大權仍操在你的監督老師身上。你的工作是來幫忙實行這些程序。要有耐心。

11. 在教室中要有期待困難的情況,而且要文刻加以"解決"它。

12. 當在做任何寫作的工作時,需用正確的正檔或用草檔。(參看下二頁手冊內之例題)。

年齡與發育階段：

　　知道怎樣去期望一個小孩,對這些與小孩相處的志願者是有莫大的幫助。我們與那些其他人（固森,蓋賽,埃格妖更美）的經驗,亦編輯出簡單的形容一般五歲至八歲小孩的行為。

　　當然一個小孩不會在他的生日時,突然,像魔術般的改變他的行為。這下面的年齡與形容,必須要有個伸縮性。或且很有用處,假如能在個人的差異範圍之內來衡量的話。

五歲的年齡：

　　喜歡學習。
　　是在快樂的平衡狀態中。
　　不喜歡被嘲弄。
　　非常的依賴父母。
　　喜歡一致和熱衷於快樂。

六歲的年齡：

　　非常活潑與精神充沛。
　　表現個性上的極端,在一瞬間,
　　　　愛與歡樂可能轉為恨與嘲弄。
　　要人家完全注意他。
　　喜歡誇耀,誇大和愛開玩笑。
　　第一次得到嘲弄的經驗與名字的叫喚。

六歲的年齡（繼續）

可能有一些害怕，特別是在晚上。

對他的行為常會責備他人。

脫離他依賴父母的傾向，而表現出反抗（甚至於一個愉快的建議都會觸怒。）

發現他的同伴是很重要的。

從競爭上，可能經歷到情緒上的壓力。

喜歡開始新的工作，但很少去完成它。

發覺很難接受嚴格的遊戲規則。

七歲的年齡：

有時能表現高度的效能，但有時亦表現出很大的學習阻礙，毫無恆心。

認識自己行為的限制，並會好好的接受。

經歷到自己智力之突飛猛進──這常常引起他對自己要求太多。

喜歡成人的讚同，並樂於介乎大人們與家庭中。

喜歡單獨，但有時感覺被排除或覺得憂傷。

退卻而更為憂悶，但仍然很愉快的享受高度的遊戲活動。

可能感覺其他人在欺騙，而他自己一個人是很誠實。

感覺別人"挑逗他" —— 他對別人的感覺更為很敏感.

對鉛筆西的藝術材料.喜歡保持整潔.

喜歡完成一件工作.

八歲的年齡:

是很熱誠.

是帶戲劇性而傾向於誇張

對他自己的能力可能會估計過高,負擔過份困難的工作而挫折.

不將一件工作從頭做到尾.

會覺得自己是一個失敗者而批評自己.

需要鼓勵來消除挫折之感.

精神集中在別人所想與所做的事.

常與另外的小孩發展成親切的關係.

喜歡收集東西.而與其他朋友交換.

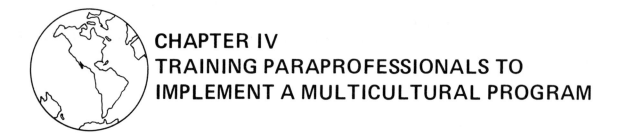

CHAPTER IV
TRAINING PARAPROFESSIONALS TO
IMPLEMENT A MULTICULTURAL PROGRAM

Once the physical setting is established, the teachers have planned the curriculum, and the volunteers have been recruited, your volunteer training sessions may begin. Since the volunteers will be implementing the program which has been planned by the teachers, it is imperative that good communication is maintained and that training sessions be carefully planned.

We have found that if we spend sufficient training time during the first culture of the year, we are able to send written lesson plans for successive cultures to each volunteer and they are then able to attempt the lesson at home as preparation for their classroom presentation.

In these later lesson plan packets, we also include packages of supplies which may not normally be available in their homes: i.e., rye flour, masa harina, popsicle sticks, powdered tempera...

In your general training session, it is imperative that you discuss all of the following items:

1. The objectives and goals of the multicultural program.
2. Developing awareness and attitudes.
3. How children learn.
4. Methods utilized in presenting art activities.
5. Methods utilized in presenting cooking activities.
6. Methods utilized in presenting recreation experiences.
7. Specific plans for the initial cultural experience.

OBJECTIVES
AND GOALS

It is important to make the volunteers aware of the teaching objectives and goals of the multicultural program. This helps them to better understand the importance of proper preparation and presentation. We have isolated several important objectives. As you individualize your program, you may identify additional goals.

In these times of emerging ethnic pride, many laws have been passed to help minorities; however, correcting prejudices is not just an intellectual pursuit. It is largely a matter of the heart — involving attitudes and perceptions.

It is imperative that children develop good feelings about themselves and others. Ethnicity should be a source of pride, not of disparagement. It is necessary to strengthen the children's appreciation of individual differences. This enables them to value differences rather than view them as something to make fun of, as children frequently do.

A major goal in promoting multicultural awareness is to infuse the entire school with a feeling of brotherhood.

DEVELOPING
AWARENESS
AND ATTITUDES

A goal of the program is to expose the children to the similarities and differences of many cultures. While the children are involved in these activities, it is a perfect opportunity to talk about attitudes. It is important that the volunteers be made aware that things that are said can have a positive or negative impact on feelings of acceptance.

Extreme generalizations about a culture should be avoided at all cost. Statements such as, "All people with green hair are lazy," have no place in a multicultural program. Furthermore, each culture supplies diverse experiences; and it becomes the responsibility of the volunteer not to limit this diversity.

Since it is impossible to capture this diversity entirely, we have limited our discussion to three areas of each culture which lend themselves best to the practicalities of the school and classroom situation. We realize that these alone cannot totally capture the cultural wealth of any group of people.

Your room environment may include pictures or exhibits of traditional costumes of a culture. When children are viewing these exhibits, it provides opportunity for them to discuss the differences between traditional and modern dress. The volunteer should mention that, throughout the world today, many people dress in a similar manner.

The cooking experience provides a perfect opportunity to discuss the similarities among cultures. For example, when cooking Mexican Tortillas, or Indian Pekee Bread, the volunteer should tell the children about similar breads of other cultures, for example Chinese Mandarin Pancakes, Norwegian Lefse, and Ethiopian Injera Flat Bread. In Chapter V you will find a chart which will assist you in drawing parallels from the cultural activities that are provided in this book.

HOW CHILDREN
LEARN

A brief discussion of the various ways a child learns will be helpful to the volunteer. An effective volunteer realizes that children mature at different rates. A child may experience success in many areas of learning and still be unsuccessful in some specific areas.

It enhances the volunteer's techniques if he is aware that learning occurs through auditory, visual, and tactile channels and that some children rely more on one mode than another.

The volunteer needs to know how to deal with a child's frustration, if it occurs. Some possible ways to facilitate the handling of frustration are: modify the activity to match the ability of the child, allow the child to complete the activity to his satisfaction rather than to meet adult standards, give the child the opportunity to discontinue the activity, or use a variety of assisting techniques where the volunteer becomes the helpful assistant.

In all activities, the volunteer should be encouraged to specifically praise the child's efforts rather than the final product. For example, rather than saying, "That's a pretty picture," a volunteer might comment, "Your pink sun really makes the sky look happy," or "The colors that you've chosen give your picture a warm feeling."

METHODS
UTILIZED IN
PRESENTING
ART ACTIVITIES

The teaching of elementary art techniques does not require that the volunteer be an artist. It is primarily a matter of guidance and encouragement at this level. Artistic freedom of expression may be a means to several goals: a feeling of self-confidence, an avenue of self-expression, a better understanding of the world.

Children are perceptive. Be certain that you show concern and equal appreciation for all members of the group.

Some children need a longer period of time before beginning the creative process. They need some degree of privacy without adult intervention. However, there will be occasions when the volunteer will need to give sympathetic assistance to the slow starter. In giving this assistance, be certain that the child still does his own work.

The volunteer should be cautioned never to allow freedom of expression to lead to the dismissal of good work habits. Certain standards should be followed in the use of materials and in the work area. Proper labeling (as discussed in Chapter II) can alleviate many clean-up problems.

HANDOUT: HOW TO PRESENT ART EXPERIENCES

The volunteer need not be an artist.

The volunteer will give guidance and encouragement.

Give suggestions only when requested. A child will take more pride in his *own* work.

If you appreciate one artist's attempts, find a way to express individual appreciation to all artists.

Neatness is important. An uncluttered work area is less confusing for all.

COMUNICADO: COMO PRESENTAR LAS EXPERIENCIAS DE ARTE

El voluntario no necesita ser artista

El voluntario dará dirección y ánimo

Dé sugestiones solamente cuando el niño se las pida. Un niño llevará más orgullo con su *propio* trabajo.

Si usted aprueba los esfuerzos de un artista, trate de hallar una manera de expresar la aprobación individua a todos los artistas.

La limpieza general y el órden son muy importantes. Un sitio de trabajo sin desorden da menos confusión para todos.

講義：如何提供藝術的經驗

志願者不必是一個藝術家。

志願者將給於指導及鼓勵。

請求時才給建議。一個小孩因自己做的工作而更會感到自豪。

假如你能欣賞一個藝術家的嘗試，也同樣的表達個人的欣賞方法而
　　推及到所有的藝術家上。

一個不混亂的地方，才能使大家工作得好，故整潔是非常重要的。

METHODS UTILIZED IN PRESENTING COOKING ACTIVITIES

The cooking experience provides the best opportunity to clarify the similarities and differences of peoples. Many similar foods are eaten throughout the world. Most children are familiar with a burrito and the volunteer may tell them that the Chinese, Ethiopians, and Norwegians roll their flat breads, in a similar way, with other foodstuffs inside.

In our experience, we have found that the students are very anxious to cook and eat the product of their efforts. Our concern that they might not enjoy the taste of some of the recipes was needless. However, if the child does his own cooking, he is generally interested in sampling the results.

Not only is cooking an enjoyable activity for the student; it provides a multitude of learning experiences. Reading, math, and science skills are strengthened during cooking activities.

The recipe should be displayed in rhebus form so that each individual (in grades K-3) can have the feeling of reading it for themselves. The volunteer helps to build the child's vocabulary with each new recipe. Here is a sample recipe in rhebus form.

Cooking may supplement math learnings by providing informal measuring experiences. The volunteers should have the children go to the food supply center in pairs so that the children may help each other count while measuring. This helps to insure proper measurement and a successful end product.

Cooking becomes both an art and a science. During the cooking experience, children become aware of certain scientific principles. This occurs when they observe changes in texture while they are mixing and cooking various ingredients. Health and nutrition may also be discussed while cooking.

Careful organization of the cooking center portion of your multicultural center will facilitate successful cooking experiences.

COOKING RULES

1. Mixing should be done while you are seated at the table.
2. Two children at a time may use these centers:
   Food Supply Center
   Cooking Center
   Hand Washing Center
   Dish Washing Center
3. Avoid moving quickly. Look around before moving.
4. Partners help each other.

LAS REGLAS DE COCINAR

1. El amasar debe hacerse cuando está sentado a la mesa.
2. Dos niños juntos pueden usar estos centros:
     El centro de provisiones de alimento
     El centro de cocinar
     El centro de lavar las manos
     El centro de lavar la vajilla
3. Evite moverse rápidamente. Mire por todas partes antes de moverse.
4. Los socios se ayudan el uno al otro.

烹飪規則

1. 應該在自己的坐位上攪拌好東西。

2. 一次祇能有二位小孩使用下列的中心：
   食品供應中心
   烹調中心
   洗手中心
   洗碗中心

3. 避免移動太快，環顧四周後才移動。

4. 同伴中互相幫助。

Four clearly-labeled, distinct centers should be maintained for food supply, cooking, hand washing, and dishwashing. The food supply center should be located on an easily accessible, low table, large enough to accomodate all the ingredients to be measured. The cooking center must be located near an electrical outlet and should be isolated to avoid accidents while the children are near the heat source. Two similar centers are needed for hand and dish washing. Three pans need to be prepared for each

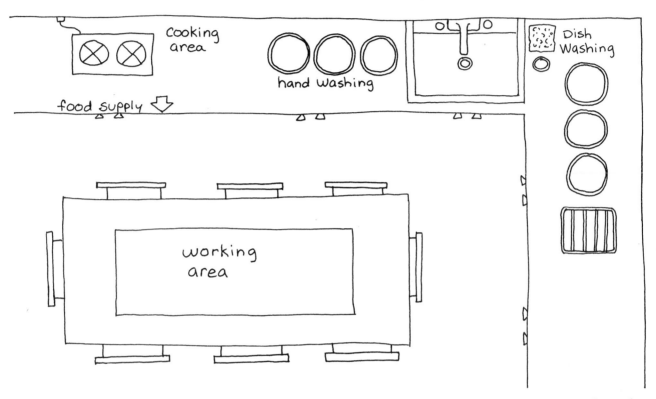

center. We have used three-pound coffee cans for washing purposes. They are free and store easily, and placing the plastic lid on the bottom of each coffee can prevents rusting. Proper disinfecting techniques are important especially when hot water is not available to your center. The three pan method for hand and dish washing may be organized in the following manner:

Pan No. 1: Water + Dish Washing Detergent

Pan No. 2: Water + 1/3 Cup Bleach

Pan No. 3: Water. Paper towels are used for hand drying and a drainer is used for dishes.

HANDOUT: HOW TO PRESENT COOKING EXPERIENCES

Cooking is both an art and a science.
A cook enjoys sampling his own achievement.
Rhebus Recipes make reading easy:

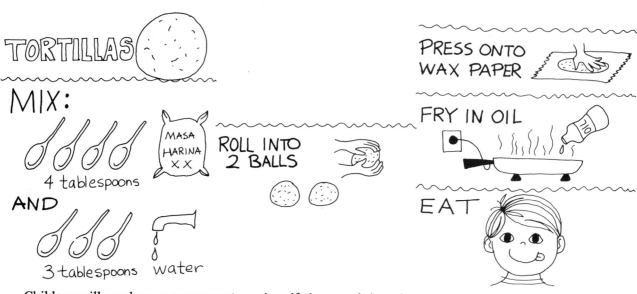

Children will produce more accurate recipes if they work in pairs.
Cleanliness is very important for both hands and dishes.

The three pan method for washing is:

Pan No. 1: Water + dish washing detergent
Pan No. 2: Water + 1/3 cup bleach
Pan No. 3: Water + drainer or paper towels

COMUNICADO: COMO PRESENTAR EXPERIENCIAS DE COCINAR

La cocina es tanto arte como ciencia

Un cocinero se goza en probar su propia realización

Las recetas de Rhebus facilitan la lectura

Los ninos produciran recetas mas exactas si trabajan en parejas

La limpieza es muy importante tanto a las manos como a la vajilla

El método para lavar las tres cazuelas es lo siguiente:

  cazuela no. 1: agua y detergente de lavar.

  cazuela no. 2: agua y una taza con una tercera parte de blanqueo.

  cazuela no. 3: agua y desaguadero o toallas de papel.

講義：如何提供烹飪經驗

烹飪是一種藝術，也是一種科學。
一個廚師享受於品嚐他所做的好菜
利玻斯 (Rhebus) 食譜易於了解

學生們如能兩人一組工作的話，則更能準確的做出食譜上的食品。
清潔手與碟子仍是重要的。
三盆式的洗碗法：
　　　第一盆： 水加洗碗用肥皂水
　　　第二盆： 水加 1/3 杯漂白劑
　　　第三盆： 水加過濾劑或毛巾紙

STANDARD MEASURES

METRIC MEASURES

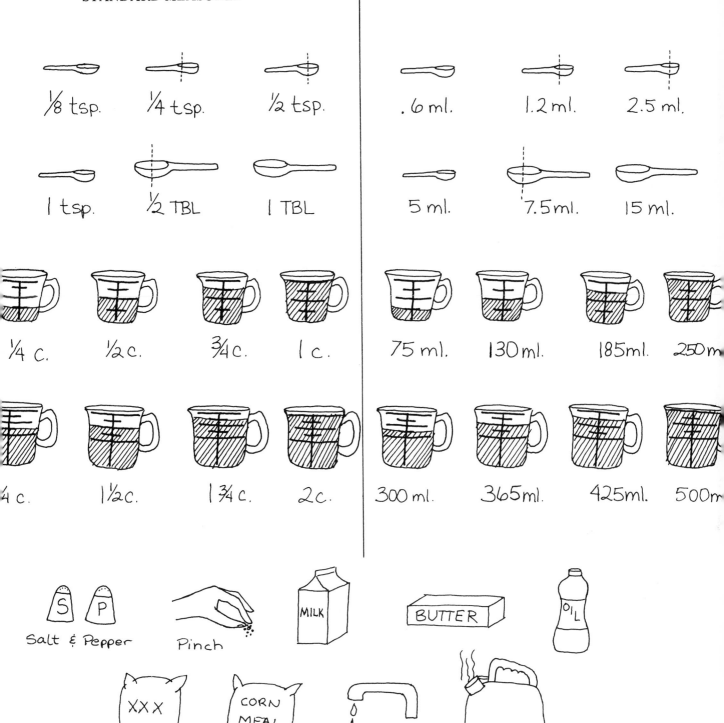

⅛ tsp.   ¼ tsp.   ½ tsp.

.6 ml.   1.2 ml.   2.5 ml.

1 tsp.   ½ TBL   1 TBL

5 ml.   7.5 ml.   15 ml.

¼ c.   ½ c.   ¾ c.   1 c.

75 ml.   130 ml.   185 ml.   250 m

4 c.   1½ c.   1¾ c.   2 c.

300 ml.   365 ml.   425 ml.   500 m

Salt & Pepper   Pinch   MILK   BUTTER   OIL

Flour   CORN MEAL   WATER   HOT WATER

IDEAS FOR RHEBUS RECIPES

METHODS UTILIZED IN PRESENTING RECREATION EXPERIENCES

Work and play are often viewed by adults as dichotomous entities. For children, however, play is a form of learning. Throughout history, many peoples have viewed gaming as experiences in learning skills and as strategies necessary for their existence. There are innumerable opportunities for the development of cultural awareness during the learning of games. Children will frequently find that a game from a different culture is similar to a game played in their own neighborhood.

Games relate to real life situations, while offering a variety of skills experiences. Chance and competition further enhance the attractiveness of games to the child. The volunteer should use games to emphasize all three: the fun, instruction, and competitions involved in the study of a culture. It is important to be moderate, however, with elements of chance and competitive style. It should be the responsibility of the volunteer to guide the game toward as true a reality of the culture it purports to model.

When presenting recreational experiences, the volunteer might be encouraged to follow a plan of learning every game and attempting it prior to its presentation. The idea of the game should be briefly explained to the children so that they know what is expected of them. It is preferable to demonstrate games and recreational experiences rather than giving only verbal directions.

The volunteer can keep the presentation moving at an interesting pace by planning ahead which games he will use and by arranging for easy transitions between them.

Each volunteer must be reminded that children possess a varying degree of physical coordination. Some children will demonstrate great readiness while others may appear to possess poor coordination skills. Pressuring them to demonstrate skills they don't possess may result in frustration.

Control may be successfully maintained by the volunteer's use of dramatic pauses to gain the full focus of the group. A volunteer who learns to vary his voice level from soft to loud at the appropriate time may find this effective. Keeping the group moving on to new experiences also provides a means to control.

When children are playing games where there is a distinct winner, the volunteer should make an effort to help each child deserve the honor.

A reluctant joiner should be invited in and then, if he still prefers not to participate, he should be allowed to watch nearby. Many young children learn best by watching an experience and duplicating it later in a less-threatening atmosphere. After ignoring the watcher for a brief period, the volunteer may slowly draw him in by offering his hand or verbally including him.

HANDOUT: HOW TO PRESENT RECREATION EXPERIENCES

For Children:
>   Play is a form of learning.

Try to emphasize all three:
>   Skill building
>   Chance and competition (be moderate)
>   Fun of participating

As the adult volunteer, you should:
>   Learn every game before presenting it
>   Explain the idea of the game
>   The children will learn best when you demonstrate
>   Plan how you will move on to the next activity. Plan ahead!

Remember:
>   Every child develops at a different physical rate — be understanding
>   Vary your voice level (a whisper gains control more quickly than a loud voice)
>   Use dramatic verbal pauses to gain attention
>   If one idea fails, move on to the next
>   Help everyone have a chance to win
>   Reluctant joiners often learn by watching others. Give them a chance to watch before inviting
>   them to join.

COMUNICADO: COMO PRESENTAR EXPERIENCIAS DE RECREO

PARA LOS NIÑOS:
El juego es una manera de aprender.
Trate de poner énfasis en todos los tres:
Establecer destrezas
Suerte y competencia (sea moderado con éstas)
El divertimiento de participar
COMO EL VOLUNTARIO ADULTO USTED DEBE:
Aprender cada juego antes de presentarlo
Explicar la idea del juego
Los niños aprenderán mejor cuando usted demuestre el juego
Planee como usted seguirá con la próxima actividad.¡ Planee de antemano!
ACUÉRDESE
Cada niño se desarrolla a un paso diferente físico — sea comprensivo
Varie el nivel de su voz
Use pausas dramáticas en hablar para ganar la atención
Si una idea sale sin éxito, siga con otra
Ayude a todo el mundo para que tenga la oportunidad de ganar.
Los maldispuestos muchas veces aprenden por mirar a los otros.
Déles la oportunidad de mirar antes de invitarlos a ingresar en el juego.

講義：如何提供康樂方面的經驗：

對小孩：

> 遊戲們是一種學習

試試看去加強這三種：

> 技能上的建立
> 机會與競爭（必須溫和的）
> 參加的興趣

做為一個成人的志願者，你必須：

— 在提供前，必須先學會每一種遊戲。

— 解釋遊戲的目的

— 當你示範表演時，小孩子們將學的更好。

— 計劃你如何進展到下一個活動，要預先有計劃！

記住：

— 了解每個小孩的生理發育進展不同。

— 變化你的說話音調。（細語比粗聲更有效果）

— 用戲劇性的措詞來增加注意力。

— 如果一個方法無效，試試另種方法。

— 幫助每一個人都有得勝的机會

— 煩厭的參加者，常因觀賞別人而學習到。在邀請他們前，先給他們觀賞的机會。

SPECIFIC PLANS FOR THE INITIAL CULTURAL EXPERIENCE

To help insure the success of the multicultural center, the three initial cultural experiences should be viewed as a training period for the volunteers.

Regardless of the children's readiness levels, those three initial multicultural experiences in art, cooking, and recreation must be carefully chosen for their simplicity. As the volunteers gain confidence in their ability to present new activities, their presentation techniques will gain sophistication. The teachers and multicultural coordinator may then feel that the children and volunteers are ready for more complicated cultural lessons. For example, it is preferable to introduce the mixing techniques necessary to making tortillas before introducing the creaming of ingredients for Ghana cakes. We also encourage frying in small amounts of grease before attempting deep fat frying.

The importance of providing "hands on" step-by-step experiences for the volunteer as well as for the child cannot be over-emphasized. We have found that a prerequisite to multicultural volunteering must be the volunteer's attendance at the original training session. Then the volunteers have the opportunity to experience how beneficial it is to play the games, cook the food, and create the artistic endeavor prior to actually teaching a lesson concerning that experience.

The aide-trainer will need to reinforce this "do before teaching" attitude and stress that each volunteer will thereafter be able to spend school time helping children. Future aide-training, for subsequent cultures, should then be self-motivated.

CHAPTER V
CLASSROOM CONTINUITY AND
ANNOTATED BIBLIOGRAPHY

CLASSROOM CONTINUITY AND ANNOTATED BIBLIOGRAPHY
INDEX

THE IMPLEMENTATION OF LEARNING

The modern day teacher is responsible for implementing all school learning programs. Effective utilization of aides is an important and sometimes difficult task to initiate and maintain. By effectively using these paraprofessionals as an extension of himself, the teacher can offer more experiences to a greater number of children in the same period of time.

One of the first responsibilities of the teaching team is to establish an effective room environment. The room environment in the Multicultural Center is important for motivational set; however, more enthusiasm is developed if this environment is extended into the regular classroom. Some suggested resouces to enrich the classroom environment are available in Chapter II, under the heading of Donations.

There are many avenues you can pursue in the introduction of multicultural education or when dealing with a specific culture.

In developing the set of lessons, a logical progression would be from self-awareness of the child, in relation to his family, his school, and his community, to the child's global awareness of his and other communities and cultures.

Many techniques may be utilized to supplement the cognitive learning that results from the experiences offered in the Multicultural Center. Visual and auditory presentation techniques might encompass records, tapes, films, filmstrips, folktales, community resource speakers, etc.

Classroom discussions, utilizing the inquiry method, are an effective way to stimulate interest and precipitate the drawing of parallels. Suggestions to aides and drawing of parallels between the cultural experiences offered in this text are presented in chart forms in this chapter. Parallels should be drawn with other cultures whenever possible.

SPECIFIC VOLUNTEER TRAINING

There is a direct and positive correlation between explicit planning and program success. Many problems can be avoided when the lesson plans that are given to the paraprofessionals include consideration of any pitfalls. Effective presentation should be the ultimate goal.

We have included sample presentation plans for three multicultural experiences. Those included on the following pages are:

Mexico — an art experience (Ojo de Dios)

Greece — a cooking experience (Baklava)

Native Americans — Recreation experiences and games

 MULTICULTURAL CENTER LESSON - MEXICAN ART - OJO DE DIOS

I.   Background Information

The custom of making an Ojo de Dios is believed to have begun among the Indians of Jalisco and Nayarit. It was made by the father of an infant to bring a long and healthy life to the child. When the child was born, the father wove the center eye. An additional eye was added on each birthday until the child's fifth birthday.

Ojo de Dios seems to be a universal symbol. The all-seeing eye, with some nuance of meaning, is a recurrent theme around the world. Amazingly similar variations are found among the Aborigines of Australia, in homes in Africa, Egypt, Ireland, Native North Americans, Scandinavia, Tibet as well as Mexico.

Today, Ojos de Dios are made in many designs and shapes. They can be seen hung on walls, in windows or as mobiles; worn as a hair ornament and other types of jewelry; or carried as a good luck charm, if sufficiently small.

II.   Preparation to be done by volunteers:
   A.   All supplies for this lesson will be pre-arranged on the tables. Note this arrangment with the children so the room may be easily cleaned at the end of the lesson. Supplies include: Scissors, Yarn, Popsicle Sticks and Nametags.
   B.   In free time, do some of step No. C-1 ahead of time to use with children who do not manipulate well and find this step too frustrating.
   C.   Familiarize yourself with volunteers information card about Ojo de Dios.

III.   Direct children in this order:
   A.   Discuss routine and clean-up. Draw their attention to where items are stored.
   B.   Children should work in pairs.
   C.   Review together the bulletin board of step-by-step directions.
      1.   Cross two popsicle sticks in middle, tie with yarn to keep sticks spread apart.
      2.   Weave yarn over one leg then under and around same leg. Go to next leg and weave same way.
      3.   Knot different colors together and continue weaving.
      4.   Place your nametag on string and tie the end.
   D.   Have each child begin to make his Ojo de Dios. Watch each step carefully before each goes on to the next step.
   E.   Some children may need help with step number one but that is the only step that you should do completely for them and then only if necessary.
   F.   Encourage children to try other Ojos de Dios at home.
   G.   As completed, display by pinning on blue hanging cloth in middle of room.
   H.   Floor and room should be cleaned before children return to rooms. Those finished first may help others and/or return to room early.

 MULTICULTURAL CENTER LESSON - GREEK COOKING - BAKLAVA

I. Background Information
    Ancient Greeks are thought to have begun the art of cooking nearly 3,000 years ago. A Greek, Archestratus, wrote the first cook book more than 2,000 years ago and Greek cooking has influenced many cuisines.

    Greek cooking is generally simple. A complete meal may be made from quickly cooked vegetables served with lemon and olive oil.

    Greeks rarely eat dessert after dinner. They prefer their sweets, pastries and rich desserts, during the early evening (about 5 P.M.). Many Greek desserts are soaked overnight in syrup or honey.

II. Preparation done by volunteers.
    A. Pick up the following items from the refrigerator in the teachers' lounge: ice cubes, margarine, cold syrup from previous day and filo*.
        *About filo: filo is a paper-thin pastry dough made with salt, flour, water, and skill. It will be stored in the refrigerator in individual packages for the day, cut into 9x9 inch squares. Filo can easily dry out and become crisp. Be certain that it is wrapped in a damp towel at all times and that the children are not given their filo until they are completely ready to begin.
    B. Preheat oven to 375 degrees and melt margarine in pan.
    C. Special note: in order to stay within our time limit, while still providing the entire Baklava experience for our children, we first make the Baklava and place it in the oven and then prepare the nuts and syrup for the following group of children. Therefore, the experience is there, although reordered. The syrup must be chilled in ice cubes before pouring it over the baklava.
    D. Prepare three pans for handwashing and three duplicate pans for dishes.
        Pan No. 1 - Dishwashing detergent and water
        Pan No. 2 - 1/3 cup purex and water
        Pan No. 3 - Plain water and paper towels for drying
    E. Prepare each place with margarine tub, paper towel, and square of wax paper.
    F. Familiarize yourself with background information.

III. Direct children in this order:
    A. Discuss safety and clean-up (see chart of rules).
    B. Supervise hand washing.
    C. Give background information of Greek foods.
    D. Read bulletin board recipe together.
    E. Practice folding the filo by using a 9x9 inch square of paper.
    F. Distribute one square of filo to each child. If triangle wrap is too difficult, accept whatever they will find effective.
        FOLLOW THESE STEPS:
        1. Fold filo in thirds to form strip.
        2. Brush filo with melted margarine.

3. Place one heaping teaspoon of crushed walnuts at one end of filo strip.
4. Fold nuts into filo. Use a triangle fold. Keep nuts inside.
5. Place triangle on baking pan and brush top with melted margarine.
6. Bake at 375 degrees for 15 minutes. While Baklava is baking, make syrup and crush chopped walnuts.
7. SYRUP: 2½ cups sugar
             2 cups water
             Juice of one lemon

    Bring to boil and simmer ten minutes. Refrigerate (or chill by placing pan in bowl of ice cubes).
8. Soak hot Baklava in cold syrup for five minutes, turning frequently.

G. When Baklava is removed from oven it should be served in the margarine tubs and about 2 tablespoons of syrup should be poured over it. The children should spend about five minutes turning their Baklava over and over in the syrup.

   At this time, the volunteer should explain that generally Baklava is allowed to soak in the syrup for about 12 hours and that this yields an even sweeter dessert.

H. The children may eat their Baklava directly from the margarine tubs. Paper towels are very necessary at this time.

I. Each child should wash his margarine tub and clean his place at the table.

J. Volunteers prepare for the next group and spin syrup container in ice to insure adequate chilling of syrup.

K. At end of day: PLEASE UNPLUG ALL ELECTRICAL APPLIANCES.

IV. SPECIAL REMINDER: Electrical fires, should they occur, may not be doused with water without danger of electrical shock. Use the can marked FIRE — it contains baking soda which may be successfully used to extinguish electrical fires.

 MULTICULTURAL LESSON: NATIVE AMERICAN RECREATION

I.   Background Information

Native American children did not attend any formal school so they had many free moments. Most children were game lovers and enjoyed many sports and ceremonial games. Athletes were honored as highly as warriors. Native Americans are credited with the invention of the game Lacrosse.

American Indians played games both for enjoyment and to build skills, strength, and stamina of the players. The Cherokee Indians called their games "the little brother of war" because they believed that games made their boys into better warriors. Some games, such as spear fighting and mud throwing, were rough and dangerous.

The Indians enjoyed games of chance as well as games of dexterity. The children often played games with the adults but there were special children's games too. Generally, boys and girls played separately and sometimes they would play the same game with different rules. Some games taught animal stalking or egg hunting. Some common games were similar to blindman's buff, follow the leader, hide and seek, ring-around-the-rosy, tug of war, top spinning, pop gun play, stick ball, and make-believe games.

II. Preparation done by volunteers
   A.   Familiarize yourself with background information and all game rules so your presentation will be spontaneous.
   B.   Materials will be arranged on counter.

III. Lesson Presentation
   A.   Ask children to close their eyes. When all eyes are closed, ask them to think about their favorite game. Have them continue to keep their eyes closed. Suggest that when you touch them on the shoulder they name their favorite game aloud. After they have had a chance to tell about their favorite game, the volunteer may begin to tell about Native American games. Move about table letting each set of partners learn a game while the others watch. Do this method of presentation until all games have been demonstrated.
   B.   After the demonstration of all games, the children should be given a few minutes to try a game and then pass it around the table in a clockwise direction to the next set of partners. Do this until all games have been tried. These are the games to be introduced:
      1.   First play this group game. Native Americans used a blanket for this game, you can use a table. Choose someone to be "it". The rest of the players sit around the table with their hands under the table. They pass a stick around while "it" counts to 10 with his back turned. "It" then faces the group and guesses who has the stick. If he guesses correctly, the person bearing the stick becomes "it" and the previous "it" joins the circle of players. Play this game about four times. Explain that if there is time at the end you will play this game again. (Do so later if you feel that there is time.)
      2.   Tell children this: Native Americans kept score on games by using sticks. Generally two players would try for the best of seven games. Seven sticks would be placed in front of them and as a game was won, the winner took one stick. This continued until

all seven sticks were awarded. (This works well for guessing games.)

One player hides an object in one of two balls of grass. The other player tries to guess which grass ball contains the object. (Two players take turns and play for best of seven games).

3.   Native American children played a game using fern leaves. The child who was able to collect the most fern leaves one-by-one, while holding his breath, was the winner. We invented a derivative of this game. The children were given a piece of heavy cardboard and ten clothespins. Holding their breath, they clip all the clothespins one-by-one to the cardboard and down again to the holding tray. Each player has a possible 20 point score.

C.   Children may return to rooms playing the Native American game of Silence: the last person to make any sound wins; therefore, the children must return to their classrooms on tip-toes and without making any sounds. Tell them that there may be more than one winner and that the winners will know who they are when they arrive at their room and are sitting in their desks.

WORKSHOP SUGGESTIONS

The detail of the lesson plans and the quantity of necessary workshops will depend on the background of your paraprofessionals. Workshops should, at any rate, be included as often as possible, since they provide an excellent opportunity to clarify techniques and share successes. Workshops may also prove to be an excellent opportunity to promote professionalism on the part of the entire teaching team.

Workshop sessions may be divided into three major areas of emphasis: social, problem solving, and the presentation of new techniques. The teacher representative of a successful center must consciously provide for the three aforementioned experiences. A time for socializing provides a necessary period of catharsis. Also, people who feel comfortable together, obviously will work together in a more effective way. A discussion or question and answer period will undoubtedly ensue. The paraprofessionals should be encouraged to discuss any and all problems and their successes should be openly recognized and shared.

The third and final portion of each workshop should include an effort to formally provide the paraprofessional with specific techniques for the presentation of multicultural programs. Obviously not all helpful lesson presentation techniques can be included in a concise, easy-to-read, two-page article. As it is for both children and adults, information gained through experience is better assimilated than information merely heard or read. Providing the paraprofessional with an opportunity to experience a lesson, prior to his presentation of the lesson, can be an effective and necessary teaching technique. We encountered an example of this necessity when we began to demonstrate the Ojos de Dios to a group of paraprofessionals. Many of the adults experienced great difficulty in duplicating the weaving technique of the Ojos de Dios; while perfecting this skill, they developed a greater understanding of how the child might be aided. The group leaders had the opportunity to model methods of dealing with learning difficulties on a first-hand basis. The volunteers observed the group leaders handling this problem. They were able to benefit from the explanation which emphasized another channel of learning.

The realization that some students need a kinesthetic approach was illuminated when the group leaders were observed physically guiding a volunteer's hand until the volunteer was able to duplicate the pattern unaided.

A relaxed atmosphere with an opportunity to explore and practice skills is as important to adults as it is to children. Furthermore, believing in the team approach to learning is one of the greatest attributes that a team leader may possess and share with his paraprofessionals.

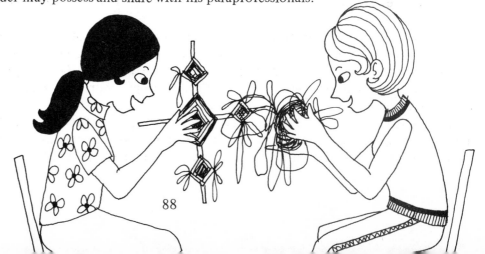

BITS AND PIECES

It would be extremely interesting, for more mature children, to construct the arts, cook the foods, and play the games in exactly the same way that their ancestors did. But with many of the activities in this book, an exact duplication of the activity is not possible. Some of the original materials, techniques and designs have been altered to fit the needs of the five to eight year old child and some of the directions have been simplified for ease of construction to increase the pleasure when creating.

When materials are not available in your area, attempt to make a reasonable substitution. The recipes found in this chapter may be helpful when making substitutions for items listed in the craft and food sections.

Later in this chapter you will find educational and community sources for multicultural information and a chart to aid in the drawing of parallels. We have included an annotated bibliography in this chapter. The materials listed are the most recent publications available in this field. Teachers are encouraged to use this source to update existing bibliographies found in other sources. If you are unable to find these multicultural materials in your area, they are available from Children's Book and Music Center in Los Angeles, California.

Most of the sixty-seven cooking activities provided in this text have been designed as individual portion recipes. This offers the child an opportunity of producing something that is totally his own. However, the treatment of some of these recipes necessitates group effort.

INTRODUCTORY AND CULMINATING ACTIVITIES

The introductory and/or culminating experiences that are planned for each culture may vary extensively. At one time, only a classroom may be involved; at another time, the program may be school-wide.

Introductory and culminating activities may take the form of dancers, drama groups, or speakers representative of a particular culture. There are many sources, outside of the school, for community people who are interested in sharing their cultural experiences. Some suggested sources for cultural information might be foreign students, cultural groups, churches, youth groups, travel groups, Embassies and Consulates.

Two activities which are best adapted to the culmination of a unit of cultural study are meal and party planning or holiday celebrations. The planning and preparations for a meal or party should include food, as well as decorations, music and entertainment. It is well to remember that any holiday may be celebrated on any day of the year and need not be confined, for study purposes, solely to the day on which it is actually celebrated by a particular cultural group. Some customs regarding holidays are discussed on the following pages in this chapter, under the specific headings for that holiday. Most holiday celebrations should include decorations, parades, and costuming.

INTRODUCTION
TO HOLIDAYS

There are many ethnic holidays which are celebrated in the United States. These days are observed by groups who maintain some ties to the land from which they or their ancestors originate. Since every individual in the United States, except the Native American, is a descendant from some foreign-born ancestor, each of us is a part of some ethnic group.

Every child loves to celebrate holidays. This is a perfect way to culminate the study of a culture. It is also another way to illuminate the similarities of various cultures. The holiday can be explained, a holiday meal planned and prepared, and appropriate games played and ethnic decorations made.

Specific days that are observed by people in other nations are called national holidays. Most of these national holidays represent some significant day in the history of the country, or the birthday of some national hero, or the day the country's independence was declared.

INTRODUCTION TO CHINESE HOLIDAYS

China's history suggests that it is one of the most ancient countries of the world. Most of the Chinese holidays traditionally center upon the worship of ancestors and nature. Since the Communist Party has controlled China, many festivals have been stopped and some have been changed to fit more closely with the Communist ideals. The Chinese New Year (Spring Festival), however, is still very important. The Communist government discourages any ancestor worship and prefers that Communist heroes be honored. People still celebrate with new clothing, special foods, and by attending special theater performances. The market sells colorful kites, masks, and candy that looks like long sticks of sugar-coated berries.

Some new Communist festivals are: National Day, October 1, founding of Peoples' Republic of China; May Day, May 1, to honor working people; Army Day, August 1, to honor China's Military forces.

 LI CHUM

Li Chum is celebrated in early February and celebrates the promise of springtime. This is a fun holiday and the most widely celebrated of the nature holidays. The ox or water buffalo is very important in this celebration. Everyone participates in a parade. Each participant carries a small clay buffalo. A large paper and bamboo construction of a buffalo is carried at the head of the procession. The buffalo are destroyed in a ceremony at the temple so that their spirits may enter heaven as a plea for a prosperous season. The evening ends in candlelight with many people attending plays and weddings. Li Chum is considered to be a very lucky day for weddings. Plum-blossom parties are also popular on this day.

 NEW YEAR

New Year's Festival is celebrated in early February. In addition to being the new year, this is the birthday celebration day for all Chinese. No matter when a baby is born in the previous year, he is considered to be exactly one year old on New Year's Day. Preparations begin early for this fifteen-day festival. It is believed to be extremely important to begin the new year with a clean home, a freshly painted red gate, lanterns, firecrackers, and new shoes. Special foods are made for both the living and the dead. Flags, banners, and costumes are readied for this religious and historical celebration. It is important to note that evil spirits are always driven away by fire, loud noises, and the color red. Firecrackers are a special part of this celebration. Children make paper chariots for the Kitchen God (T'sao Wang) to travel to heaven to report sweet things about the family to the Jade Emperor.

New Year's Eve is very quiet and people stay in their own homes with paper seals on the door. The first day of the new year is dedicated to ancestor worship and people go to their temple to worship Buddha, praying for happiness, prosperity, and good fortune for the coming year. Families prepare delicious dishes to enjoy and celebrate the new year. During the second day of the celebration, married daughters go back to their own mother's home in order to exchange gifts. The remaining fourteen days are for fun and feasting. Children are given treats of oranges, sweets, and rice cakes. The traditional Dragon Play is presented. On the 15th day, the Feast of the Lantern is celebrated — this is especially fun for children. It is celebrated with firecrackers, lanterns, and a large paper dragon that is carried by as many as 100 men.

 CHING MING

Ching Ming is celebrated in early April. This holiday celebrates the arrival of Spring. It is also a happy day to remember deceased ancestors. There are often picnics and tree planting ceremonies as well as sacrifices of food and money to one's ancestors.

GLOSSARY TO CALENDAR OF CHINA

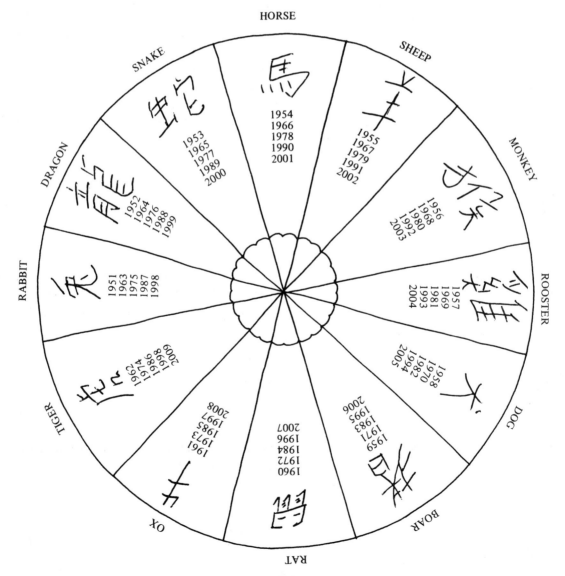

 INTRODUCTION TO GREEK HOLIDAYS

There are numerous holidays celebrated in Greece. Most of the festivals are of a religious nature because 98% of the Greek population belongs to the Greek Orthodox Church and the government has traditionally been closely tied to the church. When the Turks ruled Greece, they allowed the church leaders to control the educational, religious, and governmental affairs. These religious holidays are peoples' festivals as well and they include feasts, music, and fireworks. The people dance and sing to music provided by flutes, clarinets, castinets, and bouzakis (a stringed instrument similar to a mandolin).

Greece has been called the "cradle of democracy" because it developed this form of government thousands of years ago. A Greek festival from ancient times is now celebrated worldwide. This is the Olympic games. The opening ceremony of the Olympic games is highlighted by the lighting of the Olympic flame. The flame is lit by a torch from a fire in Elis, Greece, where the first Olympic games were held hundreds of years before the time of Christ.

Children participate, in a very special way, in three Greek holiday celebrations. During Epiphany, Easter and Christmas eves, groups of children make early morning visits to the homes in their community. At this time they sing a special tune, *Calanda,* accompanied by the playing of metal triangles. Greek families consider it good luck to receive the children's visits and in return they offer the children money and sweets. To persons from the United States, this Greek custom appears to combine caroling with our Halloween custom of trick or treating.

 GREEK INDEPENDENCE DAY

Greek Independence Day is observed on March 25. This date marks the beginning of a revolt in 1821 that led to Greek independence. In the United States, Greek Americans celebrate this holiday in traditional Greek ways. Colorful costumes from the various regions are worn in parades and in musical celebrations.

 SAINTS CONSTANTINE AND HELEN DAY

Many of the festivals in Greece celebrate the patron saints of villages. The festival of Saints Constantine and Helen, held on May 21, also marks the beginning of summer.

 PASCHA (EASTER)

To celebrate Easter in Greece, families attend church. Everyone carries a lighted candle home to light his oil lamp, which is placed in front of a religious picture in his home. They eat barbecued lamb and Easter sweets.

Children enjoy breaking painted, hard-boiled eggs by knocking them against each other. The egg is a symbol of life and happiness to the Greeks, but they believe that they must break open the egg to let the blessings escape.

 OCHI DAY

Ochi Day celebrates the rejection of Mussolini's ultimatum to Greece during World War II. It is celebrated on October 28.

 INTRODUCTION TO ISRAELI HOLIDAYS

Although Israel is a free country that welcomes all faiths, nine out of every ten Israelis are Jewish. Due to the large ratio of persons in one faith, the religion of the Jews plays a large role in the life-style of all Israelis.

National holidays are celebrated with parades, gay decorations, singing, and dancing. Non-secular holidays are often more serious and symbolic. Special holiday foods are included in all celebrations.

 ISRAELI NEW YEAR

Israeli New Year is called Rosh Hashanah and is celebrated sometime in September, the date changing from year to year depending on the Hebrew calendar. "Rosh" means "head" and "shanah" means "year". Rosh Hashanah lasts for ten days. The tenth day, called Yom Kippur, or day of atonement, is the day on which one must seek forgiveness for mistakes and resolve to live a better life.

Most New Year's celebrations of other cultures are noisy and joyous, however the Jewish New Year is a solemn, quiet, serious observance. Friends greet each other on this holiday with, "May you be inscribed for a good year." By saying this, they are wishing that what is written in the Book of Life will be good for that person.

 PASSOVER

Passover is a celebration of the Jews' liberation from slavery. This holiday is usually celebrated in April and it is one of the oldest festivals of freedom in the world.

The entire holiday is based on the Passover story of Moses leading the Jews from the domination of Egypt's Pharoah. Each Jew is encouraged to celebrate Passover as if he were an actual participant in the Exodus thousands of years ago.

The holiday is celebrated with a meal that is also a religious service. Special foods are served — matzoh, unleavened bread, horseradish, haroseth (mixture of chopped apples, nuts, cinnamon, and wine), shank bone of lamb, roasted egg, and parsley. All these foods are representative of the Jewish experiences during Passover.

Some families enjoy searching for breadcrumbs, which have been hidden throughout the house by the father. The family searches by candlelight and the bread crumbs are burned in the ceremony the next morning.

The father's chair is provided with a pillow to show the Jews' deliverance from slavery. During ancient times, only those people who had their freedom were allowed to lean or sit comfortably while eating.

This holiday is called Passover because it is when the Angel of Death *passed over* the homes of all Israelites who had marked their door with the blood of the lamb.

 PURIM - FESTIVAL OF LOTS

In Israel, many elaborate Purim celebrations are held. Some cities have festive, three-day celebrations with many activities including parades, parties, and dramatic presentations. Masquerading is one of the favorite Purim customs. Purim parties and masquerade balls are very happy occasions. People dance, sing, make noise, masquerade and exchange presents. In Israel, effigies or puppets are made of the characters in the story. A common gift that children give or receive is special holiday foods such as poppy seed candy and Hamantashen.

 SUCCOTH

This holiday is celebrated in late September or early October. This is a very happy, ancient festival. It has religious significance and is somewhat similar to the Thanksgiving Day celebrated in the United States.

The name for this holiday comes from the Hebrew word "succot", which means "booths". During harvest season, the Jewish people lived in little booths in the fields so that they could more efficiently gather their crops. These booths also signify the temporary huts used by Jews during the forty years of wandering after their exodus from Egypt.

It is celebrated by each family building a special booth which is decorated with fruits and flowers. During this holiday, the family eats all of their meals at a table inside their gaily decorated booth.

Succoth, generally celebrated in September, begins five days after Yom Kippur and is observed for eight to nine days. This holiday has three names and each help to explain the purpose of this festival: Feast of Booths, Festival of Ingathering (of the harvest), and Feast of Thanksgiving or Rejoicing.

The last day of Succoth includes a synagogue parade of both adults and children carrying flags and the Torah scrolls. Often the children are encouraged to make their own flags and banners in preparation for the holiday. During Succoth, food is also distributed to families in need.

 INTRODUCTION TO JAPANESE HOLIDAYS

Festivals or holidays in Japan are called Matsuri(s) and are a very important part of Japanese life. The main national holidays are the Emperor's Birthday on April 29, and Constitutional Memorial Day on May 3.

 CULTURE DAY

November 3 is a national holiday in Japan. This holiday was established to encourage Japan to cherish its old culture and to help create a new one. On this day, meetings are held throughout Japan to discuss and promote cultural appreciations and to honor those who have contributed to the culture of Japan.

 HINA-MATSURI (GIRL'S DAY)

In Japan, March 3 is known as Girl's Day and is celebrated with a doll festival. Long ago, dolls were not considered toys but rather were symbols of man's spirit. Today this holiday is merely a symbolic display of court dolls. Girls enjoy exchanging visits on this day and serve party refreshments while they dance and sing or listen to music.

 JAPANESE NEW YEAR - OSHOGATSU

This holiday begins January 1st and lasts from three to seven days. This is a happy time of new beginnings. Houses are clean, all bills are paid, and as many families as can buy new clothing. Friends and relatives exchange gifts and visits. Homes and stores are decorated with arrangements of bamboo, pine boughs, and red berries. Additional decorations are made from straw, ferns, and oranges. Special foods of the season include mochi, small rice cakes used in the Festival soups, and toso. A poem card game is played during this special time and boys enjoy kite flying while girls play battledore and shuttlecock.

 O-BON

The celebration of the Feast of the Lanterns includes a launching of floating candles, Bon dances at the Buddhist temple, special foods, and lanterns lit in memory of those deceased. It is a gay event in which the Buddhist priest leads the dancing.

It is, however, an important religious time. The O-Bon is a memorial festival which has been observed by Japanese Buddhist families ever since the introduction of Buddhism into Japan about 1300 years ago. It is a three-day reunion of the living with the spirits of the dead. The purpose of this festival is to perpetuate the memory of ancestors and to stimulate ancestor worship and filial piety.

 TANGO-NO-SEKKU (BOY'S FESTIVAL)

May 5 is a day on which Japanese families celebrate the good growth and health of the boys in their family. Each family flies large carp streamers from tall large poles in their garden. Carp banners symbolize the strong and courageous aspects of character. Kite flying is often an important part of this festival. During this festival special rice cakes are made and wrapped in oak or iris leaves. The special scent of these leaves lingers in the rice cakes.

 INTRODUCTION TO MEXICAN HOLIDAYS

The most common Mexican celebration is the fiesta (festival). Every village has its own patron saint with an annual fiesta in which the patron saint is honored. Village fiestas generally combine religious worship with shopping and recreation. A typical fiesta may include music, songs and dances; parades, eating and drinking, fireworks, gambling, cockfights and bullfights are especially popular. Colored tissue paper flowers and shapes decorate the church where many go to light candles and pray.

In the larger towns fiestas resemble the carnivals of the United States. Often they are less religious and mechanical rides (Ferris wheel and merry-go-round) are a focus of the celebration.

Most of the Mexican holidays include fiesta-type celebrations in addition to the activities that are also listed as special observances of that particular holiday.

 EL GRITO

Mexico's national holiday is "El Grito", Independence Day, celebrated on September 16. It is celebrated in memory of the day a priest named Hidalgo called the people to revolt against the Spanish rulers. On this day, the president of Mexico rings the Independence Bell, the same bell Hidalgo rang to call the people of Dolores together. On this day people repeat the Grito de Dolores, the famous plea of Father Hidalgo, who became known as the "Father of Mexican Independence". This day is celebrated by military parades, band concerts, and fireworks.

 VIRGIN OF GUADALUPE

The Mexicans generally celebrate many fiestas, most of which are connected with their religion, which is predominantly Roman Catholic. There is a patron saint for every town, that they honor with a fiesta. The largest fiesta of this type honors the Virgin of Guadalupe (December 12), the patron saint of all Mexico. A fiesta frequently includes lots of fireworks, special sweets, bright paper flower or banner decorations and sometimes piñatas. A piñata is a clay pot in the shape of an animal, covered with paper-mâché and tissue paper. It is filled with candy and small toys and hung from a tree limb or rafter so that it can be raised or lowered. Children are blindfolded and try to hit it with a stick and break it to spill out all the toys and candies.

 CINCO DE MAYO

Cinco de Mayo is a holiday that is celebrated more extensively by Mexican Americans than it is by Mexican nationals. It celebrates the May 5, 1862 defeat of the French Army of Napoleon.

 LAS POSADAS (CHRISTMAS IN MEXICO)

In Mexico, Las Posadas are celebrated nine days before Christmas to commemorate the journey of Mary and Joseph from Nazareth to Bethlehem, searching for posadas (lodging) each night.

The posadas take place in the form of a group of people who form a procession with lighted candles as they parade down the street. The posadas are from December 16th through the 24th culminated by a fiesta which is climaxed by breaking a piñata.

In most of the major cities now, gifts are exchanged on Christmas eve and Christmas morning. Those who prefer to celebrate in the traditional way, exchange gifts on the "Day of the Kings". This holiday is called Epiphany in the Christian culture.

The children of Mexico do not have a Christmas tree. Instead, they have a "Nacimiento" which is a nativity scene.

ALL SAINTS AND SOULS DAY

This holiday is celebrated November 1st and 2nd. The celebration of All Souls Day in Mexico has many interesting Aztec and Mayan embellishments. It also is similar to European traditions of many Italian and Spanish villages. In the United States in New Orleans, many families go to the cemeteries with baskets of food to enjoy a picnic in the cemetery. The celebration begins the last week in October and lasts through the first week in November.

In Mexico, the candy stores, bakeries, and gift shops display and sell confections and toys for "El Dia de Los Muertos", The Day of the Dead.
A special play, *Don Juan Tenorio,* is presented in the theatres. It is the story of a wicked man who is saved by the pure soul of Doña Ines, who loved him.

 INTRODUCTION TO NATIVE AMERICAN HOLIDAYS

Today many Native American groups celebrate their own, as well as, the holidays of other neighboring groups. At one time, however, each group was totally different from each of the others.

Many Native American holidays are private affairs and visitors are not welcome. These are times for worship and for the observance of sacred customs. The people of the group chant songs learned from their parents and perform ancient and sacred dances.

 INTER-TRIBAL INDIAN CEREMONIAL

Every August, the groups of Native Americans from all over the United States, meet in Gallup, New Mexico for the Inter-Tribal Indian Ceremonial. As many as twenty groups are represented. This ceremonial is like a big fair with races and dance contests. Each group exhibits their handicrafts for sale. This fair attracts many visitors who enjoy buying souvenirs and viewing parades, sports, and dances.

 SHALAKO FESTIVAL

The Zuni Indians of New Mexico grow corn on their desert land. Every drop of rain is precious and important to this group of Native Americans who celebrate to honor the Shalako, messengers of the rain spirits, December 1st. This festival includes chants, prayers, and special dances. The men dance and wear masks representative of the rain spirits and tie bells to their knees. This is an important festival for which the Zuni people prepare the entire year.

 NEW YEAR

A long time ago, before the calendar that we know today was used, Native Americans used seasons as their calendar. The most important time of year for the Choctaw Indian people was late July or early August when the corn ripened. This time marked the beginning of a New Year for them and the rituals practiced during this time could be considered a New Year celebration.

At this time, old fires were extinguished and new ones ignited as a symbol of a new beginning. It was important that all members of the group settled differences at this time and past mistakes were forgiven.

The New Year was celebrated by performing the Green Corn Dance, and to insure a year of peace, new laws were made at this time.

 INTRODUCTION TO WEST AFRICAN HOLIDAYS

African holidays vary greatly from one community to another in Western Africa. Many of the holidays deal with tribal rituals and ceremonies. Chanting, singing, and dancing are common for all celebrations.

Although many Africans have moved to the cities, and have changed their lifestyles to adjust to apartment living, they continue to maintain close contact with their tribal group or relatives. Many city dwellers return frequently to the farm or bush country in order to visit their families or perform tribal duties.

 ODUM TITUN (Ō-DOOHM TĒ TOOHN)

This Nigerian wintertime festival marks the beginning of the new year. It also follows the harvest season. Two foods are a specialty of this holiday: Fu-fu (a combination of yams and cassava), and Tuwo (a combination of guinea corn and maize). Both are served with fricassee sauce. There are ceremonial dances and drum music during the serving of the feast.

 ASHURA (AH-SHOO-ROO)

This New Year's festival is celebrated in Morocco, in Northwest Africa, on the tenth day of Muharram. During this festival, the people sprinkle water over themselves and their possessions. This is a ceremony of cleansing so the new year will have a clean start.

ABOAKYER (AH-BŌ-AHT-SHEH)

This holiday is celebrated in April or May. The Effutu people in Ghana celebrate a deer-hunting festival to bring God's blessings on their food supply. During this festival, great numbers of men and boys (over the age of seven) participate in the deer hunt and wear colorful costumes. When the first live deer is caught, it is proudly presented to the chief. Then the celebration continues with drum music and dancing.

FESTIVAL
PARALLELS

A study of holidays easily becomes a study of mankind. All men are united in the sharing of common seasonal festivals. It is, for example, possible to equate the reasons behind the manner in which the people of the United States celebrate Thanksgiving with the Israeli celebration of Succoth. Succoth also has other festival elements which are somewhat similar to an Independence Day, or the Jews' escape from Egypt. The May Day celebration of the United States shares common elements with Boy's Day of Japan. Some common celebrations commemorating the opportunity to begin anew are Chinese New Year, Rosh Hoshanah in Israel, and Oshoogatsun in Japan.

MULTICULTURAL
FOOD SUPPLIERS

If special ethnic foods are not available in your area, you may write any of the stores listed below to request specific amounts of certain items.

Arranaga Vincent Co., Inc.
(Mexican food supplies)
2424 E. 12th
Los Angeles, California
(213) 624-2943

Boys Market
(Israeli food supplies)
3750 E. Anaheim
Long Beach, California

Eilot Market
(Israeli food supplies)
Fairfax
Los Angeles, California

Falafel Works
(Israeli food supplies)
4316½ E. 4th St.
Long Beach, California
(213) 433-3227

New Meiyi Market
(Oriental food supplies)
1620 W. Redondo
Gardena, California
(213) 323-7696

Nishimoto Trading Co., Ltd.
(Oriental food supplies)
1884 E. 22nd
Los Angeles, California
(213) 747-4111

Plowboys Market
(Mexican and Oriental food supplies)
11869 E. Carson
Hawaiian Gardens, California
(714) 865-4511

S & J Importing Company
(Greek and Middle Eastern food supplies)
1770 Pacific Avenue
Long Beach, California
(213) 599-1341

Yamasaki Market
(Japanese food supplies)
1566 Santa Fe Avenue
Long Beach, California
(213) 437-7730

INTERNATIONAL FOOD PROGRAM

CSM (corn, soya and milk) is a food supplement. Since it was developed in 1966, over 1½ billion pounds have been distributed in over 100 countries. Because CSM has a variety of vitamins, minerals and protein needed for healthy life, it is the main food substance used by CARE in their overseas food program.

Corn meal may be substituted for CSM in any recipe. CSM is not available in any store in the United States or Canada. It may be ordered from Krause Milling Company, P.O. Box 1156, Milwaukee, Wisconsin 53201.

VEGETABLE SOUP - STEW (CSM BASIC RECIPE)

In the following recipe if you add yams, corn, squash, yucca or platano, it is similar to the sancocho of many Latin American countries. If you use less water and make it a stew instead of soup, it resembles Quisado of the Philippines. With even less water (semi-solid form) it can be compared to Foo Foo of West Africa and it would be similar to pilau of the Middle East. When the water is reduced to a minimum and the product is dry enough to be eaten with the fingers, it resembles Indian Uppitu or Upama. In this version, the only vegetable ingredients used are onions and chili, and the CSM is fried until browned in the fat before the water is added, and the mixture is highly seasoned and spiced. Upama is dry enough to be eaten with the fingers.

INGREDIENTS:

½ C.	(120ml.)	Oil, butter or other fat
1 C.	(240ml.)	Sliced carrots
1 C.	(240ml.)	Sliced celery
1 C.	(240ml.)	Coarsely chopped onion
2 C.	(480ml.)	Potatoes, peeled and cut up
2 C.	(480ml.)	Cut-up or canned tomatoes
2 C.	(480ml.)	Cabbage, spinach or other green vegetable
½ to 3 Quarts	(240 ml. to 3.8 l.)	Water
1 C.	(240ml.)	CSM (or corn meal) mixed with cold water
		Salt, pepper, seasonings

PROCEDURE:
1. Put oil in large pan, add onion, carrots, celery and potatoes and stew gently for ten minutes.
2. Add tomatoes and cook for another five minutes.
3. Add water and seasoning, bring to boil.
4. When boiling add cabbage or spinach.
5. Cook until all vegetables are tender. Stir in CSM mixed with cold water.
6. Bring to boil again and cook for five to ten minutes.

YIELD: 15 to 20 servings.

COMMUNITY
RESOURCES

If these community resources are not in your geographic area, perhaps knowing the names of these groups can help you to discover some on your own.

Multicultural:
The International Institute
435 S. Boyle
Los Angeles, California

Chinese:
Chinese American Citizens Alliance
415 Bamboo Lane
Los Angeles, California

Committee to Conserve Chinese Culture
P.O. Box 75727
Los Angeles, California 90075

San Fernando Valley Chinese Cultural Association
15035 Delgado Drive
Sherman Oaks, California 91403

U.S. China Peoples Friendship Association
2700 W. 3rd Street
Los Angeles, California 90057

Greece:
The Local Hellenic Societies will refer you to the best resources in your area.

St. Nicholas Orthodox Cathedral*
2300 W. 3rd Street
Los Angeles, California

Israel:
Jewish Federation Council
6505 Wilshire Blvd.
Los Angeles, California

Local Jewish Community Centers will refer you to the best resources in your area.

Japan:
Japanese American Cultural Society
368 E. lst Street
Los Angeles, California

Japanese Art and Culture Institute
1218 Menlo Avenue
Los Angeles, California 90006

Japanese Chamber of Commerce of Southern California
125 Weller Street
Los Angeles, California 90012

Japanese Cultural Society of America
355 E. 1st Street
Room 207
Los Angeles, California 90012

Japanese Folk Dance Association
1750 W. 27th
Los Angeles, California

Mexico:
Centro Cultural Cabrillo
Department of Spanish and Portuguese
University of California at Los Angeles
Los Angeles, California 90024

Plaza de la Raza
3540 N. Mission Road
Los Angeles, California

Native American:
Los Angeles Indian Center
1111 W. Washington Blvd.
Los Angeles, California

West Africa:
African Study Center Educational Service
10341 S. Western Avenue
Los Angeles, California

Afro-American Cultural Education Center
3860 Crenshaw Blvd.
Los Angeles, California

Inner City Cultural Center
1308 S. New Hampshire Ave.
Los Angeles, California

*Churches representing any culture are always a good source or starting point when looking for community resources.

EDUCATIONAL
SOURCES

Some educational sources for the purchase of multicultural books and audio-visual materials are listed here. See individual company catalogues for detailed selections.

Anti-Defamation League of B'nai B'rith
6505 Wilshire Blvd.
Suite 814
Los Angeles, California 90048

Bowmar
622 Rodier Drive
Glendale, California 91201

Children's Book and Music Center
5373 Pico Blvd.
Los Angeles, California 90019

Educational Activities
P.O. Box 392
Freeport, New York 11520

Institute for Cultural Pluralism
Resource Center
School of Education
San Diego State University
San Diego, California 92182

Lakeshore
8888 Venice Blvd.
Los Angeles, California

Lawswing Press
750 Adrian Way
San Rafael, California 94903

Lerner Publications Company
241 First Avenue, North
Minneapolis, Minnesota 55401

McGraw-Hill Book Company
Western Regional Office
8171 Redwood Highway
Novato, California 94947

QED
2921 West Alameda Avenue
P.O. Box 1608
Burbank, California 91507

Scholastic Records and Books
904 Sylvan Avenue
Englewood Cliffs, New Jersey 07632

Albert Whitman and Company
650 West Lake Street
Chicago, Illinois 60605

HOW TO USE THE ANNOTATED BIBLIOGRAPHY

This annotated bibliography has been compiled from a selection of the most recent books in the field of Multicultural education. If these books are not readily available to you in a nearby teacher's supply or catalogue store, you may find them in Los Angeles at Children's Book and Music Center.

A.   MULTICULTURAL MATERIALS

American Dream Mural Packets. Available at Children's Book and Music Center, 5373 West Pico Blvd., Los Angeles, California, 90019.
> Packets for bulletin board and other uses for: Polynesia, American Dream, Black America, Mexico, and Africa.

Burnett, Bernice. *The First Book of Holidays.* New York: Franklin Watts, 1974.
> The author describes the origins and ceremonies of ethnic holidays and festivals of other nations.

Caesar, Irving. *Sing a Song of Friendship.* MC367, Record, Bowmar.
> A collection of children's songs of world friendship and individual rights.

Children Around the World. MC158, Poster Set.
> Set of 12: 11x14 inch posters of children of China, Japan, Mexico, Nigeria, Peru, and Sweden.

De Pree, Mildred. *A Child's World of Stamps.* New York: Parents Magazine Press, 1973.
> A collection of 150 postage stamps that relate to children of the world. By examining the stamps from other parts of the world, children may discover that the pleasures of childhood are similar the world over.

Dignity of Man Foundation. *Dignity of Man.* Walnut Creek, California: Dignity of Man Foundation, 1974.
> Photo essay: A group of 31 photos to be used to explore the dignity of man on a global scale. Bilingual

Evans, Eva. *People Are Important.* New York: Golden Press, 1951.

> Teacher may choose selected passages to read to students. It describes similarities and differences of children in various cultures.

Follow the Sunset. MC322, Record.
> A collection of lullabies from all over the world.

Hallum, Rosemary and Newhart, Edith. *Multicultural Folktales.* MC404, Set of three filmstrips with 3 cassettes.

Box of:	(Africa)	*Why do Monkeys Live in Trees?*
	(China)	*The Magic Brush*
	(Mexico)	*The Mountains*

Cassettes and filmstrips may be introduced with the use of a discussion guide folder.

Horner, Deborah. *Masks of the World*. New York: Charles Scribner's Sons, 1977.

> Masks from nine cultures that are ready to be cut out and worn by children in dramatic play. These masks are modeled from actual masks in the collection of the National Mueum of Natural History, Smithsonian Institute.

It Could Be A Wonderful World. MC329, Record.

> Songs of world friendship.

It's A Children's World. MC330, Record.

> Beautiful narrations of stories from many cultures.

Joseph, Joan. *Folk Toys Around the World*. New York: Parents Magazine Press, 1972.

> Teacher reference in primary. Color illustrations of 23 toys from many lands. Instructions are at an advanced level but many may be adapted to primary level.

Maz, Julian. *Why People Are Different Colors*. New York: Holiday House, 1971.

> Book to be read to class. The author explains what causes biological differences of varied races in a manner that makes it easier for the child to see that we are a single human species that has more similarities than variations.

Moncure, Jane. *One Little World*. Elgin, Illinois: The Child's World, 1975.

> A picture book in verse that reveals that despite outward differences people everywhere are essentially the same. Easy text that a primary student can read by himself.

Outstanding American People. (33 separate stories). New York: Thomas Y. Crowell Company, 1970's.

> A series of books listed by various authors and titles. Biographies for the more mature primary readers or for teacher reference.

Quakenbush, Robert and Buch, Harry. *The Holiday Song Book*. New York: Lothrop, Lee, and Shepard Company, 1977.

> Teacher resource. A collection of words and music for American holiday celebrations — includes American Indian Day and Hanukkah. Brief descriptions of each holiday are included.

Raynor, Dorka. *Grandparents Around the World*. Chicago: Albert Whitman and Company, 1977.

> A photo essay of children from various cultures around the world with their grandparents.

Schreiner, Nikki. *My Ancestors Are From Everywhere - Kits 1, 2, 3, and 4*. Palos Verdes Estates, California: Touch and See. 1975.

> Sets of activity cards from 29 countries with suggested activities branching into all areas of the curriculum. These will generally appeal in grades 4 thru 6.

Simon, Norma. *All Kinds of Families*. Chicago: Albert Whitman and Company, 1976.

> A picture book that acknowledges that families do not always exist in the traditional manner. The book stresses the supportive function of the family even though it may have a different structure.

Sing a Song of People. Bowmar Book: M517.

> A songbook combining what is included in three Bowmar multicultural records.

Temko, Florence. *Folk Crafts for World Friendship*. Garden City, New York: Doubleday, 1976.

> Includes colorful, simple instructions for handicrafts from all over the world. Easily readable for grades 4 thru 6 — easily adapted for primary.

Told Under the City Umbrella. MC264, Book.

> A collection of stories for children's listening about city children of many cultural groups.

Vegetable Soup Activities. MC266, MC267.

> Some of these ethnic activities are appropriate for primary children.

Whitman, Jerry and Others. *Sing a Song of Neighbors*. MC369, Bowmar Record.

> Multicultural songs in English and some in original language.

Simon, Norma. *Why Am I Different?* SG547.

> Stresses how differences enhance our experience.

World Culture Series. Sound Filmstrip Sets. MC427.

 This excellent series introduces people, their cultures, and musical traditions around the world. Each set includes a record or cassette, two film strips, and a teacher's guide. The series includes:

   North American Indian Songs
   Folk Songs of Israel
   Folk Songs of Many People
   Folk Songs of Africa
   Folk Songs of Our Pacific Neighbors
   Children's Songs of Mexico

B. FOLKLORE MATERIALS: CHINA

Asian Cultural Centre for UNESCO. *Folk Tales from Asia for Children Everywhere*. New York: Weatherhill, 1977. Books 1, 2, 3, 4, 5, 6.
 Six volumes of folktales from all of Asia. Delightfully presented for children's listening.
Chritie, Anthony. *Chinese Mythology*. New York: Paul Hamelyn, 1968.
 Teacher reference. A scholarly presentation of Chinese myths, legends, and ancient art pieces.
Hsiao, Ellen. *A Chinese Year*. New York: M. Evans and Company, Inc., 1970.
 Teacher reference for early childhood. Follows Nansan and Ai-lan, children of China, and their family through a year of experiences. Includes many cultural insights.
Kimishima, Hisako. *Ma Lien and the Magic Brush*. AM68.
 Story of a boy, in China, who outwits a Mandarin with his magic paintbrush.
Marn-Ling and the Chinese Musical Instruments. AM246, Record with photos of instruments.
 A record which tells the story of a Chinese girl who discovers and plays Asian musical instruments. Includes color photographs of the instruments.
Marn-Ling Sees the Chinese Lion Dance. AM247, Record with Photos.
 A Chinese girl attends a New Year's festival. Includes songs and dance instruction.
McKenna, Siobhan. *Chinese Fairy Tales*. AM241, Record. AM242, Cassette.
 Several Chinese fairy tales are presented on this recording.
Pellowski, Anne. *Chinese Folk Tales*. AM243, Record. AM244, Cassette.
 Chinese legends, proverbs, rhymes, and folk tales.
Reit, Seymour. *Rice Cakes and Paper Dragons*. New York: Dodd, Mead, and Company, 1973.
 Photographs and story, appropriate for the more mature reader, tell of a Chinese-American girl's daily life and her celebration of Chinese New Year.

C. FOLKLORE MATERIALS: GREECE

Jones, Jayne. *The Greeks in America*. Minneapolis, Minnesota, Lerner Publication Company, 1969.
 Teacher reference. Brief summary of early Greece, immigration to America, plus obstacles and achievement.

D. FOLKLORE MATERIALS: ISRAEL

Ausubel, Nathan. *Pictorial History of the Jewish People*. New York: Crown Publishers, Inc., 1953.
 Teacher reference. Black and white photography and text describe the Jewish people in the past 2,000 years.
Ausubel, Nathan (ed). *A Treasury of Jewish Folklore*. MC115.
 A wealth of material for children's listening. It includes hundreds of stories and songs representing the traditions and legends of the Jewish people.

Brodsky, Beverly. *Jonah*. New York: Lippincott, 1977.

Third graders may enjoy reading about Jonah. Beautiful water color illustrations accompany this ancient story of Jonah and the Whale.

Cone, Molly. *Purim*. New York: Thomas Y. Crowell, 1967.

Third graders will enjoy reading this tale of Purim and its celebration of Spring and happiness.

de Leon, Moses. *The Alphabet of Creation*. MC101.

Beautiful illustrations re-tell this ancient mystical tale of creation. Picture book for listening.

Dor, David. *Israeli-Yemenite Folklore in Song and Dance*. MC132, Record.

Dance directions are included with most of the songs on this record.

Glass, Henry. *Around the World in Dance*. MC301, Record.

Dances from: Belgium, England, Israel, Nigeria, United States.

Lawrence, Esther. *Songs of the Jewish People*. MC136, Record.

This record includes many authentic songs of the Jewish culture in Yiddish, Hebrew, etc. Some English.

Lisnoski, Gabriel. *How Tevye Became a Milkman*. MC429, Book.

Tale of a Jewish milkman who loves mankind.

Rubin, Ruth. *A Treasury of Jewish Folksongs*. New York: Schocken Books, 1964.

A large collection of songs from Israel in Hebrew with English translations.

Rubin, Ruth. *Jewish Folk Songs*. MC134, Record.

Songs from Ruth Rubin's Treasury of Folksongs — includes descriptive notes.

Singer, Isaac. *Why Noah Chose the Dove*. MC124, Book.

A Jewish interpretation of the animal's dialogue as they approach Noah's ark.

Singer, Isaac. *When Shlemiel Went to Warsaw and Other Stories*. New York: Doubleday, 1968.

Line drawings accompany eight folktales translated from the Yiddish. These tales have universal appeal and are appropriate for children listening.

Singer, Isaac. *Zlateh the Goat and Other Stories.* New York: Harper and Row, 1966.

Children will enjoy listening to the seven folk tales which are included in this delightfully illustrated book (illustrations by Maurice Sendak). This folklore originated in Middle Europe.

Singer, Isaac. *Naftali the Storyteller and His Horse, Sus and Other Stories*. New York: McGraw-Hill Ryerson, Ltd., 1976.

Children will enjoy listening to this collection of nine delightful stories which offer insight into life in the Jewish home and community.

Steiner, Eric. *Jewish Folksongs*. Melville, New York: Belwin Mills, 1975.

Words and music for Jewish folksongs. A brief description precedes each song.

Zemach, Margot. *It Could Always Be Worse*. New York: Pearl Pressman Liberty, 1976.

Children will enjoy listening to this delightfully told and illustrated Yiddish folk tale.

The Music of the Jewish People. MC112, Book.

A complete study of the Jewish musical tradition. It includes many illustrations and over 100 musical examples.

E.   FOLKLORE MATERIALS: JAPAN

Asian Cultural Center for UNESCO. *Folk Tales from Asia for Children Everywhere*. New York: Weatherhill, 1977. Books 1, 2, 3, 4, 5, 6.

Six volumes of folktales from all of Asia. Delightfully presented for children's listening.

Bartoli, Jennifer. *The Story of the Grateful Crane*. Chicago: Albert Whitman and Company, 1977.

This Japanese folktale tells a classical story of how kindness is repaid. Beautifully illustrated. Appropriate for children's listening.

Berger, Donald. *Folk Songs of Japanese Children*. Tokyo, Japan: Charles E. Tuttle Company, Inc., 1969.

A super collection of Japanese tales, games, songs, and music. All music includes complete explanations and are presented in English, phonetic Japanese, and calligraphy.

De Forest, Charlott. *The Prancing Pony*. New York: John Weatherhill, Inc., 1971.
An extensive collection of nursery rhymes found widely throughout Japan.

Favorite Songs of Japanese Children. AM262 Record, AM263, 264, two filmstrips with record or cassette.
Fifteen songs in Japanese and English with shamisen and koto accompaniments. Song book with words and music is available.

Folk and Fairy Tales of Japan. AM268, two cassettes.
A delightful collection of many Japanese folk tales.

Matsutani, Miyoko. *How the Withered Trees Blossomed*. New York: J.B. Lippincott Company, 1969.
This beautifully illustrated book is presented in Japanese tradition and reads back to front. Calligraphy is included in this somewhat tragic tale.

McDermott, Gerald. *The Stonecutter*. New York: The Viking Press, 1975.
A Japanese folk tale about a man's foolish desire for power. Illustrated with design motifs of traditional Japanese printmaking.

Piggot, Juliet. *Japanese Mythology*. New York: Paul Hamelyn, 1969.
Teacher's reference. A scholarly presentation of Japanese myths, legends, and ancient art pieces.

Price, Christine. *Asian Folk and Fairy Tales*. AM200, Record. AM201, Cassette.
Recorded folktales from India, Japan, and Korea.

Sasaki, Jeannie and Uzeda, Frances. *Chocho is for Butterfly*. Available at Children's Book and Music Center, Los Angeles, California.
A Japanese-English pre-primer in simple bright colors. An enjoyable and easy introduction to the Japanese language.

Uchida, Yoshiko. *The Rooster Who Understood Japanese*. New York: Charles Scribner's Sons, 1976.
This delightful tale of a Japanese-American girl and her pet rooster is appropriate for children's listening.

Uyeda, Frances and Sasaki, Jeannie. *Fold, Cut, and Say the Japanese Way*. Available at Children's Book and Music Center in Los Angeles, California.
An excellent book for the primary student. Includes many crafts and activities of Japan, i.e., Zori, Carp, and good luck tree with seeds for actual planting.

Yolen, Jane. *The Seeing Stick*. New York: Thomas Y. Crowell Company, 1977.
A modern tale told in the classical Japanese folktale manner. Tells how an old man teaches the emperor's blind daughter to see. Beautiful wash crayon and pencil drawings are an integral part of the equally beautiful text.

F.   FOLKLORE MATERIALS: MEXICO

Cancioncitas Para Chiquintines. SP516, Book.
Book and record feature piano arrangements for each Spanish-language song.

Campos, Anthony. *Mexican Folk Tales*. Tucson, Arizona: The University of Arizona Press, 1977.
A collection of twenty-seven delightful tales of Mexican origin. Appropriate for children's listening.

Canciones y Juegos Infantiles. Materials Acquisition Project. 2950 National Avenue, San Diego, California 92113. Fortuna Discos, Mexico.
All Spanish record with games for children.

Children's Songs of Mexico. SP122-125, record, filmstrips, and book.
Bilingual presentaion of fun-to-sing Mexican songs.

Ferrer, Chucho. *Cri-Cri y Sus Nuevos Amigos.* RCC, S.A. de C.V.; Available at Children's Book and Music Center, Los Angeles, California.
> Record with fun Spanish songs for children.

Flores, Gloriamalia. *Special Events in the Barrio: Volume One: Los Dias de Los Muertos.* Los Angeles: Self-Help Graphics and Art, Inc., 1976.
> Oversize book with large line drawings depicting the holiday — The Day of the Dead. The bilingual text is appropriate for child's reading level.

Gonzales, Dolores (ed.). *Canciones y Juegos de Nuevo Mexico.* SP508, Book.
> Bilingual presentation of songs and games of Spanish-speaking children.

Juegos Meniques Para Chiquitines. SP518, Book.
> Spanish finger plays with some English instructions.

Katz, Lucinda Lee (comp.). *Bilingual/Bicultural Multi-Cultural Resources.* ERIC/ECE, Urbana, Illinois, 1974. ERIC Clearinghouse on Early Childhood Education, University of Illinois, 805 W. Pennsylvania Avenue, Urbana, Illinois 61801.

Kent, Jack. *The Christmas Piñata.* SP5, Book.
> Picture book of Mexican village life.

Kouzel, Daisy and Thollander, Earl. *The Cuckoo's Reward, El Premio Del Cuco.* Garden City, New York: Doubleday, 1977.
> This beautifully illustrated bilingual folktale is appropriate for children's listening. This tale deals with envy, vanity, bravery and self-sacrifice.

Latin American Children Game Songs. SP206, Record.
> Bilingual presentation of children singing songs from the Mexican culture.

Lindsey, David. *The Wonderful Chirrionera and Other Tales from Mexican Folklore.* Texas: Heidelberg Publishing, 1974.
> A delightful collection of Mexican folklore.

Martinez, Jimmie and Watters, Arlene. *Us, A Cultural Mosaic.* San Diego, California: San Diego City Schools, 1977.
> Interesting collection of activities which may be helpful to teachers when planning programs and activities.

Mexican Folk Dances. PE620, Record.
> Instrumentals of Mexican folk dances with diagrams and instructions for learning.

Mistral, Gabrula. *Crickets and Frogs.* New York: Atheneum, 1977.
> Woodblock prints accompany this delightful bilingual tale which is popular throughout Mexico and other Spanish-speaking countries. This tale of a cricket's search for his identity is appropriate for the young child's reading level.

Nava, Louisa (prod.). *Lectura Con Gabriela.* Recorded by Gabriela De La Paz. Copyright: 1977 by Louise Elaine Nava, 22439 Robin Oaks Terrace, Diamond Bar, California 91765.
> Record of fun Spanish songs. Designed to aid reading in Spanish.

Nicholson, Irene. *Mexican and Central American Mythology.* New York: Paul Hamlyn, 1967.
> Teacher resource for art and mythology. Illustrations are drawn from seven cultures — Maya, Olmec, Zapotec, Mixtec, Totanac, Toltec, and Aztec.

Nine Days to Christmas. SP12, Book.
> For children's listening. Set in a modern Mexican city.

Para Chiquitines. SP522, Book.
> Book to accompany record of songs, verses and fingerplays.

Politi, Leo. *Little Leo.* New York: Scribners, 1951.

Politi, Leo. *The Nicest Gift.* New York: Charles Scribner's Sons, 1973.
> Chicano tale of Christmas in Los Angeles when the family dog disappears. Beautifully illustrated and utilizes numerous Spanish words. Appropriate for children's listening.

Politi, Leo. *Three Stalks of Corn*. New York: Charles Scribner's Sons, 1976.

    A Chicano tale of a small girl and her grandmother who live in a barrio in California. Explains why corn is precious to culture and includes some corn recipes.

Prieto, Mariana. *Play It In Spanish*. New York: The John Day Company, 1973.

    Seventeen games and action songs from many Spanish-speaking countries including the words and music in both English and Spanish.

Rohmer, Harriet and Anchondo, Mary. *How We Came to the Fifth World. Como Vinimos al Quinto Mundo*. San Francisco, California: Children's Book Press, 1976.

    One of a series of paperback bilingual myths and legends from various Spanish-speaking cultures. Color illustrations and text describe an Aztec myth of the creation and destruction of the first four of our five worlds.

Sandoval, Ruben. *Games, Games, Games, Juegos, Juegos, Juegos*. Garden City, New York: Doubleday, 1977.

    Bilingual text and photographs of Chicano children at play. Game rules are included.

Sayer, Chloë. *Crafts of Mexico*. New York: Doubleday, 1977.

    Teacher resource. Beautiful, colorful photo illustrations of Mexican folk crafts. Text offers detailed knowledge of authentic folk arts.

Schreiner, Nikki. *Mexico*. Palos Verdes Estates, California: Touch and See, 1976.

    Mural and book packet. Line drawings may be duplicated for one teacher's classroom. Brief stories accompany the material and are appropriate for child's reading level.

Singer, Jane and Singer, Kurt. *Folk Tales of Mexico*. Minneapolis, Minnesota: T.S. Denison and Company, Inc., 1969.

    A collection of ten Mexican folk tales. Appropriate for children's listening.

Songs in Spanish for Children. SP211, Record.

    A collection of songs in Spanish about counting, animals, months of year. An illustrated booklet is included with Spanish songs and English vocabulary.

Stevens, Cat. *Teaser and the Firecat*. New York: Four Wind Press, 1972.

    A simple, imaginative picture book that can be read by the Spanish or French speaking student. Young readers are delighted to discover the ease of translation.

Tallon, Robert. *ABCDEFGHIJKLMNOPQRSTUVWXYZ in English and Spanish*. New York: The Lion Press, 1969.

    Bilingual alphabet book. Colorful illustrations. Pronunciation guide includes aid for both Spanish and English.

The Toy Trumpet. SP14, Book.

    Clever illustrations tell the story of a small boy's life in his village.

Treasury of Mexican Folkways. SP504, Book.

    Teacher reference. Includes myths, customs, folklore, and tradition as well as songs and dances of Mexico.

Vasquez, Mario (ed.). *Our First Ancestors*. Los Angeles: A.B.C. Pride Publications, 1974.

    A bilingual coloring book which depicts the Mexican culture.

Vela, Irma. *Bailes a Colores*. Records or Cassettes. Available from: American Universal Artforms Corporation, Box 2242, Austin, Texas 78767.

    Consists of Units I, II, III, with manuals, step chart, records (or cassettes) and various other informative materials.

Versitos Para Chiquitines. SP520, Book.

    Spanish verses of El Chorrito, A Brincar, etc.

G. FOLKLORE MATERIALS: NATIVE AMERICAN

Aliki. *Corn Is Maize, the Gift of the Indians*. New York: Thomas Y. Crowell Company, 1976.
    The author relays the account of the amazing plant that Native Americans discovered, nurtured, and then shared with the rest of the world.

American Indian Tales for Children. Retold by Anne Pellowski. NA506, Record.
    A collection of six fun-to-hear Native American folk tales for children.

Amon, Aline. *Talking Hands*. Garden City, New York: Doubleday and Company, Inc., 1968.
    A very simple and clearly illustrated text of Native American sign language. The author includes sample sentences to describe the life of a typical Plains boy. It also shows how you can use signs today in everyday activities.

Ballard, Louis. *American Indian Music for the Classroom*. NA500-502, Records, Cassettes, and Transparencies.
    A scholarly presentation of Native American music with visual aids.

Baylor, Byrd. *Before You Came This Way*. New York: E.P. Dutton and Company, Inc., 1969.
    Prehistoric Native American lifestyle is imagined by the original story of petroglyphs on canyon walls.

Baylor, Byrd. *The Desert Is Theirs*. New York: Charles Scribner's Sons, 1975.
    A story of the Papagos Indians with illustrations that eloquently shows the oneness of the desert people and their land.

Baylor, Byrd. *Hawk, I'm Your Brother*. New York: Charles Scribner's Sons, 1976.
    A modern tale about a Native American boy who wants to fly.

Baylor, Byrd. *They Put On Masks*. New York: Charles Scribner's Sons, 1974.
    Beautifully illustrates and describes the Native American use of masks.

Baylor, Byrd. *When Clay Sings*. New York: Charles Scribner's Sons, 1972.
    The author and illustrator create a picture of the earlier Native American way of life, by putting together pieces of prehistoric pottery.

Bernstein, Margery and Kobrin, Janet. *Coyote Goes Hunting for Fire*. New York: Charles Scribner's Sons, 1974.
    A California Native American myth about how animals discovered fire. First told by the Yano Indians and retold by the authors so that young children can read the myth themselves.

Bernstein, Margery and Kobrin, Janet. *Earth Namer*. New York: Charles Scribner's Sons, 1974.
    A California Native American myth about the origin of the earth. First told by Maiden Indians and retold by the authors so that young students can read the myth themselves.

Bernstein, Margery and Kobrin, Janet. *How the Sun Made a Promise and Kept It*. New York: Charles Scribner's Sons, 1974.
    A Canadian Native American myth of how the brave beaver freed the sun and of the promise the sun made in return. First told by Bungee Indians and retold by the authors in simple form for easier reading level.

Bernstein, Margery and Kobrin, Janet. *The Summer Maker*. New York: Charles Scribner's Sons, 1977.
    A Native American myth about how the first summer came to be. First told by the Ojibway Indians and retold by the authors for the 6 thru 9 year old child.

Blood, Charles and Link, Martin. *The Goat in the Rug*. New York: Parents Magazine Press, 1976.
    A picture book with authentic Navajo designs and locales to help tell the story of traditional Navajo weaving.

Blue-Wings-Flying. NA131, Book.

    Good insight into Hopi Indian culture and legends. Easily used with young children.

Burland, Cottie. *North American Indian Mythology*. New York: Hamlyn Publishing Group, 1975.

    Teacher reference. A wide-ranging survey of the mythology of various groups of Native Americans. Each chapter begins with a description of the geographical background of the group because the outlook on life and, therefore, mythology was influenced by environment.

Crowder, Jack. *Stephannie and the Coyote*. Bernalillo, New Mexico: Jack Crowder, 1969.

    A bilingual book in Navajo and English with a pronunciation chart and glossary. It tells the story of a Navajo child's typical day and family with colorful photos.

Fregois, Claudia. *A Gift*. Englewood Cliffs, New Jersey: Prentice-Hall, Inc., 1976.

    A modern tale that can be read to young children with illustrations utilizing Native American motifs.

Hall, Geraldine. *Kee's Home*. Flagstaff, Arizona: Northland Press, 1976.

    A Navajo bilingual primer, that also introduces the Navajo language to English-speaking children. Each language is printed in a separate color. Each page of text is faced with a beautiful illustration depicting Navajo lifestyle.

Hofman, Charles. *American Indians Sing*. New York: The John Day Company, 1967.

    Teacher reference. The text presents the significance of music in Native American lives, their musical instruments, the importance of dance in ritual and ceremony, and gives examples of their song-poetry.

McDermott, Gerald. *Arrow to the Sun*. New York: The Viking Press, Inc., 1974.

    An adaptation of the Pueblo Native American's tale of the universal myth of the hero-guest. Mr. McDermott captures the qualities of Pueblo art to aid in retelling this myth.

McGovern, Ann. *If You Lived with the Sioux Indians*. NA228, Book.

    Describes Sioux life in detail.

Niethammer, Carolyn. *Daughters of the Earth*. New York: Collier Books, 1977.

    The text includes Native American folklore concerning women from birth to death.

Rockwell, Anne. *The Dancing Stars*. New York: Thomas Y. Crowell Company, 1972.

    An Iroquois legend of the creation of a familiar constellation retold in easy words and delightful illustrations.

Sleator, William. *The Angry Moon*. NA102, Book.

    The legend of a villainous moon with illustrations adapted from Tlingit design.

Sounds of Indian America. NA544, Record. NA545, Cassette.

    Music and dances of the plains and southwest Native Americans. Packet includes seven pages of color photographs of dancers. Especially appropriate for primary students.

H.   FOLKLORE MATERIALS: WESTERN AFRICA

Aardema, Verna. *Who's in Rabbit's House?* New York: The Dial Press, 1977.

    This African folktale provides delightful listening for children. Animal masks are worn by the people to depict this tale.

Aardema, Verna. *Why Mosquitoes Buzz in People's Ears*. New York: The Dial Press, 1975.

    This delightful picture book for children's listening is an authentic animal tale of Western Africa.

Adoff, Arnold. *Big Sister Tells Me That I'm Black*. New York: Holt, Rinehart and Winston, 1976.

    Children will enjoy reading this delightful, poetic tale of a black boy in America.

African Fables. BL500, Record.

    Two volumes of African fables suitable for young children.

African Village Folktales. BL506, Record. BL507, Cassette.

    Records or cassettes of African folktales from many different regions.

Dietz, Betty and Olatunji, Michael. *Musical Instruments of Africa*. New York: The John Day Company, 1965.

Teacher reference. Black and white photographs accompany this detailed description of the songs, instruments, and music of Africa.

Feelings, Muriel and Feelings, Tom. *Jambo Means Hello*. New York: The Dial Press, 1971.

Outstanding illustrations provide insights into East African life. Provides an awareness of the people and the environment that created the Swahili language.

Feelings, Muriel and Feelings, Tom. *Moja Means One*. New York: The Dial Press, 1971.

A Swahili counting book that beautifully portrays the African way of life.

Folk Songs of Africa. BL457, Record.

A collection of African songs for children. Includes: Kum Bah Yah, work songs, and children's songs.

Gerson, Mary-Joan. *Omoteji's Baby Brother*. New York: Henry Z. Walch, Inc., 1974.

Children will enjoy listening to this tale of Nigerian life and customs in which a young boy chooses a special gift for his newborn brother's naming ceremony.

Giovanni, Nikki. *Spin a Soft Black Song*. BL737, Book.

Poetry for and about children from the black perspective.

Greenfield, Eloise. *Africa Dream*. BL253, Book.

A picture book poem fantasy about a black child's visit to Africa. The beautiful pictures depict the rich culture of African life.

Haley, Gail. *A Story, A Story*. BL586, Book.

A retold African tale that has won a Caldecott Award.

Jenkins, Ella. *Jambo and Other Call and Response Songs and Chants*. SG246, Record.

Call and response songs and counting in Swahili. All of the Ella Jenkins' records are delightful. Some other titles are:

> Adventures in Rhythm
> And One and Two
> Call and Response
> Counting Games and Rhythms for Little Ones
> Little Johnny Brown
> My Street Begins at My House
> We Are America's Children

Jenkins, Ella. *The Ella Jenkins Songbook for Children*. New York: Oak Publications, 1966.

Music and lyrics for many of Ella Jenkin's most popular songs.

Jones, Bessie. *Bessie Jones: So Glad I'm Here*. BL311, Record.

A record of songs, games, and stories from the Georgia Sea Islands.

Jones, Bessie, Hawes, Bess. *Step it Down*. PT170, Book.

Teacher reference. Excellent source for Afro-American heritage folklore — games, songs, stories.

Keats, Ezra. *John Henry*. New York: Pantheon Books, 1965.

A modern tale of a black American folk hero.

Langner, Nola. *Rafiki*. New York: The Viking Press, 1977.

This tale of a little girl with big ideas is set in Eastern Africa. The illustrations are delightful. Appropriate for children's listening.

McDermott, Gerald. *Anansi the Spider*. New York: Holt, Rinehart, and Winston, 1972.

Anansi, the spider, is a great folk hero of Western Africa. In this delightful story the child may read of Anansi's experiences with fish and falcon.

McDermott, Gerald. *The Magic Tree*. San Francisco: Holt, Rinehart, and Winston, 1975.

This beautifully illustrated tale is appropriate for children's listening. It is a tale of family difficulties set in Mid-Africa.

Musgrove, Margaret. *Ashanti to Zulu*. BL250, Book.

Using the letters of the alphabet from A to Z, the reader is introduced to 26 African peoples.

The beautiful illustrations and brief text that accompanies each letter depicts a custom important to each of the peoples.

Pearl Primus' Africa. BL173, 3 Records. BL174, 3 Cassettes.

Teacher reference for primary grades.

Singing Games from Ghana. BL476, Record with book.

Songs from Ghana with accompanying book which contains melodies, words and easy directions.

ART RECIPES

A. DOUGH - which will get very hard

INGREDIENTS:

2 C.	(480ml.)	Table salt
2/3 C.	(160ml.)	Water

PROCEDURE:

1. Mix and heat ingredients above in saucepan. Measure 1 C. (240ml.) cornstarch, loosely packed; ½ C. (120ml.) cold water; and food coloring, if desired.
2. Mix these ingredients together and add to hot mixture in saucepan.
3. Stir until it leaves sides of pan and forms a ball.

B. FINGERPAINT

INGREDIENTS:

1 C.	(240ml.)	Water
1/3 C.	(80ml.)	Cornstarch
	—	Glycerine
		Food Coloring

PROCEDURE:

1. Bring water to a boil and dissolve starch and stir two together.
2. Let mixture cool again and store in cool place.

C. PAPIER MÂCHÉ - SHREDDED

MATERIALS:

Newspaper, torn in strips

Dry wallpaper paste or 3 Tbs. (45ml.) flour and 1 pint (480ml.) water. Boil until mixture is thick as heavy cream, then add ½ tsp. (2.5ml.) salt.

PROCEDURE:

1. Tear newspaper into strips and soak in hot water in a rust-proof container for 24 hours.
2. Mash soaked paper until it is pulpy. Squeeze out excess water.
3. Add dry wallpaper paste powder to mixture and include some salt to prevent souring.

D. PAPIER MÂCHÉ - FOR STRIP WORK
INGREDIENTS:

    Newspaper torn in strips
    Paste mixture shown in "C"

PROCEDURE:

1. Tear newspaper or paper toweling into strips ½" wide.
2. Dip each strip into paste mixture.
3. Apply strips diagonally onto surface of mold. Apply additional strips in a criss-cross fashion for 5 or 6 layers.
4. If the mâché is to be removed from the mold, apply a liberal covering of vaseline or petroleum jelly to the surface of the mold.

E. PASTE FOR A GROUP
INGREDIENTS:

2 C.	(240ml.)	Flour
4½ C.	(4.2 l.)	Boiling water
1½ tsp.	(7.5ml.)	Oil of wintergreen
2 C.	(240ml.)	Cold water
2 tsp.	(10ml.)	Powdered alum

PROCEDURE:

1. Mix flour with cold water. Slowly add boiling water and stir.
2. Cook in double boiler (over low heat) until smooth.
3. Add alum and stir until smooth.
4. Remove from stove, add oil of wintergreen when mixture is cool.
5. Store in covered jars in a cool place.

F. SAWDUST PASTE
INGREDIENTS:

½ C.	(120ml.)	Flour
3 C.	(2.8 l.)	Water
3 Tbs.	(45ml.)	Powdered alum
3 Tbs.	(45ml.)	Powdered glue
1 Tbs.	(15ml.)	Oil of cloves
		Sawdust

PROCEDURE:

1. Blend flour and water. Add remaining ingredients. Blend well.
2. Add sawdust (about 2 C. or 240ml.) until mixture is easily formed by pressure.

G. WHEAT PASTE FOR A GROUP
INGREDIENTS:

2 C.	(480ml.)	Boiling water
1 C.	(240ml.)	Wheat flour
½ C.	(120ml.)	Salt (for preservative)

PROCEDURE:

    Stir all above ingredients together well.

H. HARDENING PLAYDOUGH

INGREDIENTS:

3 C.	(720ml.)	Flour
1 C.	(240 ml.)	Salt
1 Tbs.	(15ml.)	Powdered alum
4 Tbs.	(60ml.)	Salad oil
1½ C.	(360ml.)	Boiling water

PROCEDURE:

1. Add all ingredients, except boiling water.
2. Vigorously mix in boiling water.
3. Knead dough on wax paper.
4. Food coloring may be kneaded into the dough.
5. This dough dries hard when left in air.

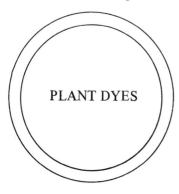

PLANT DYES

African women have passed their recipes for vegetable dyes from generation to generation. The children learn about dyes and colors by gathering roots, leaves and flowers for their mothers to make their dyes.

You may want to make plant dyes for the raffia you will use in your weaving. Dyeing involves two processes. First, you prepare the "mordant" which allows the fiber to absorb the color and make it fast. Secondly, you prepare and use the dye to give the fiber color.

The easiest mordants to obtain are alum or white vinegar and cream of tartar. You dissolve several tablespoons of the mordant in a cup of cool water, then add this mixture to the bucket of hot water you will use for "mordanting". You must have the fiber in the mordant for at least two hours. Remove the fibers and squeeze out excess water. Sometimes different mordants produce different shades of the same color.

After mordanting your raffia fiber, you soak it in the dye bath of very hot but not boiling water. You leave it in the bath until it is a shade or two darker than you want because it will dry lighter. When the fiber is not quite dry, it is most flexible and easiest to use.

Saffron (Yellow): Alum mordant. Boil a few pinches of dried saffron in a little water for half an hour. Strain the liquid through a clean cloth (an old pillow case is good for this) into the bath for dye.

Marigold and Golden Marguerite (Orange): Alum mordant. Collect a large number of flowers. Boil for an hour or longer. Strain liquid into the bath.

Onion (Orange): Alum mordant. Collect several brown skins from cooking onions. Cover with water and cook for at least one hour. Strain.

Dahlia and Zinnia (Red): Boil petals of flowers for an hour and strain.

Dandelions (Magenta): Gather several whole plants. Cover with water and boil for two hours. Strain.

Black Walnut Hulls (Brown): No mordant required. Cover a pot full of hulls with water. Leave overnight. Boil for two hours, then strain into bath for dye.

PARALLELS OF ART IN CULTURES FOUND IN THIS TEXT

	CHINA	GREECE	ISRAEL	JAPAN	MEXICO	NATIVE AMERICAN	WEST AFRICA
MASKS	Lion's Head, 13	Masks for Greek Play, 152		Masks for Nō Drama, 209	Masks, 236	Masks, 262	Masks, 295
BARK PAINTING					Bark Painting, 234 Amatl Witchcraft Dolls, 233	Pictograph Painting on Hides, 264	
EMBROIDERED CLOTH		Embroidered Cloth, 147	Stitchery, 183				
FAMILY EMBLEM	Chinese Chops, 126			Family Crest, 205			
FANS	Fans, 127			Fans, 207			Fans, 292
GOD'S EYE					Ojos de Dios, 236	Warrior's Eye of God Amulet, 272	
MOSAICS		Straw Painting, 155			Yarn Painting, 242	Sand Painting, 265	
PUPPETS		Karagiosi Puppets, 149	Purim Puppet, 181				
SHAKING MUSICAL INSTRUMENTS			Musical Instruments Made of Plants, 180		Maracas, 235	Gourd Rattles, 260	
POTTERY	Lacquered Plates, 128	Painted Earthenware, 154			Painted Paper Plates, 237 Pottery, 239	Rolled Clay Bowl, 264	Papier Mâché Bowl, 297
KITES			Kites, 178	Kites, 208			
BATIK				Batik, 200			Batik, 290

PARALLELS OF COOKING IN CULTURES FOUND IN THIS TEXT

	CHINA	GREECE	ISRAEL	JAPAN	MEXICO	NATIVE AMERICAN	WEST AFRICA
PAPER COOKING	Paper Chicken, 138	Lamb in a Bag, 162		Tori No Gin-Gami Yaki, 215			
FLAT BREAD	Mandarin Pancakes, 137		Pita Bread, 191		Tortillas, 249	Navajo Fry Bread, 276 Pekee Bread, 277 Tse Aste, 278	
DEEP FRIED FILLED PASTRY	Spring Rolls, 140 Fried Wonton, 136 Teem Gok, 140				Chimichangas, 244		
FILLED FLAT BREAD	Mandarin Pancakes, 137 Filled with Hot Chili Beef, 137	Baklava, 158 Tiropetes, 165	Falafel, 187		Quesadillas, 248 Tacos, 249		
FRIED VEGETABLES OR FRUITS		Drachma Fried Potatoes, 159	Fruit Fritters, 188	Tempura, 219			Fried Plantain, 300 Cassava Chips, 299
FRITTERS		Patatokeftehes, 164	Latkes, 191	Egg Rolls, 215			Akara, 298 Banana Fritters, 299
DEEP FRIED CAKES					Churros, 245 Naquis, 247		Ghana Cakes, 301
SOUP		Lemon Soup, 162 Lentil Soup Fassoulada Soup, 163		Egg Soup, 216			Groundnut Soup, 301

PARALLELS OF RECREATION IN CULTURES FOUND IN THIS TEXT

	CHINA	GREECE	ISRAEL	JAPAN	MEXICO	NATIVE AMERICAN	WEST AFRICA
GAMES OF TAG	Blindman's Tag, 141	Pebble, 168		Japanese Tag, 223 Hunting the Treasure, 223 Occupations, 224	Colores, 251 Encantados, 252		African Blindman's Buff, 303 Cat & Rat, 303 Hen and Wildcat, 304 Mulambilwa, 305
SENSORY MOTOR	Chopstick Pickup, 142 Rice Bag Jacks, 142		Bli Yadayim, 193 Peanuts in the Bottle, 197	Fuku Warai, 221 Juggling, 223		Cat's Cradle, 280 Cup on a Stick, 281 Fruit & Nuts, 282	Jumping, 305
RHYTHM GAMES	Chinese Stick Rhythms, 141					Game of the Moccasin, 282 Stick Passing, 285	
HIDE AND SEEK		Hide, 167 Krifto, 167	Hide and Seek, 194				
MATH AND LOGIC GAMES	Fist Throwing, 142 Odd or Even, 142			Five Eyes, 221		Cherrystones, 280 Papago, 284	Jarbadach, 304 Owari, 305
TARGET GAMES	Square Throwing, 143		Lag B'Omer, 195		La Pelota, 252	Arrow Game, 279 Arrow Through the Hoop, 279 Ball and Ring Game, 279 Ring Stick Game, 284	Nsikwi, 305
BALL GAMES		Circle Ball, 167		Yemari, 223		Ball Race, 279 Buckskin Ball, 279	Handball, 304
DRAMATIC PLAY			Hail O' King, 194		Coyote and Sheep, 251 Colores, 251 Juan Pirulero, 252		Game Trap, 304
FOLLOW THE LEADER GAMES				Hana, Hana, Hana, Kuchi, 221 Big Lamp, Little Lamp, 221			Simon Says, 306

CHAPTER VI
CHINA

INDEX

ABOUT CHINA

In 1912 the Ch'ing Imperial Dynasty of China was overthrown. At this time, the Republic of China was established. After 37 years of foreign invasion and inner conflict, mainland China became the People's Republic of China. In 1949, the government of the Republic of China moved to the island of Taiwan. Although modern political ideologies have separated the original physical boundaries of China, culture and common traditions still abound.

People of Chinese descent may be found throughout the world. During specific periods in history, large groups of Chinese moved to Vietnam, the Philippines, Hawaii, and other parts of the United States (particularly California and New York). The migration of peoples is one way in which man has been able to share his cultural resource with others.

For our study of China's folklore we will deal with traditional folkways as they are enjoyed by people of Chinese ancestry throughout the world.

INTRODUCING THE ARTS OF CHINA

There are many traditional Chinese art forms for ivory, bronze, jade, and wooden carving. Porcelain, silk and lacquerware are also very popular.

The people of China produce items both of quality and crafts for fun and festivals. Today, Chinese artists are being encouraged to develop greater skills and to revive the old techniques such as the carving of precious stones.

124

BREAD DOUGH FIGURES

BACKGROUND: At one time, Kwangchow was a center for doughmen. These doughmen would walk down the streets selling personally designed figures of small animals and people fashioned from bread dough. The walking doughman would dry his crudely-fashioned, brightly-colored figures in the sun. Today, when these figures are produced in the workshops a slow oven is used to facilitate the drying process.

MATERIALS:

This recipe doesn't keep well unbaked. Bake as soon as possible.

1 C.	(240ml.)	Flour
¼ C.	(60ml.)	Salt
7 Tbs.	(105ml.)	Water

PROCEDURE:
1. Mix the dough together and knead until workable.
2. Form into any shape or figure.
3. Bake in 350°F, 176°C oven for 1 hour.
4. Food coloring or powdered poster paint may be added to the dough as you knead and mix, or figure may be formed, baked, and then painted with brightly colored paints.
5. If the dough figure is very thick, poke a hole in the underside of base to prevent cracking.

 CHINESE CHOPS

BACKGROUND: All business transactions, personal legal documents, check writing, financial notes, etc., require the stamp of a personalized chop of the people involved. The chop has the same effect and meaning as a signature does in western countries. The chop that is used by a person on official papers must be registered in advance at the local government office. An expert is often required to read the complicated calligraphy on a chop. A person may choose to use several chops but only one style of his chop may be registered. It is against the law, and will be prosecuted as forgery, if some one tries to forge another person's chop or intends to take advantage of that chop.

The Chinese have eight different calligraphy styles so a chop can be carved in eight different ways according to the individual's taste.

A chop is also the way the Chinese sign their name on art work. The chops are printed in red ink. They are usually made from bamboo, ivory, soapstone or jade if it is a very special chop.

You can make your own chop by carving your initials or Chinese name on a small eraser. Try several designs. When you have chosen your official chop, mark it with the special symbol (⪦) in the lower left-hand corner.

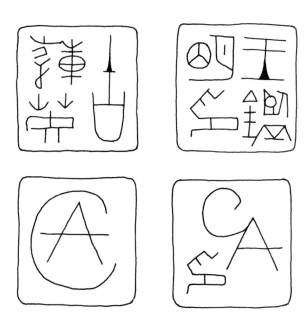

 FANS

BACKGROUND: Fans are now largely a Chinese export item. At one time, however, fans were used daily by almost all the people of China. They were used both for their cooling effect when creating new air currents and as an extension of the hand when gesturing. Special fans may be used by the well-dressed woman in order to improve her appearance. A special kind of fan is made of algum and has delicate wood carving work on it. When this kind of fan is waved in the air, the essence of a perfume-like smell will be spread in the surrounding area.

Chinese honeycomb fans are fun to make and represent a papercraft that was invented by the Chinese. Fans are produced by glueing this delicate papercraft to bamboo slats.

MATERIALS:

> Ten strips of tissue paper, 1X10 inches
> (Inserts between new ditto masters may be saved and used if tissue is not readily available)
> White glue
> Que-Tips (for applying glue if not in applicator bottles)
> 2 ice cream sticks (or coffee stirrers, or bamboo sticks)
> Cellophane tape

PROCEDURE:

1. Apply glue as illustrated by 5 dotted lines.
2. Lay second strip on top of first and apply glue between previous applications, as indicated by four arrows.
3. Continue layering strips and applying glue in alternate positions until all strips are joined.
4. Allow this to dry thoroughly.
5. Open the dry strips and crease in opposite direction to form diamond shapes. Press firmly.
6. Glue ice cream sticks to flat sides and tape at bottom.
7. Open fan 360° so that the 2 ice cream sticks touch and fan is opened to a circle.

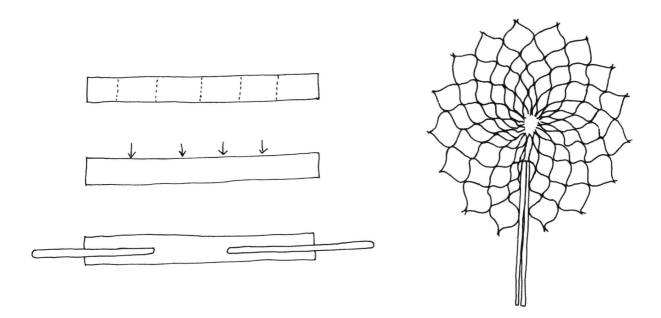

 LACQUERED PAPER PLATES

BACKGROUND: Chinese lacquerware is produced by coating a wooden object with as many as forty layers of varnish. This is a time-consuming process since each layer of varnish must be completely dry before the next coat is added. We limited our applications to two in order to offer an enjoyable activity to children.

MATERIALS:

>Paper plate
>Poster paints and brushes
>White glue
>Carbon paper

PROCEDURE:

1. Paint the paper plate a solid color and allow to dry.
2. Use carbon paper to transfer one of the Chinese designs to your plate or create your own design.
3. Paint the design and allow it to dry.
4. Paint the entire plate with at least two coats of white glue — allow plate to dry between coats.

PATTERN FOR LACQUERED PAPER PLATES AND LANTERNS

 LANTERNS

BACKGROUND: Lanterns are used by many people in China to add enjoyment to festivals and celebrations. For centuries, lanterns have been made of jade, glass, tissue or rice paper, or silk. Some Chinese lanterns have combined textile arts with dramatic lighting.

MATERIALS:

  Oatmeal or salt box. (If these are not available, form poster board into cylinders)
  String
  Scissors, hole punch
  Felt-tip markers
  Shiny fabric to resemble silk (tissue paper may also be substituted)

PROCEDURE:

1. Cut 2 to 4 rectangles out of an oatmeal box (after removing the outer paper).
2. Cut a piece of fabric large enough to fit inside the cylinder and overlap slightly.
3. Trace around the Chinese design patterns (or draw some designs of your own).
4. Use felt-tip markers to add vibrant colors.
5. Glue the fabric into the inside of the oatmeal carton and carefully stretch it so it will not dry wrinkled.
   (Younger children may need to glue the fabric to the outside of the cylinder to simplify the process.)
6. Punch holes on each side of the lantern and tie a string to aid in hanging.

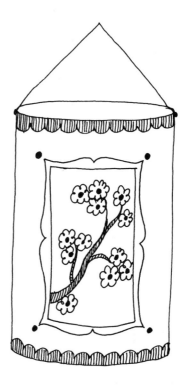

LION'S HEAD OR DRAGON'S COSTUME

BACKGROUND: In many parts of China, both dragon's and lion's head costumes are worn during parades and holiday celebrations. The costumed lion dances through the streets as he bounces to the beat of the music.

MATERIALS:

> Large cardboard box
> Poster paints and brushes
> Sheet dyed a bright color
> Tissue paper
> Assorted art scraps

PROCEDURE:

1. Paint and decorate a large cardboard box to resemble the head of an animal, i.e., dragon or lion.
2. Attach, to the head, a sheet which has been dyed a bright color.
3. Use 2 to 3 children under the box and sheet to dance and join in the parade.

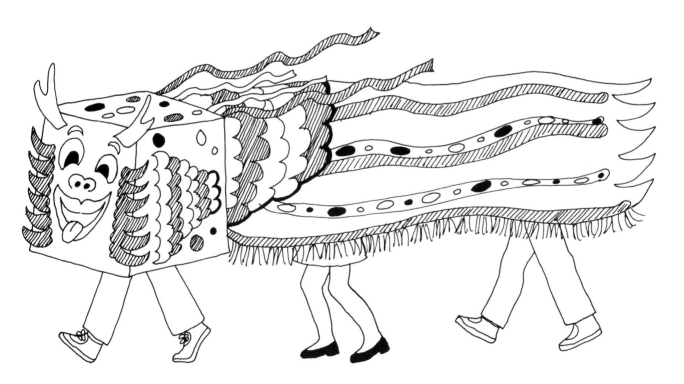

 PAPER CUTS

BACKGROUND: Many Chinese families have a family member who is particularly skilled at paper cutting. Paper is a favorite decoration during many Chinese holidays and red lacy-looking paper cuts are a common sight throughout China and among Chinese-Americans.

MATERIALS:

        Colored tissue paper

        Patterns of various paper cuts

        Scissors and pencils

PROCEDURE:

1. Trace one of the patterns on to your colored tissue paper.

2. Carefully cut on all the heavy lines and cut and remove those sections which are to be thrown away.

3. Your paper cut may be hung to fly freely in the breeze or it may be mounted on a piece of sturdy paper for display.

PATTERNS FOR PAPER CUTS

RED ENVELOPES - LI SEE

BACKGROUND: During the Chinese New Year celebration, red envelopes, containing money, are given as gifts. Married adults are usually the givers, while children, single adults, and the very elderly receive these money gifts as greetings. Very small coins, like pennies, nickels, and dimes, are given during funerals; consequently, these coins should not be included in a red envelope which is used for festive times when one wishes to express wishes for good luck or happiness. Red envelopes are decorated with gold calligraphy. White envelopes are used at funerals. Both of these envelopes are used much like greeting cards are used in the United States.

MATERIALS:

>Red paper cut into 6" squares
>Small rectangles of paper to make play money
>Tape
>Gold ink and brushes or crayons

PROCEDURE:

1. Place play money near center of red paper square.
2. Fold C up slightly and then once again.
3. Fold corners D and B toward center, overlapping slightly, and tape in place.
4. Fold A down to complete envelope and tuck into place.
5. Decorate with good wishes in gold.

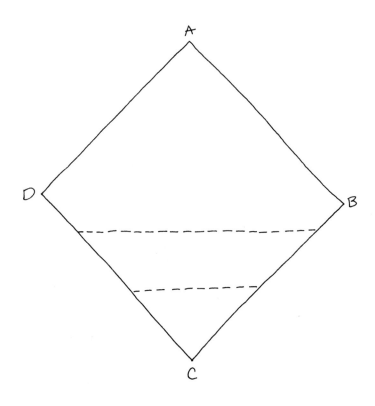

 INTRODUCING THE COOKING OF CHINA

Modern Chinese cooking has evolved out of what were distinctly regional cooking styles. Due to the vastness of China and the great range of its climates, these styles were each unique. The five early styles were Peking, Honan, Szechwan, Canton and Fukien. Today four more general schools of cooking are referred to: northern (Peking, Shantung and Honan); coastal (Fukien and Shanghai); inland (Szechwan and Yunnan); and southern (the area around Canton).

Since China's history includes so much hunger and hardship, it is particularly admirable that the culture has developed its fine art of cooking. When a Chinese dish is prepared, more than just the sense of taste is considered. The colors must be pleasing to the eye, the ingredients must be of uniform size, and the food should have a pleasant aroma.

When a person is planning a meal, the dishes are chosen for contrasts in colors, textures, and tastes. A proper dinner includes one fowl, one fish, one meat dish and the appropriate vegetables. Desserts are practically unknown in China. In Chinese-American restaurants, however, this is not the case. Often a fortune cookie is served at the end of the meal.

When your group is planning a Chinese meal, the children will enjoy writing their own fortunes. Here are a few suggestions. Have the children write their own Chinese fortunes, put them in a bowl and have each child choose one.

Chinese Fortunes:

Opportunity knocks only once. Be alert.

What is done cannot be undone.

Better be left alone than in bad company.

Don't let your time disappear without a gain.

Every man is the architect of his own fortune.

Putting things off is robbing yourself of chance.

ALMOND COOKIES - HSING-JEN-PING

BACKGROUND: Almond cookies are the traditional sweet offered in Chinese-American restaurants. The Chinese eat very few desserts immediately following a meal. Most of their sweets are served at tea time. In Northern Chinese cooking, pine nuts are frequently used. Substituting these for blanched almonds would also be good.

INGREDIENTS:

½ C.	(120ml.)	Flour
1/8 tsp.	(.6ml.)	Baking soda
3 Tbs.	(45ml.)	Sugar
¼ C.	(60ml.)	Shortening (lard is best)
1 Tbs.	(15ml.)	Beaten egg
¼ tsp.	(1.2ml.)	Almond extract

1 drop yellow food coloring

2 blanched almonds (cut in half lengthwise)

PROCEDURE:
1. Sift flour and baking soda together.
2. Cream shortening and sugar.
3. Add the beaten egg and almond extract.
4. Mix thoroughly.
5. Gradually add the flour and soda mixture and mix well.
6. Roll a teaspoon of dough into a ball.
7. Press flat on ungreased cookie sheet.
8. Brush each cookie with beaten egg and press almond half into the center of each cookie.
9. Bake at 350°F, 176°C for 15-18 minutes.

 FRIED WON TON

BACKGROUND: Fried Won Ton is an example of "deem sum". Deem sum means "touch the heart" or "dot heart" and implies a snack or appetizer.

INGREDIENTS:

2 Tbs.	(30ml.)	Chopped shrimp
¼ tsp.	(1.2ml.)	Minced parsley
¼ tsp.	(1.2ml.)	Chopped green onion
¼ tsp.	(1.2ml.)	Chopped water chestnuts

4 drops of pressed ginger or 1/8 tsp. (.6ml.) dried ginger

| ½ tsp. | (2.4ml.) | Soy sauce |

2 Won Ton skins

PROCEDURE:
1. Mix carefully the first 6 ingredients.
2. Place the shrimp mixture on the won ton skin.
3. Moisten 2 edges of the skin with water.
4. Fold skin in half to form a triangle.
5. Press edges to seal.
6. Deep fat fry 1 to 2 minutes at 370°F, 190°C.
7. Drain.

HOT CHILI BEEF FILLING FOR MANDARIN PANCAKES

BACKGROUND: Mandarin pancakes are usually filled with duck. Another variation is a chili filling, similar to the Mexican burrito. The proper way to fill and eat a Mandarin pancake is to spread the pancake on a plate. Then you put two to three Tbs. (30-45ml.) filling or Peking duck in the center. You roll the pancake up. You place the roll in your left hand if you are right-handed. This frees your right hand for the use of chopsticks on other dishes. Support the end of the pancake from underneath with your thumb and small finger.

INGREDIENTS:

1 lb.	(454gms.)	Boneless beef sirloin (cut in paper-thin strips)
3 Tbs.	(45ml.)	Soy sauce
1 Tbs.	(15ml.)	Sherry
2 tsp.	(10ml.)	Cornstarch
½ to 1 tsp.	(2.5 to 5ml.)	Liquid hot-pepper seasoning (optional)

PROCEDURE:
1. Combine the soy sauce, sherry, cornstarch and hot pepper.
2. Add the meat and stir for a few minutes.
3. Heat 3 Tbs. (45ml.) oil over highest heat in fry pan.
4. Add meat mixture. (Be careful — this may splatter.)
5. Cook, stirring constantly, until meat looses pink color.
6. Place a little filling on Mandarin pancake, roll it up and fold one end up to hold in the pieces.

 MANDARIN PANCAKES

BACKGROUND: The Mandarin Pancake is another example of the many kinds of flat bread found in cultures throughout the world. It has been called a Chinese tortilla.

INGREDIENTS:

¼ C.	(60ml.)	All-purpose flour
3 Tbs.	(45ml.)	Boiling water
Sesame oil or salad oil		

PROCEDURE:
1. Put flour in margarine tub.
2. Add water and mix with chopsticks or a fork.
3. Work dough until it sticks together and then knead it on a lightly floured board or wax paper for 10 minutes until very smooth.
4. Cover and let stand for 30 minutes.
5. Cut the dough in half.
6. Shape each section into a ball and flatten slightly.
7. Roll each ball to 3" diameter on a lightly floured board.
8. Brush the top of one pancake with sesame oil and cover with the other pancake.

9.   Press the two rounds lightly but firmly together to align them.
10.   Roll the double pancake to 7" - 8" diameter on a lightly floured board.
11.   Fry on a medium-high, ungreased frying pan turning every 15 seconds until pancake is blistered by air pockets, is slightly translucent, parchment colored and feels dry. Pancake should not brown; if overcooked, it becomes brittle.
12.   Remove from pan and gently pull the two halves apart.

 PAPER CHICKEN

BACKGROUND: This recipe represents the Chinese method of cooking in cellophane paper. This method is utilized to keep all the moisture in the meat and to keep out all the oil.

INGREDIENTS:

1" pieces of boned and skinned chicken (one chicken breast should be enough for twelve children)

2 tsp.	(10ml.)	Soy sauce
2 tsp.	(10ml.)	Sherry or chicken broth
2 tsp.	(10ml.)	Salad oil or sesame oil
Slivers of ginger root (optional)		
¼ tsp.	(1.2ml.)	Grated fresh ginger
Cooking oil		

6" squares of foil or parchment paper

PROCEDURE:
1.   Bone and skin chicken and cut into 1 x 1 x ½ inch slices.
2.   Marinate pieces in soy sauce, broth, oil and ginger for 10 minutes.
3.   Place one drained piece of chicken in the center of the foil.
4.   Fold the foil over the chicken to form a triangle.
5.   Very carefully seal the foil so that no oil can seep into the chicken.
6.   Fry the packages for 2 minutes in deep oil at 350°F, 176°C.

RED BEAN POPSICLES - HUNG DOW BING

BACKGROUND: This is a very nutritious snack, because the red beans are healthful. The red beans are available only in Asian markets. If you are lucky enough to have this resource, the children will love this snack.

INGREDIENTS:

1 lb.	(.45kilo)	Smooth red beans (available in Asian markets)
Water to cover beans		
½ C.	(120ml.)	Brown sugar (more if you prefer a sweeter taste)
Popsicle sticks		

PROCEDURE:
1. Wash and drain beans.
2. Put in a large pot and cover with water.
3. Bring to boil, then add the sugar.
4. Cover pot, turn heat to low and simmer 2½ to 3 hours.
5. Allow the beans to cool slightly, then pour the mixture through a fine sieve into a large bowl.
6. Transfer to an ice cube tray and place in freezer.
7. When the mixture starts to congeal, insert popsicle sticks.

 SINGING RICE

BACKGROUND: This rice snaps, crackles and pops when hot food is poured over it. Legend says that a chef invented it from leftovers when he had to feed an emperor unexpectedly. The dish was such a success that the chef was hired to cook for the emperor's court.

INGREDIENTS:

1 C.	(240ml.)	Long grain rice
4 C.	(960ml.)	Water
2 tsp.	(10ml.)	Salt
Salad oil for deep frying		

PROCEDURE:
1. A day in advance put rice, water and salt in a two-quart saucepan. Let stand one half hour.
2. Bring to boil, cover and simmer thirty minutes.
3. Drain.
4. Spread evenly on a heavily greased cookie sheet.
5. Bake at 250°F, 121°C for 8 hours, turn rice occasionally with spatula.
6. Deep fry at 425°F, 218°C for 4 minutes.
7. Drain.
8. Transfer to warm serving platter or soup bowl.
9. Pour hot soup or entree over rice at table. (Rice, food and containers must be hot for rice to sing.)

SPRING ROLLS (OR PANCAKE ROLLS)

BACKGROUND: Spring rolls are soft pancakes offered to the diner, who then chooses the filling from a variety of foods laid out in front of him. He fills his pancake with the ingredients of his choice and rolls it up (turning up and in on one end). The fillings are usually shredded cooked meats and quick-fried crunchy vegetables. The pancakes get their name because they are served most often in the spring when the vegetables are best.

Because preparing spring-roll wrappers from scratch is such a precise culinary operation, we suggest that you use the ready-made variety. These are available at a Chinese market.

INGREDIENTS:

1 Tbs.	(15ml.)	Lard or shortening
¼ lb.	(.11kilo)	Shredded pork
¼ lb.	(.11kilo)	Bean sprouts
2 Spring onions (cut in 1" segments)		
1 Tbs.	(15ml.)	Soy sauce
1 tsp.	(5ml.)	Sugar
6 Spring-roll wrappers		

PROCEDURE:
1. Heat shortening in frying pan.
2. Add the pork and stir-fry for 2 minutes.
3. Add all other ingredients except wrappers and stir-fry for 2 minutes.
4. Place an equal portion on each of the wrappers.
5. Roll from the bottom two thirds of the way, then roll the rest of way.
6. Moisten edge with beaten egg and press down.
7. Deep fry the rolls in hot oil for about three minutes.
8. Drain.

 TEEM GOK

BACKGROUND: Teem Gok is an example of "deem sum". Deem sum means "touch the heart", or "dot heart", and implies a snack or appetizer.

INGREDIENTS:

¼ tsp.	(1.2ml.)	Brown sugar
¼ tsp.	(1.2ml.)	White sugar
¼ tsp.	(1.2ml.)	Coconut meal
2 peanuts, chopped		
Won ton skins		
Oil		

PROCEDURE:
1. Mix the first four ingredients.
2. Place mixture in center of won ton skin.
3. Moisten two adjacent edges with water.
4. Fold skin into triangle.
5. Seal the moistened edges.
6. Fry in hot oil for one minute at 375°F, 190°C.
7. Drain.

 INTRODUCING THE RECREATION OF CHINA

Many Chinese enjoy opera, movies, education, and political studies.

The government encourages physical fitness which includes swimming, volleyball, basketball, and ping-pong. Children spend their Sunday leisure time listening to storytellers, shooting marbles, and kicking shuttlecocks to see who can keep them airborne the longest.

 BLINDMAN'S TAG

This game is for three or four players. One player is "it" and wears a blindfold. All other players attempt to touch "it" without being caught. If "it" tags any player, that player automatically becomes "it".

 CHINESE STICK RHYTHMS

This game is for two players. The equipment is one or two rhythm sticks for each player. Players work out patterns and rhythms by hitting each other's and own sticks together.

 CHOPSTICK PICKUP

This game is for two players. The equipment is one bowl and a pair of chopsticks for each player. Five marbles are given to each player. The players are to use chopsticks to move the marbles from one bowl to the other. Hands may not touch the marbles; however, if a marble drops on the floor, the player may use his hand to pick up the marble and place it in the original bowl so he may begin again.

 FIST THROWING

This game is for two players. Two children face each other and count aloud and together: "One, two, three, four." On the fourth number, each child may call out any number between one and ten. The child who guesses closest to the total number of fingers extended on the two players' hands is the winner. Winners may accumulate points for a championship.

 LAME CHICKEN

This game is for two or more players. The equipment is ten ice cream sticks or tongue depressors spaced one foot apart in an even row. The player must hop over each of the sticks on one leg. After hopping over the ten sticks, he picks up the tenth stick and hops back over the remaining nine sticks. This continues until all the sticks are picked up or the player touches his other foot to the ground or touches his foot to any of the sticks.

 RICE BAG JACKS

This game is for two or more players. The equipment is five 3 inch fabric squares filled with 1 tablespoon of rice (or sand) and tied with string. During his turn, a player holds the five rice bags in his hand and drops them to spread apart on the table. He then throws up one rice bag and catches it, while picking up another rice bag from the table. Players should alternate turns until one player is able to complete the five-bag catch.

 SHUTTLECOCK GAME

1.   Fold a piece of 12 inch wire (not too stiff) in half.
2.   Loop the wire through the center hole of a metal washer or coin.
3.   Twist the wire around three short feathers from a feather duster until the feathers stand upright.
4.   Decorate the base with colorful pieces of paper or cloth.
5.   Have a contest with a friend. See who can keep the shuttlecock in the air the longest by kicking it up with the side of his foot.

SQUARE THROWING

This game is for two or more players. Place two one-foot squares adjacent to each other. Each player must have a lagger (rock, coin or trinket). Player No. 1 places his lagger in one of the squares. Player No. 2 stands some assigned distance away and attempts to throw his lagger at Player No. 1's lagger. He may accumulate points in this manner to any desired total:

    5   Direct hit
    3   Same square
    2   Adjacent square
    1   Outside square

CHAPTER VII
GREECE

INDEX

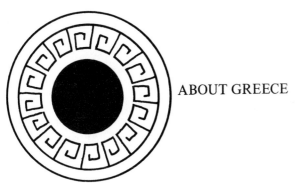

ABOUT GREECE

Greece is a democracy in southeastern Europe. It is a mountainous area that is surrounded by water on three sides. It is, therefore, a prominent seaport in its part of the world. The ruins of ancient Greece attract daily visitors to Greece.

The national language is Greek. Most of the alphabets throughout Europe and the Americas have been based on the Greek alphabet. Greeks are known for their respect for learning; consequently, many wealthy Greeks have founded institutes of learning both public and private.

For our study of Greek folklore we have offered activities from both ancient and modern Greece.

INTRODUCING THE ARTS OF GREECE

The beauty of ancient Greek art and architecture has spread throughout the world. The Greeks viewed each item, no matter how small, as a work of art. Coins were often produced as artistic master-pieces. The classic beauty of Greek art has even been duplicated in modern art pieces. Greek scenes were often of daily life, majestic buildings, or likenesses of Greek gods.

Today, Greek handicrafts abound in the form of handwoven goods, embroideries, carved rustic furniture, ceramics, leather and metal goods, brass and silver household articles and jewelry, and carved statues.

 COINS OF GREECE

In ancient Greece, the making of coins was considered to be a highly skilled art. In the 600's B.C., each community made its own coins. Gods and goddesses from mythology were a popular motif. Some ancient Greek works of art have deteriorated in the past 2,000 years; however, coins made well over 2,500 years ago can still be found in museums throughout Athens.

Simulated Greek coins may be made in the following way.

MATERIALS:

Posterboard	Permanent black felt-tip marker
String or yarn	Scissors and pencils
Heavy aluminum foil	Tissue or rags
Circle patterns or compass	Toothpicks
White glue	

PROCEDURE:

1. Cut a pattern from posterboard the same size as you would like your coin to be. It will probably be larger than a 50 cent piece. About a 3 inch diameter is good.
2. Use a pencil to sketch the design of your coin. Use yarn and glue to define the lines on your coin. Use the toothpick as a tool to aid in gluing the yarn.
3. When you are satisfied with your string and yarn gluing, cover your coin with heavy aluminum foil and smooth carefully over the raised areas in order to define your design.
4. Cover the aluminum foil disk with black felt-tip marker. As you gently wipe away the black, an antique finish will remain on your coin.

 EMBROIDERED CLOTH

BACKGROUND: Colorful embroidery of fabric is a favorite handicraft of Greece. Although Greece imports some of its clothing today, many beautifully decorated pieces are found throughout the market place and are representative of domestic regional designs.

MATERIALS:

       White fabric (use burlap for young children)

       Embroidery hoops (optional)

       Colored felt-tip markers

       Embroidery thread and needles (embroidery needles have large eyes)

       Patterns and carbon paper (we keep our patterns reusable by having the children use them after they have been taped inside a plastic bag)

PROCEDURE:

1. Fringe the edges of your fabric by pulling 3-5 strings out at each edge.
2. Trace over one of the patterns using carbon paper to transfer the design.
3. Color the design on the fabric with felt-tip markers.
4. Thread a needle and place an embroidery hoop on your fabric.
5. Outline the edges of your design with the same color thread as you used felt-tip pen. Use a stitch that covers the complete outline by bringing the needle up through the backside of the fabric and then in over the top.
6. Do all knotting and changes of direction from the underside of the fabric.
7. As you complete your work, be sure to clip all the loose strings from the backside of your work or work the threads back underneath the threads which are well in place.
8. Remove your fabric from the embroidery hoop and hang or display it in a prominent place.

PATTERNS FOR EMBROIDERED CLOTH

KARAGIOSI PUPPET

BACKGROUND: Traveling puppet theaters are popular in Greece. A popular detective puppet, originally from Turkey, is called Karagiosi. Karagiosi wears many disguises — a woman, soldier, cook — but the audience always recognizes him because of his large nose and hunched back. Hashivat, his friend, helps him to solve all crimes.

The puppet theaters use leather puppets which have been treated with oil to make them transparent. Their brightly painted clothing is visible to the audience when the light shines through the puppets.

Many other countries have their favorite puppets. For example:

England — Punch and Judy
Germany — Kasperle
Italy — Pulcinella

The directions for a children's version of the Karagiosi puppet are below.

MATERIALS:

Crayons
Hole punch
Manila paper or tagboard
Paper fasteners or string
Pattern outlines
Pencil or stick
Salad oil and brushes
Spray varnish (optional)

PROCEDURE:

1. Trace the three pattern pieces on to your tagboard.
2. Color your puppet.
3. Connect points A-A and B-B using hole punch and paper fasteners or string.
4. Punch a hole in Karagiosi's shoulder. Stick a pencil through this hole to work your puppet. Some tape at the end of the pencil will keep the puppet from slipping loose.
5. Brush over crayoned puppet with salad oil. Blot with paper towel.
6. For a nice finish, the puppets may be sprayed with varnish.

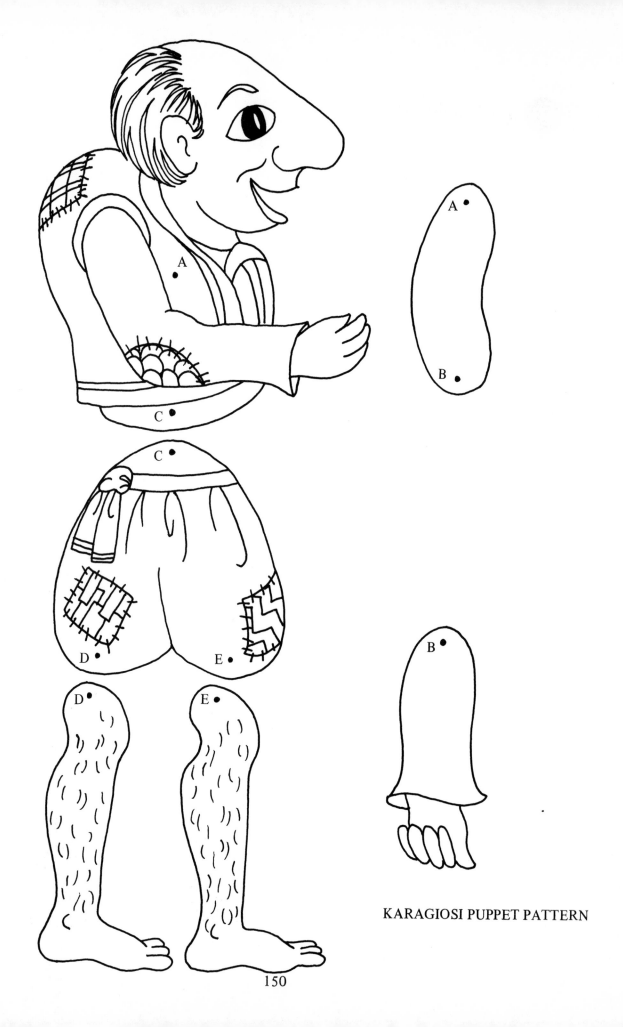

KARAGIOSI PUPPET PATTERN

150

KOMBOLOI (WORRY BEADS)

BACKGROUND: A traditional Greek art piece is Greek Worry Beads. If a Greek person is concerned over a problem, he takes out his worry beads and soothes himself. He simply holds the beads behind his back and counts them two by two. This is an effective relaxation technique. Men generally use worry beads while women display them as an art piece.

Directions for worry beads follow.

MATERIALS:

> Yarn
> Beads (old broken jewelry is fine)
> 2x4 inch cardboard squares
> Monofilament, plastic fishline (cut in 20" pieces)
> Scissors

PROCEDURE:

1. Wrap a piece of yarn ten times around the length of the cardboard square.
2. Use a small piece of yarn to tie the skein at the top of the cardboard. Wrap tape around the two ends of this yarn.
3. Cut the yarn along the bottom of the cardboard.
4. Remove yarn from cardboard.
5. Tie the strands of yarn together about 1 inch down from the top. This will form the tassel.
6. String one large bead on to the tassel, using the two pieces of yarn which have been taped.
7. Loosely string 14 beads to the monofilament.
8. Tie tassel and bead next to last bead strung.
9. String 14 more beads.
10. String nametag to worry beads.
11. Tie the two ends of monofilament (a square knot works well for this) together and cut off excess. Display on banner.

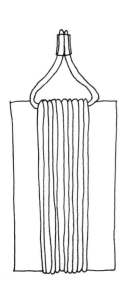

BACKGROUND: Early Greeks wore animal masks to worship their goddess of agriculture (Demeter) and their god of grapes (Dionysius). This worship use of masks later developed into a primarily theatrical use of masks. One man could then play several roles in one Greek play simply by changing masks. Greek masks were constructed of painted canvas. Sometimes a small megaphone was installed in the mouthpiece of the mask so that the actor's voice could be heard by large audiences. Special masks were made to be worn only by villains or only by the hero.

MATERIALS:

> Mask pattern
> White pipe cleaners
> White construction paper
> White styrofoam egg cartons (to form nose or eyes)
> White yarn and glue
> Cotton balls
> Hole reinforcers
> Hole punch, scissors, and string

PROCEDURE:

1. Trace mask pattern on to 8½" x 11" white construction paper. Pattern may be made into a ditto and run on white construction paper to aid in cutting.
2. Join points A-A, B-B, C-C, D-D and staple at these points to give the face contour.
3. Have partners lightly mark with white chalk or pencil where *their* eyes, nose, and mouth are located. Trace desired outlines on construction paper.
4. Cut spaces for eyes, nose, and mouth. Encourage students to utilize yarn, cotton balls, and egg cartons to glue more contour to their mask.
5. Fold side pieces by ears as marked and reinforce the punched holes with notebook hole reinforcers. Tie string through holes so mask may be attached to face.

FOLD LINE

A

A

FOLD LINE

D

C

C

C

153

PATTERN FOR MASKS FOR A GREEK PLAY

FOLD LINE

 PAINTED EARTHENWARE

BACKGROUND: Potters in ancient Greece are believed to have invented the potter's wheel. Bowls, pots, and vases were generally painted when completed and were often illustrated with scenes of everyday life and of mythology.

MATERIALS:

      Clay which will harden in air (or use one of the recipes from Chapter 5)

      Wax paper

      Poster paints and brushes

      Liquid detergent

      Shellac or inexpensive hairspray

PROCEDURE:

1. Work clay until all the air seems to be expelled.
2. Form a ball and poke a hole in the center. Use your fingers to slowly work the clay into the shape of a bowl.
3. When you have the shape you desire, begin to work out all the cracks and make the bowl smooth both on the inside and outside.
4. Paint the bowl with a mixture of tempera and detergent and allow it to dry.
5. If you wish to make your bowl look very Greek, add a Greek design or scene.
6. After the paint has dried, spray your bowl inside and out with shellac to protect the paint.

 STRAW PAINTING

BACKGROUND: It is believed that Greek straw mosaics originated in the prisons of Greece where the mattresses are stuffed with straw. Prisoners earned money by selling colorful straw mosaic scenes and containers covered with straw mosaics. Olympic events and Greek architecture offer exciting subject matter. Although broom straw or grass provides the common material for this craft, we have adapted this craft to be more appropriate for children ages 5 through 8 by using drinking straws as our raw material.

MATERIALS:

>Drinking straws
>Heavy paper
>Colored felt-tip markers
>White glue and Q-tips
>Patterns or suggested designs
>Pop-top from soda pop can

PROCEDURE:

1. Transfer the pattern to your paper by tracing over carbon paper or paste a copy of the design directly on your heavy paper.
2. Start at one corner and work away from that point in an organized manner to avoid damaging your finished mosaic.
3. Apply white glue to your design and glue drinking straws side by side to completely fill in your design.
4. When glue has dried, color the drinking straws with felt-tip markers to create a colorful mosaic effect.
5. Display your Greek straw painting by using a pop-top from a soda pop can as a hanger. Glue the flat tab to the back of your straw painting.

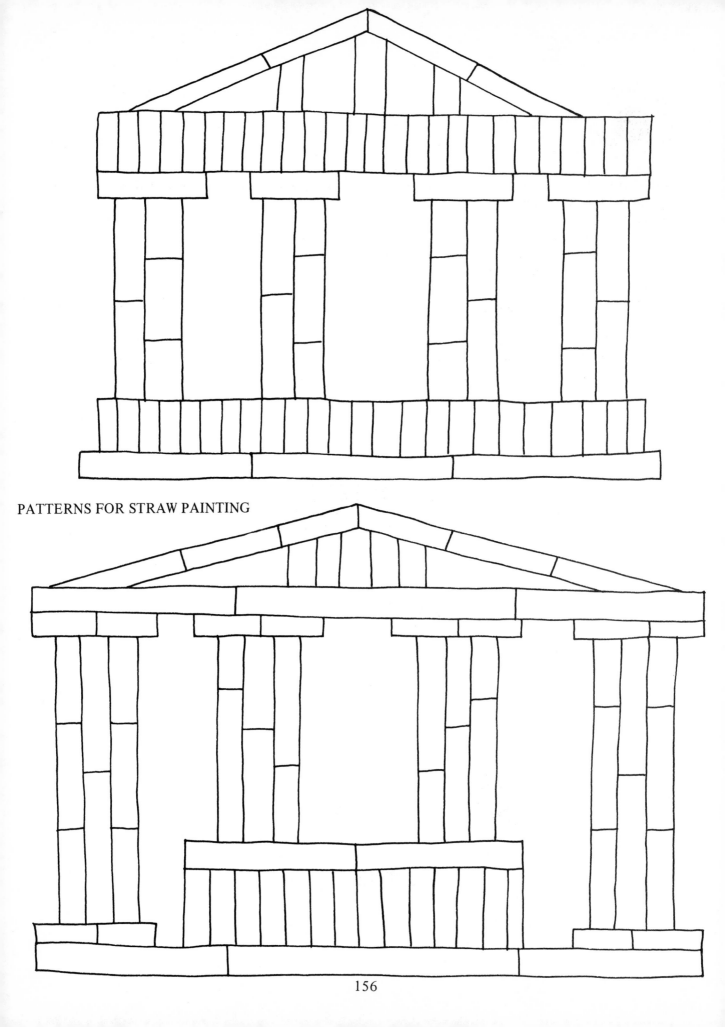

PATTERNS FOR STRAW PAINTING

156

 YO-YO

BACKGROUND: Yo-yos have been popular throughout the world. Yo-yos similar to these are made by the children of modern-day Greece.

MATERIALS:

> 4 large, flat coat buttons
> 1 paper clip (or soft wire — copper or iron)
> 5 feet of string (heavy fishing line or yo-yo string)

PROCEDURE:

1. Sew buttons together in groups of two using thread. If pairs of buttons vary in size, assemble yo-yo with smaller buttons on outside.
2. Thread the wire through the button holes and use pliers to crimp ends together.
3. Hold the yo-yo in both hands and twist one set of buttons to twist center wire together.
4. Tie cord to wire at center of yo-yo. Make a finger loop at other end. Wrap string around yo-yo.

 INTRODUCING THE COOKING OF GREECE

Ancient Greeks are thought to have begun the art of cooking nearly 3,000 years ago. A Greek, Archestratus, wrote the first cook book more than 2,000 years ago and Greek cooking has influenced many different cuisines. Today, Greek, Turkish, and Armenian dishes are often similar and it is difficult to determine the origin of these recipes because the borders of these countries have changed many times.

There are many olive and lemon trees in Greece; therefore, olives and lemons are used extensively in Greek cooking. Every-day meals are generally simple. Often a complete meal will be fresh vegetables quickly cooked, sprinkled with olive oil and lemon juice. Delicious feasts presented elegantly are also a part of the Greek cooking heritage.

Kali Orexi means Good appetite!

BAKLAVA

BACKGROUND: Greeks rarely eat dessert after dinner. They prefer their sweets, pastries and rich desserts during the early evening (about 5:00 P.M.). Many Greek desserts are soaked overnight in syrup or honey. Baklava is the best-known example of this type of Greek dessert. It is made from filo which is a paper-thin pastry dough made with salt, flour, water and skill. Filo is available in Greek markets.

INGREDIENTS:

       9"x9" square of filo

1 tsp.	(5ml.)	Crushed nuts
		Melted margarine

Syrup:

2½ C.	(600ml.)	Sugar
2 C.	(480ml.)	Water
		Juice of 1 lemon

PROCEDURE:
1. The syrup must be cold when it is poured on the hot baklava, so it should be made first and refrigerated.
2. Combine the sugar, water and lemon, bring to a boil and simmer for 10 minutes. Refrigerate.
3. Fold filo in thirds to form strip.
4. Brush filo with melted margarine.
5. Place one heaping teaspoon of crushed walnuts at one end of filo strip.
6. Fold nuts into filo. Use a triangle fold. Keep nuts inside.
7. Place triangle on baking pan and brush top with melted margarine.
8. Bake at 375°F, 190°C for 15 minutes.
9. Soak hot Baklava in approximately 2 Tbs. (30ml.) cold syrup for 5 minutes, turning frequently.

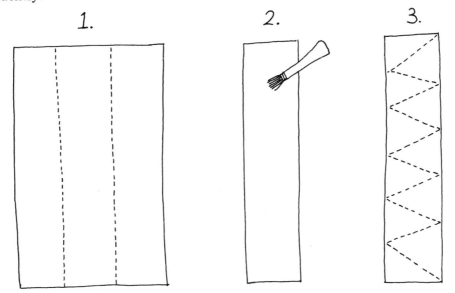

 DRACHMA FRIED POTATOES

BACKGROUND: Most meals ordered in Greece come with these potatoes, cut into round shapes like the Greek silver coin, the drachma.

INGREDIENTS:

¼ to ½		Potato
2 C.	(480ml.)	Oil for frying
		Salt

PROCEDURE:
1. Have the children peel the potatoes and slice into ½ inch rounds.
2. Dry with towel.
3. Heat oil in a large frying pan until hot.
4. Gently place potatoes in oil and fry 10 minutes or until ready. For very crisp potatoes, fry only 5 minutes. Remove from oil and place in refrigerator to chill. Reheat oil until hot again and place chilled, partially cooked potatoes in oil to finish frying for 5 minutes more.
5. Use slotted spoon to turn potatoes over and remove from oil.
6. Drain on paper towels.
7. Sprinkle with salt while hot.

EGG AND LEMON SAUCE (SALTSA AVGOLEMONO)

BACKGROUND: The Greeks use a lot of lemon and olive oil in their cooking. Often a complete meal will be fresh vegetables, quickly cooked and served with a lemon sauce. A typical sauce used to enhance vegetables is made from the water the vegetables were cooking in, enriched with olive oil, thickened with egg yolks and spiced with lemon. The following recipe is an easy-to-make version of this white sauce that could be used for the children to dip vegetables.

INGREDIENTS:

4 egg yolks		
3 to 4 Tbs.	(45-60ml.)	Lemon juice
3 to 4 Tbs.	(45-60ml.)	Hot seasoned broth

PROCEDURE:
1. Beat egg yolks until thick.
2. Slowly beat in lemon juice, then the hot broth.
3. Cook over very low heat, stirring constantly, until thickened and smooth.
4. Turn off heat, cover pan, let stand 5 minutes.
5. If a thinner sauce is desired, add more broth. Makes ½ cup (120ml.)

 GREEK SALAD

BACKGROUND: Greek meals usually include large salads which are frequently prepared at table. Often the greens are omitted from the salad.

INGREDIENTS:

¼ C.	(60ml.)	Chicory
¼ C.	(60ml.)	Romaine
1 Tbs.	(15ml.)	Cucumber, peeled and diced
1 Tbs.	(15ml.)	Tomatoes, diced
1 sliced radish (optional)		
1 Greek olive		
1 tsp.	(5ml.)	Green onion, chopped
1 Tbs.	(15ml.)	Olive oil
1½ tsp.	(7.5ml.)	Red wine vinegar or lemon
Pinch of salt and pepper mixture		
Pinch of oregano		
1 Anchovy fillet		
½ oz.	(15 gms.)	Feta cheese, crumbled

PROCEDURE:
1. Have the children chop all the vegetables.
2. Combine the vegetables in a margarine tub.
3. Combine the olive oil, red wine vinegar or lemon, salt, pepper and oregano. Shake or stir this dressing.
4. The anchovy fillet can be ground and included in dressing, chopped and put in salad or omitted.
5. Crumble the feta cheese on top of the salad.
6. Toss and enjoy.

 HALVAH

BACKGROUND: It is often difficult to determine if a particular dish (recipe) is of Greek, Turkish, or Armenian origin because the borders of these countries have changed many times and the dishes are very similar. The Turks are thought to have brought Halvah to Greece in the 1300's. Halvah is used extensively in Jewish households in the United States.

INGREDIENTS:

1/3 C.	(80ml.)	Olive oil
1 C.	(240ml.)	Semolina or white cornmeal
2/3 C.	(160ml.)	Sugar
1 C.	(240ml.)	Milk
1/3 C.	(80ml.)	Water

PROCEDURE:
1. In a heavy saucepan, heat the oil over moderate heat until a light haze forms above it.
2. Slowly pour in the semolina a thin stream, stirring constantly.
3. Reduce the heat to low and simmer for 20 minutes, or until all the oil has been absorbed and the meal turns a light golden color, stirring occasionally.
4. Add the sugar, stirring constantly
5. Gradually stir in the milk and water mixture.
6. Continue cooking about 10 minutes longer, stirring constantly until the mixture is thick enough to hold its shape almost solidly in the spoon.
7. Pour the halvah into a small (3"x 5") ungreased baking dish, spread it and smooth the top with the back of a spoon.
8. Cool until firm and then cut into 1" squares.

 KOULOURAKIA

BACKGROUND: Koulourakia is a Greek Easter sweet that is a shortbread cookie decorated with sesame seeds. It may be coiled or shaped like a pretzel.

INGREDIENTS:

1 Tbs.	(15ml.)	Butter
1 Tbs plus 1 tsp.	(20ml.)	Sugar
1½ tsp.	(7.5ml.)	Beaten egg yolks
1 tsp.	(5ml.)	Light cream
1/8 tsp.	(.6ml.)	Vanilla
¼ C.	(60ml.)	Unsifted all-purpose flour
1/8 tsp.	(.6ml.)	Baking powder
Pinch of nutmeg or cinnamon		

PROCEDURE:
1. Cream together the butter and sugar.
2. Add the beaten egg yolks, cream and vanilla.
3. Combine the flour, baking powder and nutmeg or cinnamon and add to the mixture.
4. Mix well, cover and chill until the dough is easy to work with (approximately 15 minutes).
5. Roll the dough into a coil and shape.
6. Brush top with beaten egg white and sprinkle with sesame seeds.
7. Bake at 350°F, 176°C, 8 - 10 minutes.

 LAMB IN A BAG

BACKGROUND: Ancient Greek sheepherders wrapped their meat in paper (klephtiko) to seal in the cooking odors so their enemies, the Turks, would not find them.

INGREDIENTS:

1" square piece of lamb
1 pinch mixture of salt, pepper, oregano, garlic powder and grated lemon peel
1" square piece zucchini cut lengthwise
1" square piece crookneck squash cut lengthwise
1 Mushroom

| ¼ tsp. | (1.2ml.) | Lemon juice |
| 1 tsp. | (5ml.) | Melted butter |

1 Small paper bag or 9" square piece of paper
Salad oil to coat outside of paper bag

PROCEDURE:
1. Coat outside of bag or piece of paper with salad oil.
2. Season the lamb with the salt, pepper, and spice mixture and place in the bag or on paper.
3. Mix the lemon juice and melted butter.
4. Roll the vegetables in the lemon butter and place in bag or on piece of paper.
5. Fold down bag or fold paper and secure with paper clip. .
6. Place bag or folded paper on baking pan and bake at 350°F, 176°C, 15 minutes.

 SOUPA AVGOLEMONO (LEMON SOUP)

BACKGROUND: Greece produces large flavorful lemons and Greek cooks use them in a variety of ways. They generously season their vegetables and salads with them. In salads, the lemon is used in place of salad dressing vinegar. The following recipe is for a lemon-flavored chicken soup called soupa avgolemono — this is the national soup of Greece.

INGREDIENTS:

4 cans or 48 oz.	(1440ml. or 1.5 liters)	Chicken broth
3 Tbs.	(45ml.)	Uncooked rice
3		Eggs, beaten
3 Tbs.	(45ml.)	Lemon juice

PROCEDURE:

1. Cook broth and rice until the rice is tender, about twenty minutes.
2. Beat eggs until they are light and gradually add lemon juice, beating until blended.
3. Pour part of the hot soup slowly into the egg mixture.
4. Return this mixture to the remainder of the soup.

This recipe serves six.

 LENTIL SOUP AND FASSOULADA SOUP

BACKGROUND: Due to the abundant supplies of olive trees, olives are a large part of the Greek diet and olive oil is used extensively in their cooking. The two following soup recipes are common dishes that utilize olive oil.

LENTIL SOUP (FAHKEE)

INGREDIENTS:

3/4 C.	(180ml.)	Lentils
3½ C.	(840ml.)	Water
½ C.	(120ml.)	Tomato sauce
½ tsp.	(2.5ml.)	Salt
2½ Tbs.	(37.5ml.)	Olive oil
2 cloves		Garlic, unpeeled

PROCEDURE:

1. Empty the lentils into a dish. Look them over and remove any gravel.
2. Put the lentils into a saucepan, rinse with cold running water and drain.
3. Add the 3½ cups water and the garlic.
4. Bring to a boil. Turn to low heat, stir in the tomato sauce, salt, and olive oil.
5. Simmer gently for 50 minutes. Add water if the soup becomes too thick.

Serves three.

FASSOULADA SOUP (NATIONAL BEAN SOUP)

INGREDIENTS:

1 lb.	(454 grams)	Dried navy beans
2		Large onions, sliced or chopped
2		Garlic cloves, crushed
½ C.	(120ml.)	Olive oil
¼ tsp.	(1.2ml.)	Thyme
1 Tbs.	(15ml.)	Tomato paste
2 tsp.	(10ml.)	Salt
		Freshly ground black pepper
4 Qts.	(4.5 liters)	Boiling water (to cover)
		Juice of half a lemon
2 Tbs.	(30ml.)	Minced parsley

PROCEDURE:

1. Soak the beans overnight; drain.
2. Cook the onions and crushed garlic in olive oil until they are transparent, add thyme and tomato paste.
3. Add the drained beans, salt, pepper, and enough water to stand at least two inches above the top of the beans.
4. Cook slowly, covered, 2 to 3 hours, until beans are very soft.
5. Shortly before serving, add lemon juice and parsley.

Serves eight people.

NEW YEAR'S BREAD (VASILOPETA)

BACKGROUND: This Greek New Year's bread is a large loaf of sweet bread formed from several little balls. Blanched almonds are poked into the dough to form the numeral of the new year. It is customary to bake a coin in each loaf and slice the bread at midnight. Whoever gets the coin is blessed with good fortune in the new year.

INGREDIENTS:

¾ tsp.	(3.7ml.)	Active dry yeast
1 Tbs.	(15ml.)	Warm water
1 Tbs.	(15ml.)	Milk
1 Tbs.	(15ml.)	Butter
3 Tbs.	(45ml.)	Beaten egg
1 1/3 Tbs.	(20ml.)	Sugar
½ tsp.	(2.5ml.)	Grated orange peel
1 pinch		Nutmeg
1 pinch		Salt
¾ C.	(180ml.)	Unsifted all-purpose flour

PROCEDURE:

1. Combine the yeast with the warm water and stir to dissolve.
2. Add the next seven ingredients and stir well.
3. Add the flour slowly to the liquid, use a little less or a little more than ¾ cup flour to make the dough a workable consistency.
4. Knead the dough on a floured board for five minutes, cover and let rise for one hour in a warm place.
5. Punch down and knead again.
6. Make ½" balls and form a loaf.
7. Cover and let rise for twenty minutes in a warm place.
8. Brush top with egg yolk mixed with 1 Tbs. (15ml.) water.
9. Decorate with sesame seeds and blanched almonds.
10. Bake at 350°F, 176°C for 15 minutes.

PATATOKEFTEHES (POTATO PANCAKES)

BACKGROUND: Many different cultures make potato pancakes with a few variations. In Israel, potato pancakes are called Latkes. That recipe can be found in Chapter 8.

INGREDIENTS:

½ C.	(120ml.)	Cold mashed potatoes
2 Tbs.	(30ml.)	Beaten egg
1 tsp.	(5ml.)	Chopped onion or scallion
2¼ tsp.	(11.2ml.)	Flour
¼ tsp.	(1.2ml.)	Parsley
1 pinch		Salt
¼ C.	(60ml.)	Grated cheese, Kefaloteri or Parmesan
½ C.	(120ml.)	Oil, for frying OR use 1 cube of melted butter, if broiling or baking.

PROCEDURE:

1. Mix all ingredients in a margarine tub except fats and cheese.
2. Make patties.
3. Dip in grated cheese.
4. Fry in hot oil until brown on both sides, about 10 minutes.
5. Use a wide spatula to turn over.
6. If broiling or baking is preferred, lay patties in buttered pan, sprinkle with grated cheese and bake at 450°F, 232°C for 15 minutes, or broil until brown for approximately 10 minutes.
7. Serve plain, with yogurt or garlic sauce.

 **TIROPETES**

BACKGROUND: Vasilopitta is a Greek holiday celebrated in January, that in English means St. Basil's pie. The holiday is observed in churches and among families, where special pies made from filo dough, eggs and cheese are served. Each pie contains a coin, and the person who finds it in his slice is thought to be lucky for the whole year.

INGREDIENTS:

9x9 inch square of filo (available in a Greek market)
Melted butter or margarine

1 Tbs.	(15ml.)	Feta cheese
1 Tbs.	(15ml.)	Small curd cottage cheese
1 Tbs.	(15ml.)	Cream cheese
1½ tsp.	(7.5ml.)	Beaten egg
¼ tsp.	(1.2ml.)	Chopped parsley
¼ tsp.	(1.2ml.)	Chopped chives

PROCEDURE:

1. Cream together the feta, cottage cheese and cream cheese.
2. Add the beaten egg, parsley and chives and mix well.
3. Fold two pieces of filo in thirds to form strips.
4. Brush filo with melted margarine.
5. Place one heaping Tbs. (15ml.) cheese-egg mixture at one end of filo strip. (Add coin if desired.)
6. Fold the cheese mixture into filo. Use a triangle fold.
7. Place triangle on greased baking sheet and brush top with melted margarine.
8. Bake at 375°F, 190°C for 15 minutes.

 INTRODUCING THE RECREATION OF GREECE

Children are frequently needed for work in most Greek families. They often work very hard while helping their parents in their job.

Playtime is generally spent out-of-doors and may focus on learning job skills. Many Greek children make their own toys from pine cones and seashells. Others play with toys similar to those purchased in the United States. Flutes are often made from bamboo or bird's bones. Boys often make their own rod and tackle for fishing. Girls learn to care for children and to spin, weave, and do embroidery.

A major part of Greek life today is handicrafts, folk music, and dancing. Most of the traditional folk dances are circle dances. Traditional folk dances are always an important part of Greek holiday celebrations. In most of the dances, the dancers stand in a semicircle around a leader. They hold hands or hold the ends of a knotted handkerchief. Only the leader performs. If the leader is a man, he leaps and twists. A woman leader steps and turns primly. The other dancers in the semicircle move together, swinging with the music. The music has been handed down through hundreds of years. Some dances are regional, others such as the Tsamikos and the Kalamatianos have become national dances and are performed all over Greece. The songs are usually accompanied by a violin, a clarinet, and sometimes a lauto, which is similar to a lute.

 CIRCLE BALL

Circle ball requires two to five players. A circle is drawn in the sand or on the ground. You can use masking tape to pre-mark a circle in a carpeted area. Move the entire group to this area and ask them to sit around the circle while you explain this game.

The children take turns rolling a ball toward the circle. Each time a child rolls the ball inside the circle, he scores a point. The winner is the first person to accumulate ten points.

The size of the circle and the ball, and the distance the players stand from their target, should be determined by the age and ability of the players. Mark a suggested spot and adjust it to the child's ability. For indoor play, you can provide a homemade ball made from newspaper and masking tape. Homemade balls are still used by many children.

 HIDE

Hide requires three to ten players. A tin can is used to mark the "home" position of "it". "It" then tries to find those hiding and when he finds one of them, they race back to the can. If the hider gets to the can first and kicks it over, everyone is free. If "it" gets to the can first, he jumps over the can and says 1-2-3 on *name*. Play continues until all players are found or one player kicks the can and frees everyone.

 KRIFTO

Krifto requires four more more players. "It" should stand at home base and count to 20 while hiding his face in his arm. After 20 counts, "it" may look for those persons who are hiding. When he finds them, everyone should run back to the home base. Whoever touches home base first is the winner.

 ODD OR EVEN

This is a favorite game that was even played in ancient times. Use two players in each game and give the players ten beans each.

Player number one places any number of beans in his closed hand and asks, "Odd or even?" Player number two looks at the closed fist and guesses, "Even." If it is really an odd number of beans in the closed fist, player number one says "Give me one to make it even." On a correct guess, guesser is given one bean. Play continues until one player is out of beans.

 PEBBLE

This game can be played in or out of doors. Three to ten players are needed. Equipment needed is a goal box and a pebble. One person is "it" and the goal box is placed a set distance from "it". The others stand in line, each with one hand outstretched, palm up. "It" pretends to drop the pebble in their hands. When he actually drops it, the runner with the pebble must run to the goal and back to "it" (standing still), before any of the other children can catch him.

If he succeeds, he becomes "it" for the next game. If he is caught, the one who captured him becomes the next "it".

The child who receives the pebble may choose his own time to run, but he must start before "it" touches the last pair of hands in line. The pebble receiver tries to look unconcerned so that the others will not guess that he has the pebble.

The others watch carefully to guess who has the pebble and try to catch him.

 RIDER BALL

This game requires eight or more players. Players work in pairs and four players play catch while their partners stand behind them and hold firmly to their waists. If the rear player looses his grip, he becomes the front of the team and the game of catch continues.

CHAPTER VIII
ISRAEL

INDEX

נ

ש

אֵ

ר

ש

ג

ה

ABOUT ISRAEL

The republic of Israel began in 1948 in a land previously called Palestine, on the western edge of the area called the Middle East. Many of the towns in Israel still bear their biblical names. Not only Jews live in Israel — there are a diversity of people from Algiers, Morocco, and Europe, including Arabs and Druzes. Many ancient historical sites attract visitors from throughout the world.

Israeli culture includes the folklore of all the diverse people that represent its population. Israel is also developing its own folklore. The activities presented in this text represent a collection of both its inherited folklore and new customs.

INTRODUCING THE ARTS OF ISRAEL

All of the cities and many of the villages of Israel have their own art museums. Sculptors and artists strive to express the freedom of the people of Israel.

Many of the recent books about Israel tell of their skilled craftsmen — potters, goldsmiths, silversmiths, blacksmiths, and coin-makers. Some fashioned delicate, lacy jewelry decorated with precious stones. Many women are skilled at embroidery and basket weaving. Many of the highly skilled crafts have been passed down for several generations.

 BOOTH (SUCCAH)

BACKGROUND: Succot is a festival of thanksgiving which begins five days after Yom Kippur. In celebration of this light day festival, many Jewish families build gazebos out of branches and leaves and decorate them with fruits and flowers. In the city of Jerusalem, contests are held to choose the most attractive succah and prizes are often awarded. Many Israeli families sleep in the succah and even eat their meals there during the celebration.

MATERIALS:
> Shoe box
> Colored paper scraps
> White glue
> Scissors
> Collected leaves, sticks, and flowers

PROCEDURE:
1. Mark and cut the shoe box so that it is basically a roof with legs — as illustrated. Leave the legs large enough so that the booth will stand freely.
2. Use white glue to cover the succah with bits of colored paper, leaves, and sticks.
3. Decorate the booth on the inside also.
4. Hold a contest to determine the most attractive succah.

CHAD GADYA MOBILE (HA-GOD-YA)

BACKGROUND: Chad Gadya (an only kid) is a folksong traditionally sung during Passover. It tells the story of a man who bought a goat for two Hebrew coins. The kid is then eaten by a cat, who is bitten by a dog, who is beaten with a stick, that is burned by fire, that is quenched by water...finally, God appears and all order is restored. The progressive building of one part of the story to another is typical of much folklore, i.e., Partridge in a Pear Tree, House that Jack Built. Music for this song may be obtained through any synagogue. One version of the lyrics is included here:

(1)
An only kid!
An only kid!
My father bought
For two zuzim.
An only kid! An only kid!

(2)
Then came the cat
And ate the kid
My father bought
For two zuzim.
An only kid! An only kid!

(3)
Then came the dog
And bit the cat
That ate the kid
My father bought
For two zuzim.
An only kid! An only kid!

(4)
Then came the stick
And beat the dog,
That bit the cat,
That ate the kid
My father bought
For two zuzim.
An only kid! An only kid!

(5)
Then came the fire
And burned the stick,
That beat the dog,
That bit the cat,
That ate the kid
My father bought
For two zuzim
An only kid! An only kid!

(6)
Then came the water
And quenched the fire
That burned the stick,
That beat the dog,
That bit the cat,
That ate the kid
My father bought
For two zuzim.
An only kid! An only kid!

(7)
Then came the ox
And drank the water,
That quenched the fire,
That burned the stick,
That beat the dog,
That bit the cat,
That ate the kid
My father bought
For two zuzim.
An only kid! An only kid!

(8)
Then came the shohet*
And slaughtered the ox,
That drank the water,
That quenched the fire,
That burned the stick,
That beat the dog,
That bit the cat,
That ate the kid
My father bought
For two zuzim.
An only kid! An only kid!

(9)
Then came death's angel
And slew the shohet,
That slaughtered the ox,
That drank the water,
That quenched the fire,
That burned the stick,
That beat the dog,
That bit the cat,
That ate the kid
My father bought
For two zuzim.
An only kid! An only kid!

*Shohet – ritual slaughterer

172

(10)
Then came the Holy One, praised be He,
And destroyed death's angel
That slew the shohet,
That slaughtered the ox,
That drank the water,
That quenched the fire,
That burned the stick,
That beat the dog,
That bit the cat,
That ate the kid
My father bought
For two zuzim.
An only kid! An only kid!

The correct order of the symbols on the mobile will help the children to correctly order the song and may be used as a decoration during Passover.

MATERIALS:

Construction paper
Scissors and hole punch
Colored felt-tip pens
Coat hanger
Patterns
String

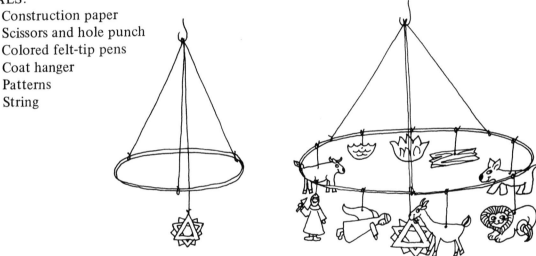

PROCEDURE:

1. Bend coat wire into a circle and attach three 20'' pieces of string as shown; adjust the placement of the string so that the circle will hang evenly. Tie a 24'' piece of string to the intersection so that the star may hang in the center.
2. Trace the 10 patterns on colored construction paper or trace the patterns with carbon paper. Cut out the patterns or make up your own designs. Add detail with felt-tip markers.
3. Punch a hole in the top of each of the ten shapes and use small pieces of string to attach the shapes to the coat hanger circle.
4. Place the shapes on the circle in order and spaced so that three shapes are arranged between each hanging string. The correct order for the Chad Gadya song is: kid, cat, dog, stick, fire, water, ox, shohet, death's angel. Hang star of David on string in center of circle.
5. Display mobile by hanging it on a hook.

173

PATTERNS FOR CHAD GADYA MOBILE

CAT

KID

FIRE

DOG

STICK

OX

WATER

SHOHET

STAR
(HOLY ONE)

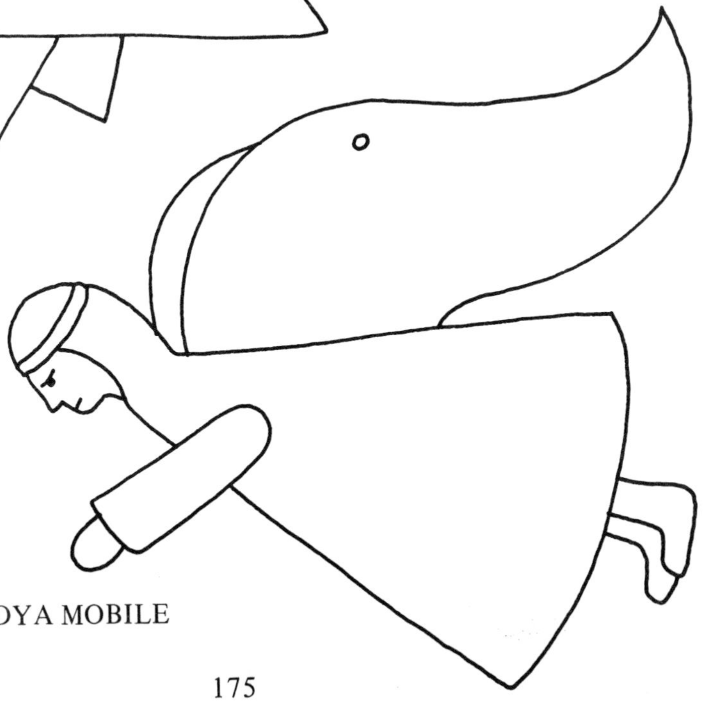

DEATH'S
ANGEL

PATTERNS FOR CHAD GADYA MOBILE

 DREIDLE

BACKGROUND: Chanukah (or Hanukkah) is a well-known Jewish holiday during which the dreidle game is played. Four Hebrew letters are placed on the four sides of a spinning top: Nun, Gimmel, Hey and Shin. These are represented by the symbols:

These symbols stand for the words: Nes, Gadol, Haya, and Sham respectively, which may be translated to mean: "A great miracle happened there." The point system for each symbol on the dreidle is as follows:

NUN
No chips won or lost.

GIMMEL
Spinner takes entire pot of chips.

HEY
Spinner takes half pot of chips.

SHIN
Spinner adds two chips to pot.

MATERIALS:
        Pattern
        Scissors
        White glue
        1/8" dowel 3" long (or substitute ice cream sticks)

PROCEDURE:
1. Cut out 24 circles to be used as markers.
2. Trace around pattern copying symbols and carefully cutting out on the heavy black lines.
3. Fold and glue dreidle together.
4. Poke 1/8" dowel through holes A and B to form top.

HOW TO PLAY THE DREIDLE GAME: Game may include two to five players. Distribute markers evenly to all players. All players put one marker in center of table. Player number one spins the dreidle and does what the dreidle tells him to do. All players put one more marker in the center of the table and player number two spins the dreidle and does what is indicated. Play continues until all markers are used. The winner is the player with the most chips at the end of the game.

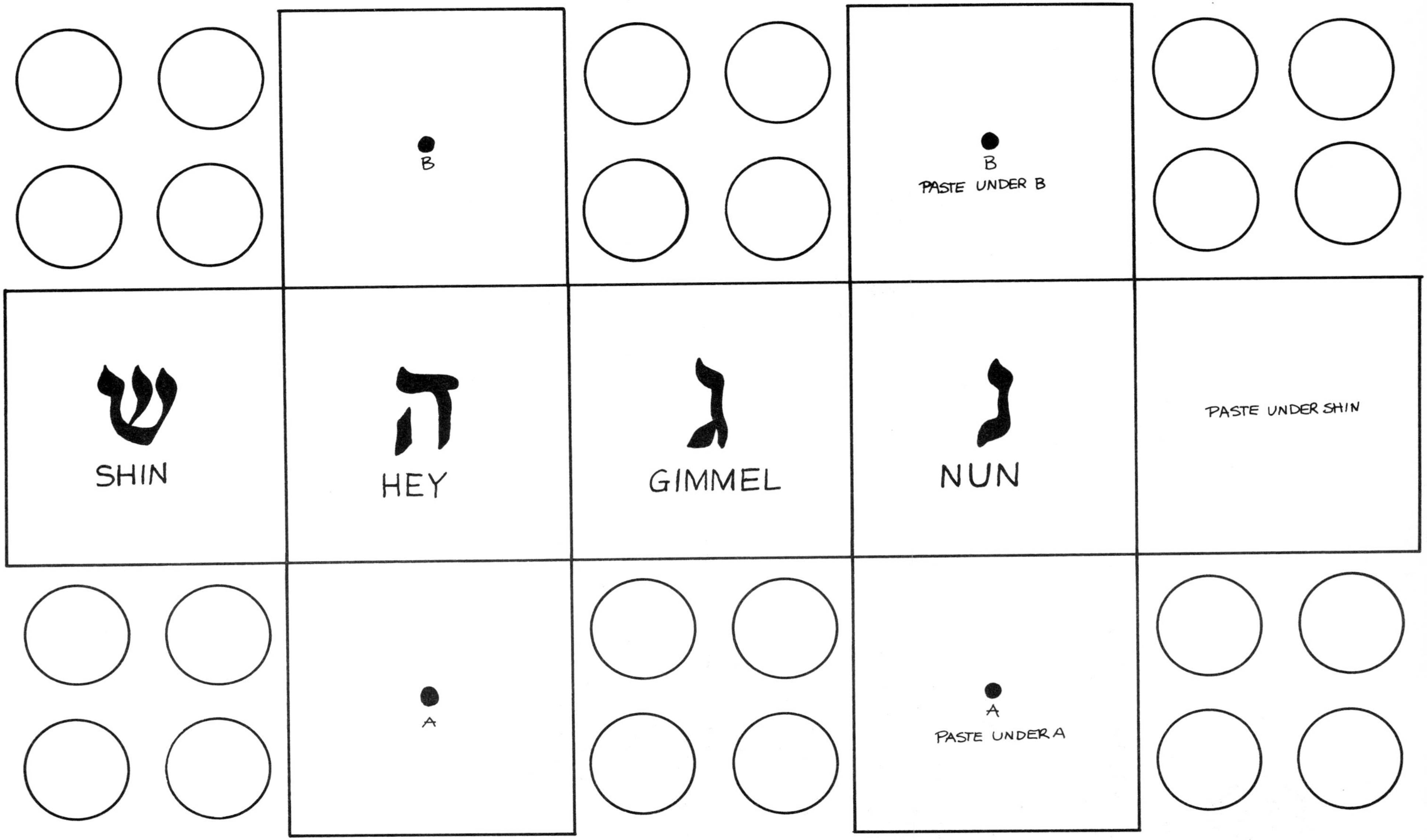

PASTE UNDER SHIN

PASTE UNDER B

● B

NUN

נ

PASTE UNDER A

● A

B ●

HEY

ה

A ●

GIMMEL

ג

SHIN

ש

DREIDLE PATTERN

 KITE

BACKGROUND: Some friends of ours, who grew up on a kibbutz near the Negev, taught us to make kites similar to those that they had made as children. These kites bear the national emblem of the six-pointed star. The Star of David is an ancient Jewish symbol and is also found on the flag of Israel.

MATERIALS:

> 6 Bamboo teriyake sticks
> White paper
> String
> White glue
> Blue felt-tip markers

PROCEDURE:

1. Using three teriyake sticks and string, form a triangle, tying the sticks in place.
2. Do number one with three more sticks.
3. Combine the two triangles by placing one upside down.
   Tie the two together at the six points where they cross.
4. Place the paper pattern over the stick form, cutting carefully on the broken lines. Or, you may now trace the stick pattern on a sheet of white paper and cut, allowing a ½" margin around the outside of the star. Cut on the outer lines.
5. Fold the excess of paper around the bamboo sticks and glue in place so that paper is folded over and glued around each outer edge.
6. Attach strings as indicated by four arrows and extend out about 12" to meet single flying string. Allow about 4 to 5 feet of kite string per child.
7. Now, fly for fun just like they do in many parts of Israel.

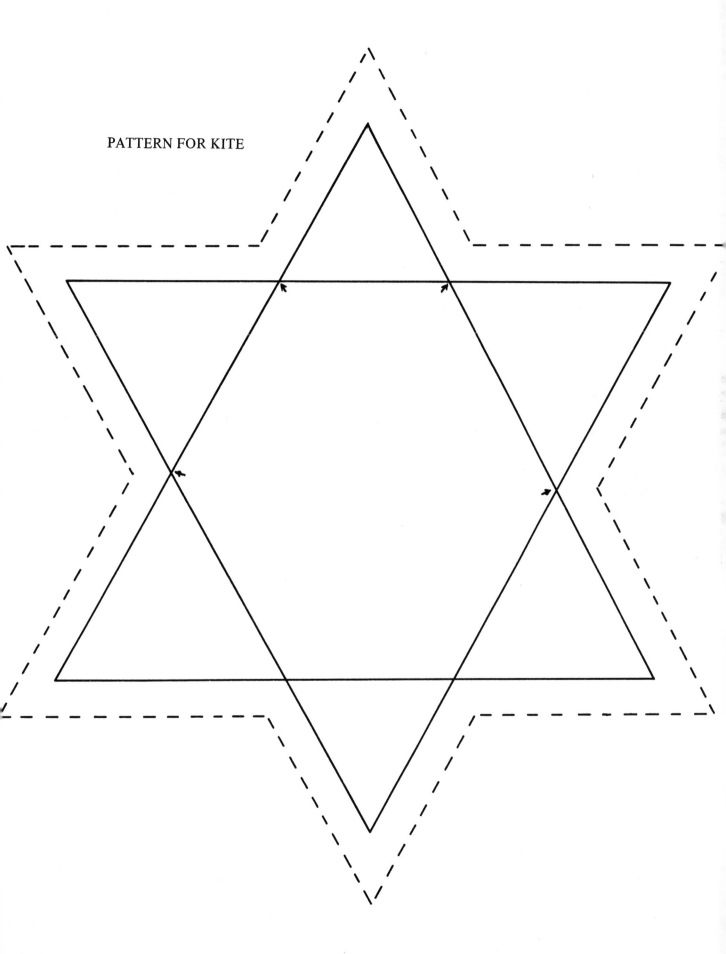

PATTERN FOR KITE

MUSICAL INSTRUMENTS MADE OF PLANTS

BACKGROUND: The Kibbutzim Council for Musical Education in Israel has edited a book by Tamar Yardeni-Yaffe which illustrates the possibilities of making instruments from plants. Tamar suggests that the child has entered a secret world of creation when he is allowed to create musically. He further emphasizes the opportunity for children to produce something beautiful from a plant that is about to wither away. The children of Kibbutz Maoz Hayim begin by making shakeable musical instruments that are culminations of a nature collection walk.

MATERIALS:
> Scissors, awl, and hammer for hole punching
> Rope and string
> Dowels and sticks
> A collection of shells, seed pods, fruit pods, and metal
> Poster paints and brushes

PROCEDURE:
1. Provide the children with a collection box of materials or arrange to have a nature collection walk prior to this craft.
2. Discuss the sounds found among the nature items. Demonstrate how seed pods may be shaken or two items may be strung together and shaken to produce a rhythmic feeling.
3. Some children may want to leave their creations a natural color while others may want to vividly decorate each item.
4. Use the awl and hammer to punch holes in any items which will be strung.
5. Complete these personalized instruments and have a musical happening.

 PURIM PUPPETS

BACKGROUND: Purim, or the Festival of Lots, is celebrated by Jews throughout the world. It is a joyous springtime celebration that is looked forward to by the children of Jewish families with as much excitement as Christian children await Christmas or as the Hindu child would await Holi. This holiday is held to honor Queen Esther and Mordecai (Esther's cousin), who together saved the Jews from the wicked Haman of Persia. During this season, Jews eat special cakes and hold dressy parties. Today during the telling of this story in synagogues, the children shout and shake rattles at the mention of Haman's name. During Purim the Book of Esther is read and the story of Queen Esther is retold many times as a pageant, play, or puppet show.

MATERIALS:

    Scissors and hole puncher
    Toilet paper rolls
    Colored paper
    Ice cream sticks
    White glue
    String
    Patterns
    Wire coat hangers
    Yarn scraps

PROCEDURE:

1. Cover a toilet paper roll with a cylinder of colored paper. Glue in place.
2. Use the paper punch to punch 2 holes (for hanging) in the top of each cylinder (place holes directly across from each other).
3. Tie some string through the 2 holes at the top of the puppet and knot. Tie a new piece of string (about 12" long) from the free string to the bent coat hanger (this is to be held by the puppeteer).
4. For a complete play you need: Queen Esther, Mordecai, Haman, King Ahasuerus, the servant, and a horse. Study the suggestions and pattern pieces so that you can make these puppets. Add touches of your own.
5. Use scissor points to punch holes for the ice cream stick arms, except for the horse. Add some white glue around the opening to keep the arms in place.
6. Plan your play.

PATTERN FOR PURIM PUPPETS

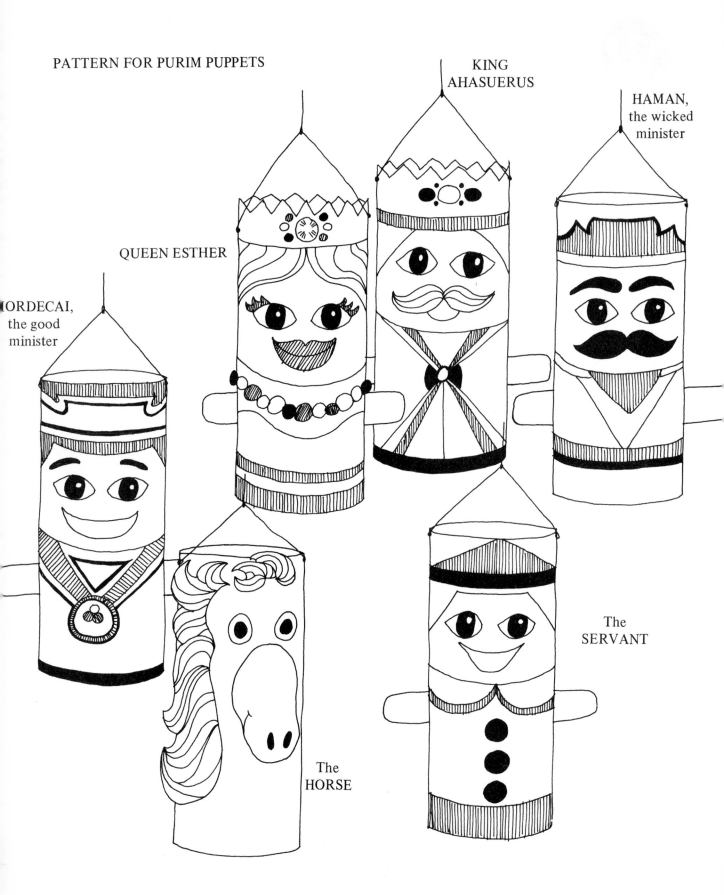

KING
AHASUERUS

HAMAN,
the wicked
minister

QUEEN ESTHER

MORDECAI,
the good
minister

The
SERVANT

The
HORSE

182

 STITCHERY

BACKGROUND: Although Israel is near Asia, the Israeli way of life is far more like life in the United States. Many of the cities are very modern and look much like any town in the United States. Many of the arts are also very similar to those enjoyed in the United States. In school and at home children are encouraged to use their time wisely and doing stitchery is one enjoyable pastime. Flowers and· designs from nature are popular motifs.

MATERIALS:

Patterns
Embroidery thread and needle
Colored felt-tip pens
Embroidery hoops, if available

PROCEDURE:

1. Transfer your design to cloth by tracing or by tracing over carbon paper.
2. Use felt-tip markers to color your design as you would like.
3. Thread your needle.
4. Use the three stitches suggested below, to outline and complete your stitchery.

STITCHERY*

I. RUNNING STITCH

Pick up an equal amount of cloth each time. Work right to left.

II. BACKSTITCH

Work from right to left, bring needle up through cloth about ¼" in front of the starting point. Go back and then come out ¼" beyond last visible point.

III. CROSS-STITCH

Produce a row of slanting stitches to form one half of each cross. At end of line, turn fabric, complete other half of each cross.

*An additional source of information: Enthoven, Jacqueline. *Stitchery for Children*. New York: Van Nostrand Reinhold Company. 1968.

 INTRODUCING THE COOKING OF ISRAEL

Tzenna (meaning austerity) is the word for food in Israel. Israeli cooking really had its origin in 1948 when Israel came into existence. People of at least eighty nationalities have come together to form the population of Israel, each bringing their recipes and traditions from the lands they left.

Israeli cooking is lumped into three categories: European, Oriental (which covers non-European dishes: Arabic, North African, Indian, and the Far East), and original dishes.

Israelis are developing original dishes, neither European nor Oriental, that utilize the plentiful products that are grown in their country. Due to modern farming techniques, Israeli farmers have increased production six-fold in the past two decades. Israel is the third largest exporter of avocados (after California and South Africa). They also raise guava, citrus fruits, mangos, vegetables, dates, rice and honey.

 BAGEL COOKIES (KA'ACHEI SUMSUM)

BACKGROUND: Bagels are traditional food eaten by Jews throughout the world. These bagels are usually eaten for Sabbath breakfast, with coffee, by Syrian Jews in Israel.

INGREDIENTS:

1 tsp.	(5ml.)	Yeast
¼ tsp.	(1.2ml.)	Sugar
2 Tbs.	(30ml.)	Warm water
½ C.	(120ml.)	Flour
2 Tbs.	(30ml.)	Melted margarine
1/8 tsp.	(.6ml.)	Salt
		One beaten egg
3 oz.	(80ml.)	Sesame seeds

PROCEDURE:
1. Place yeast and sugar in a bowl.
2. Pour over water and stir to dissolve. Place in a warm place for 10 minutes.
3. Mix flour, salt, margarine and yeast mixture to form a dough.
4. Cover dough with a towel. Put in a warm place for 2 hours.
5. After dough rises, take small ball and roll into strips 4 inches (10cm.) long.
6. Form into bagel or doughnut shape, moisten ends if needed to join ends.
7. Place on greased baking sheet.
8. Brush with beaten egg, sprinkle with sesame seeds.
9. Bake at 375°F, 190°C, for 20-30 minutes.

 CHALLAH BREAD (BRAIDED BREAD)

BACKGROUND: Challah is the traditional twisted bread always served on the Sabbath. An old tradition that goes back to the time when loaves were carried as a tribute to the priests in the Temple in Jerusalem, is that the person baking the bread breaks off a bit of dough and throws it in the fire while saying a prayer for their home and for peace for the world.

INGREDIENTS:

1 tsp.	(5ml.)	Dry yeast
1 Tbs.	(15ml.)	Warm water
¼ C.	(60ml.)	Hot water
1 tsp.	(5ml.)	Vegetable oil
½ tsp.	(2.5ml.)	Salt
½ tsp.	(2.5ml.)	Sugar
1 Tbs.	(15ml.)	Beaten egg
1 C.	(240ml.)	Flour

PROCEDURE:
1. Soften the yeast in the warm water.
2. To the boiling hot water, add the oil, salt and sugar. Stir until the sugar is dissolved.
3. Cool and when lukewarm, add the softened yeast.
4. Add the beaten egg to the liquid.
5. Add enough flour and stir and beat to make a smooth, thick batter.
6. Let sit for a few minutes (approximately 10) then add the rest of the flour to make a dough that can be handled.
7. Knead until smooth and elastic on wax paper.
8. Shape into a ball and grease the surface, place in a greased bowl and cover with a clean cloth.
9. Let rise in a warm place, until doubled in size.

10. Knead again until dough is fine-grained.
11. Divide dough into 3 portions.
12. Roll each into long strips and fasten ends together. Braid into a twisted loaf.
13. Place loaf on a greased baking sheet.
14. Cover and let rise until double in bulk again in a warm place.
15. Brush top with beaten egg with 1 tsp. (5ml.) cold water added and sprinkle with poppy seeds.
16. Bake in a hot oven at 375°F, 190°C for 10-12 minutes; then at 350°F, 176°C for 15 minutes.

 FALAFEL

BACKGROUND: Falafel is as common in Israel as the hot dog is in the United States. It is sold on many street corners throughout the country. It consists of chick-pea balls served in Pita bread with lettuce, tomato, and a sauce.

INGREDIENTS:

3 Tbs.	(45ml.)	Chick-peas (soak 12-24 hours and drain, or washed and drained canned beans may be used)
1 inch	(2.5cm.)	Piece of green onion
½ tsp.	(2.5ml.)	Beaten egg
1/8 tsp.	(.6ml.)	Lemon juice
2 tsp.	(10ml.)	Cracked wheat soaked (soak bulgar wheat 12-24 hours, drain)
2 drops		Crushed garlic
Pinch		Salt
Pinch		Red pepper

PROCEDURE:
1. Grind the chick-peas and green onion with a fine grinder.
2. Add the egg, lemon juice, cracked wheat, garlic, salt, pepper and mix well.
3. Form 3 balls, roll them in wheat flour.
4. Deep-fry at 375°F, 190°C for 1-2 minutes.
5. Drain.
6. Eat by themselves, or place in Pita bread with lettuce, tomatoes, and sauce.

 FRUIT FRITTERS

BACKGROUND: There are many varieties of latkes made in different countries, also there are many varieties enjoyed during the Chanukah season. In addition to the cheese, potato, and just plain latkes, Israelis also make fruit fritters. The batter is especially delicate, similar to a Japanese tempura, and the fruit may be any kind that is in season.

INGREDIENTS:

¼ C.	(60ml.)	Flour
½ tsp.	(2.5ml.)	Baking powder
Pinch		Salt
1¼ tsp.	(6.2ml.)	Sugar
1 Tbs.	(15ml.)	Beaten egg
2 Tbs.	(30ml.)	Milk
1 tsp.	(5ml.)	Melted margarine
		Sliced bananas, apples or other fruit

PROCEDURE:
1. Sift together flour, baking powder, salt and sugar.
2. Mix the egg, milk and melted margarine.
3. Stir the liquid mixture into the dry ingredients.
4. Blend until smooth but do not overbeat.
5. Batter should be heavy enough to coat the fruit; adjust with more milk or flour, if necessary.
6. Dip fruit into batter and deep-fry in hot fat.
7. Drain on paper towels.
8. Usually are served with confectioners' sugar sprinkled on top.

 HAMANTASCHEN

BACKGROUND: Hamantaschen are triangularly shaped, filled cookies that are traditionally served at the feast of Purim. Purim is a spring holiday celebrating the freeing of ancient Jews from the Persian prime minister Haman, who was going to have them killed. The Hamantaschen are shaped like a triangle because the wicked Haman wore a three-cornered hat.

INGREDIENTS:

Pastry:

2 Tbs.	(30ml.)	Beaten egg
2 Tbs.	(30ml.)	Sugar
2 Tbs.	(30ml.)	Melted butter
1½ tsp.	(7.5ml.)	Water
¼ tsp.	(1.2ml.)	Vanilla
1 Tbs.	(15ml.)	Lemon juice
1/8 tsp.	(.6ml.)	Baking soda
1/8 tsp.	(.6ml.)	Baking powder
Pinch		Salt
¾ C.	(180ml.)	Flour

Filling:

¼ C.	(60ml.)	Lekvar (Prune butter)
2 Tbs.	(30ml.)	Chopped nuts
½ tsp.	(2.5ml.)	Grated lemon rind

PROCEDURE:
1. Preheat oven to 375°F, 190°C and grease cookie sheet.
2. Put beaten eggs in margarine tub then beat in sugar, butter, water, vanilla and lemon juice.
3. Sift flour with baking soda, baking powder and salt.
4. Slowly add the flour mixture to the liquid mixture. Mix together until the dough forms a ball and seems stiff enough to be rolled out. Wrap dough and cool while you make filling.
5. To make filling, combine the prune mixture, lemon and nuts and mix well.
6. Put dough on a lightly floured piece of wax paper, then roll out dough until quite thin.
7. Cut out circles of dough with a cutter or the edge of a glass.
8. Place rounded tsp. (5ml.) of filling in center of dough circle.
9. Loosen dough by slipping table knife under three sides, flip dough over filling forming a triangle.
10. Pinch all seams of dough, sealing filling inside.
11. Place Hamantaschen on greased cookie sheet. Drip ¼ to ½ tsp. (1.2-2.5ml.) honey over top of each.
12. Bake until golden, about 12 minutes at 375°F, 190°C.

HAMANTASCHEN COOKIE

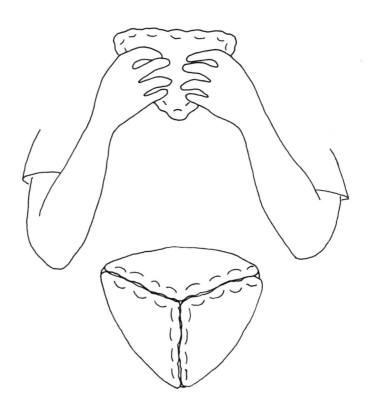

 HONEY CLUSTERS

BACKGROUND: The people of Israel come from many other lands yet all celebrate their New Year by eating foods that are cooked with honey.

INGREDIENTS:

¼ C.	(60ml.)	Flour
Pinch		Salt
1 Tbs.	(15ml.)	Beaten egg

Syrup:

½ C.	(120ml.)	Honey
¼ tsp.	(1.2ml.)	Ginger

PROCEDURE:
1. Sift the flour.
2. Mix the flour, egg and salt.
3. Knead the dough, adding more flour if it is too sticky.
4. Roll the dough into a rope 1/3" thick.
5. Cut into ½" pieces and place them on a well greased cookie sheet.
6. Bake at 375°F, 190°C for 15 minutes or until golden brown, turn the pieces with a spatula to brown both sides evenly.
7. Bring the honey and ginger to a boil in a saucepan.
8. Add the baked pieces and boil gently for 20 minutes, stirring with a wooden spoon.
9. Remove from syrup and place on a slightly greased plate.
10. Allow to cool before eating.

LATKES (POTATO PANCAKES)

BACKGROUND: Potato pancakes are made in a variety of ways in several cultures. A recipe for Greek potato pancakes (patatokeftehes) can be found in Chapter VII. Applesauce is usually served with Latkes.

INGREDIENTS:

½ C.	(120ml.)	Grated potato
1 Tbs.	(15ml.)	Grated onion
Pinch		Salt and pepper
1 tsp.	(5ml.)	Matzo meal
1 Tbs.	(15ml.)	Beaten egg
		Vegetable oil for cooking

PROCEDURE:
1. Peel and grate the potatoes and onion.
2. Drain the mixture by placing it in a towel and pressing the liquid out.
3. Place the potato-onion mixture in a margarine tub.
4. Add the salt, pepper, matzo meal and egg.
5. Mix vigorously until the ingredients are well combined.
6. Heat cooking oil in a heavy skillet until a drop of water sputters and evaporates instantly.
7. Drop 1-2 Tbs. (15-30ml.) batter into skillet and flatten it into a 2-2½" cake.
8. Fry about 2 minutes on each side, or until they are golden brown.

 PITA BREAD

BACKGROUND: Pita bread is a flat bread used extensively in Middle Eastern cooking. It is frequently filled with various stuffings and eaten like a sandwich.

INGREDIENTS:

1 scant tsp.	(4ml.)	Dry yeast
¼ C.	(60ml.)	Warm water
1/8 tsp.	(.6ml.)	Salt
½ C.	(120ml.)	Flour

PROCEDURE:
1. Sprinkle the yeast on the warm water and stir to dissolve.
2. Add salt.
3. Add the flour slowly, beating vigorously.
4. Knead the dough on a well-floured board for four minutes with greased hands.
5. Flatten dough into two 4" circles on a greased cookie sheet.
6. Cover with towel and let rise 25 minutes.
7. Bake at 475°F, 246°C 12-15 minutes.

POPPYSEED CANDY

BACKGROUND: Poppyseeds are used frequently in Israeli candies and cookies.

INGREDIENTS:

¼ C.	(60ml.)	Poppy seed
½ C.	(120ml.)	Honey
2 Tbs.	(30ml.)	Nuts

PROCEDURE:

1. Rinse the poppy seeds in a fine strainer. Drain well.
2. Chop the nuts.
3. Place the seeds, honey and nuts in a small saucepan and bring to a boil over medium heat.
4. Boil steadily for 8 minutes; if mixture browns sooner, remove from heat.
5. Spread mixture on a greased plate.
6. Cut into squares while still hot.
7. It will be chewy when cool.

INTRODUCING THE RECREATION OF ISRAEL

Israel is a new country with a mixture of modern buildings and old forts. Leisure time is spent listening to the radio and attending movies, theater, dance and concerts. Some of the favorite sports in Israel include: basketball, hiking, rowing, sailing, skin diving, soccer and swimming. Much of the time the weather is quite warm — children lead an out-of-doors life which includes picnics, camping, and excursions to historical places. A favorite party in Israel is the Kumsitz (from the German, "come sit"). At this party, the children sit around the campfire at night to sing and clap. Often the words are only "La, la, la".

The national dance of Israel is the Hora. It is a circle dance that is enjoyed by people throughout the world. It is danced to the music of "Hava Nagila" and may be found on most records and in most Jewish or Israeli books. A brief description of the dance may be found in this listing. Children living on a Kibbutz do quite a bit of singing of both children's and folk songs. Circle dances are also very popular.

City children of Israel play many games exactly as children of the United States. Some favorite party games are: Blindman's Buff, Jacks and Ball, Musical Chairs and Red Light-Green Light. Name games are common in both countries.

 BEN HUR

This game requires two even-numbered teams of two to ten players.
MATERIALS:

      Two brooms.

PROCEDURE: This is a team relay which is raced in pairs. Two players from each team straddle a broomstick with the bristles behind them. They pretend to be Ben Hur and his horse; the broom is the chariot. At a starting signal the chariot, horse and rider race to the goal and back. The winning chariot scores a point for their team. At the end of the game, the team with the most points is the winner of the game.

BLI YADAYIM

This game is for four to five for fun or four to five teams for competing.
MATERIALS:

      One rope or string about 6 feet long
      One hat for each player

PROCEDURE: Players stand in a line with both of their hands holding the rope. All play must take place without the use of hands and without anyone letting go of the rope. If teams are competing, dropping the rope constitutes a loss.

Holding the rope, the team moves to a location about five feet from home base where they find on the floor a hat for each player. Without using their hands, they must each get a hat on their head and then return to home base. The first team at home base, with each player wearing a hat, wins. Although all play must be accomplished without the use of hands, team members may help each other with any other parts of their body.

193

 DREIDLE GAME

One version of the dreidle game and directions for making a dreidle are available in the art section of this chapter.

This game requires two to four players.

MATERIALS:

One dreidle

One gift box lid which has been marked off into nine sections and numbered as shown:

PROCEDURE: Players take turns spinning the dreidle. The number that the apex of the dreidle rests on is the player's score for that turn. The first player to accumulate 100 points is the winner.

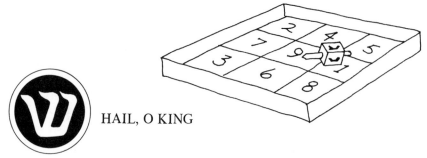

 HAIL, O KING

This game requires three to seven players.

PROCEDURE: A child is chosen to be "it". He is called "The King". While the king sits on his throne, the other players secretly choose an act or a story that they will pantomime and they assign parts. Now this dialogue takes place:

     Players: Hail, O King

     King: Where have you been?

     Players: Far away in the forest.

     King: What have you been doing there?

The players now act out their pantomime and the King must guess what story they are portraying. After the King guesses correctly or gives up, he may then choose a new King.

 HIDE AND SEEK

This game requires two to ten players.

MATERIALS:

Button or any small object.

PROCEDURE: One player is chosen to be "it" and leaves the room while a button (that he has previously been shown) is hidden by the rest of the group and a song is chosen.

When "it" returns to the room, the group begins to sing the song they have agreed upon. If "it" is close to the hidden button the group sings loudly. If "it" is far away from the button, the group sings softly.

This game is a variation of "Button, button" or "Hot and cold" which are both popular with children in the United States.

 HORA

This dance is performed to the music, "Hava Nagila". More intricate dance instructions may be found on most Israeli record albums which also contain the music. A simplified form of the dance may be tried by the children:

1. All children join hands and form a circle, arms extended. Movement is counterclockwise.
2. Right foot steps left, crossing over in front of left foot.
3. Left foot steps left.
4. Right foot steps left, crossing behind left foot.
5. Left foot steps left.
6. Right foot kicks to front.
7. Left foot kicks to front.
8. Continue numbers 2-7 until music is completed.

 LAG B'OMER

BACKGROUND: On the eighteenth day of the month of Iyar, early in the spring, Jews celebrate a holiday dedicated to the memory of a famous scholar, Simeon Bar Yohai, who refused to obey the Romans' decree that Hebrew scholars could not teach or study their holy books. Simeon escaped with his son to a cave in Galilee and lived and studied there for thirteen years. Other Jews, knowing of his hiding place, came to visit and to learn in secret once each year.

Before his death, Simeon asked his followers to celebrate rather than mourn his death. Consequently, the day he died, called Lag B'omer, is a joyous occasion for everyone, dedicated to scholarship. Children dance and sing on picnics and play with bows and arrows symbolizing the hunters' disguises of the original followers of Simeon.

In the United States, Lag B'omer is the first day of Jewish Book Week. The following game is traditionally played by children during Lag B'omer.

MATERIALS:

Seven clean, empty tuna fish cans
Twelve markers
Colored paper
Scissors
Rubber cement
Felt pens

PROCEDURE:

1. Cut out the seven illustrated circle patterns and glue one inside each of your seven tuna cans.
2. Paper clip sides of tuna cans together to form circle.

HOW TO PLAY LAG B'OMER:

1. This game requires two to four players. Use beans as markers. Each player gets six markers. Player stands four feet from target and throws his beans into the Lag B'omer cans one at a time. His score is determined by adding the number values of each can in which the beans land.
2. The highest scoring player from each complete turn receives one bean from each of the other players.
3. The winner is the player who still has beans at the end of the game.

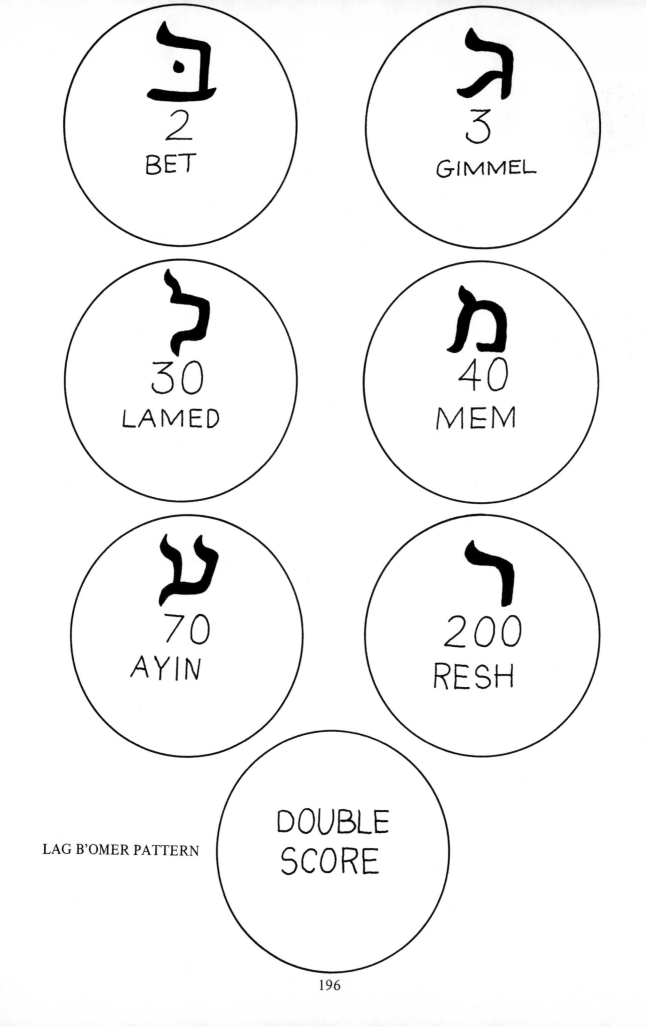

2
BET

3
GIMMEL

30
LAMED

40
MEM

70
AYIN

200
RESH

DOUBLE SCORE

LAG B'OMER PATTERN

 NAME GAME

This game requires two to five players.

PROCEDURE:
1. One player calls out any category, such as flowers, states, cars, or famous movie stars. Player number two then names as many items as he can that fall into this category.
2. The first player to accumulate fifty items from various given categories is the winner.

 PEANUTS IN THE BOTTLE

This game requires two to five players.

MATERIALS:
Bottle
10 peanuts
Chair

PROCEDURE:
1. Bottle is placed on the floor while player kneels on chair, facing bottle.
2. Player uses hand, resting on chair to drop peanuts into bottle.
3. Player who gets the most peanuts in the bottle is the winner.

CHAPTER IX
JAPAN

INDEX

ABOUT JAPAN

Japan is a country of islands (four large ones and numerous small ones) in the Pacific Ocean, along the northeastern coast of Asia. It is a mountainous country with relatively little farmland or mineral deposits.

Japan maintains a democratic government which is actually a constitutional monarchy. The emperor inherits his throne and performs ceremonial duties. He has no power in the government.

In Japan there are suggestions of both Oriental and Western influence. Japan still maintains some designs which are distinctively Japanese. Japan is famous for the high level of its craftsmanship in manufactured and artistically produced products. Some examples of these may be found on the following pages.

INTRODUCING THE ARTS OF JAPAN

Japanese people express their love of beauty (especially beauty of nature) through art in their painting, porcelain vases, lacquerware, textiles, gardens, homes and flower arrangements.

The Japanese enjoy making a few flowers and twigs look as though they are really growing. Their creative talents combine natural beauty with simple designs. Although Japan produces art which is distinctively Japanese, there is a marked suggestion of Chinese and Western influence on many Japanese creations.

Home art items include: screens, dishes, vases, clothing, writing of poetry, calligraphy (Japanese writing as often seen on the side of a painting) and artistic penmanship. It should be emphasized that the Japanese excel in painting, theater and dance, poetry, architecture, and the making of small decorative objects. Elegance, delicacy and economy of line characterize the Japanese arts.

Most paintings (on silk or rice paper) are displayed unframed as a vertical or horizontal scroll. Gracefulness of line and exotic color combinations characterize Japanese art. Take any good Japanese painting, put your finger on a particular spot, and then trace that line as it winds around until the finger is back where you started; you will feel this delicacy of line painted with no awkward angles but only sweeping curves. This is particularly noticeable in Japanese woodblock prints.

Perhaps the Japanese secret to so many artistic talents lies in the fact that the government of Japan glorifes their actors and artists, calling them "National Living Treasures". Artists are encouraged to work at their art totally without financial pressures.

199

 BATIK

BACKGROUND: Batik was originally a Chinese art. When Buddhism reached Japan from China, experts were sent through the country to teach weaving and cloth dyeing. Later, Nō and Kabuki theater encouraged dramatic color, so new ways of dyeing were sought. Yuzen is a process where the design is marked out in rice flour paste or wax to keep the dye from taking. Some designs are combined with tie-dyeing or embroidery. Yuzen dyed silks are a specialty of Kyoto. Bold designs are made for the noble families. Color, too, has status value; for example, yellow is a royal color. Some of the earliest dyes were clear blue, soft brown, and black.

MATERIALS:

Coffee cans as dye pails
Double boiler
Iron
Muslin — cut in 12" squares (prewashed and dried)
Paint brushes to paint wax on fabric

Paraffin or old candles
Plastic bags or gloves
Rit dye — a bright red is a good choice for a first
Terry cloth or old towels

PROCEDURE:
1. Cover the work area with newspaper.
2. Mix dye according to directions on box. Put in coffee cans.
3. Melt wax in top of double boiler. (Wax will catch fire if it is melted directly over flame.) Keep wax hot and liquid. The wax will be painted on the cloth to keep the dye from taking in chosen areas. Wax should go all the way through the cloth and when held up to the light, light should shine clearly through. If not, re-wax.
4. Stir dye and stir cloth into dye until you see color you want on cloth.
5. Remove cloth from dye and blot between terry cloth towels.
6. Hang cloth to dry.
7. You may continue to add wax and dyes as long as you wish. Be certain that cloth is completely dry before adding next dye. When dyeing with successive colors, use the lighter shades of dye first.
8. The heat of an iron will remove the wax from your finished batik. Set iron on "cotton" setting. Place the batik between two towels or two thick layers of newspaper. The newspapers will need to be changed frequently.
9. Allow your batik to cool and it may be fringed as a wall hanging or mounted.

 CARP

BACKGROUND: On Boy's Day (May 5) in Japan, bright carp streamers wave over each house. There are usually three carp of graduated sizes; one is black and two are red. Boys in Japan are brought up on the story of the carp, a fish which swims against the strongest currents. The carp is not a lazy fish who lies around in sunny pools but is, rather, a real fighter. Japanese boys hope they may grow up as strong and as courageous as the carp.

MATERIALS:

        Tissue paper rectangle 18" x 24" (exact size may vary)
        Small tissue paper pieces of various colors
        Tagboard — cut in 1½" x 15" strips
        Stapler
        Glue
        Pencil or chalk
        Black construction paper (for eyes)
        String in 12" lengths

PROCEDURE:

1. Fold large sheet of tissue paper in half lengthwise.
2. Draw outline of fish. Use folded side as top of fish.
3. Cut out fish through both thicknesses.
4. Cut from paper pieces: side fins, dorsal fins, eyes, and scales. Glue in place on both sides of fish.
5. Staple tagboard strip around mouth opening for stiffness (leaving ends free to attach and fit together in step 6). Tissue paper may be folded over strip to hide tagboard strip.
6. Overlap tagboard to fit. Glue together. Glue bottom edge of carp, leave mouth and tail open to catch the wind.
7. Staple 12" length of string to each side of carp's mouth so he may be hung.

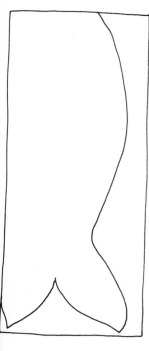
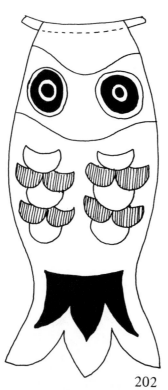

 DARUMA DOLLS

BACKGROUND: Japan is one of the world's largest toy producers, and most of these toys are of folk background. Travelers in Japan marvel at the large number of toys to be found. City streets are full of color and life, seeming to overflow with gay dolls, tops, miniature tea sets, paper toys and musical instruments.

Although the roly-poly Daruma dolls which are made without arms or legs were not originally intended as toys, today they are sometimes used as such. Daruma dolls are actually made for the celebration of the Japanese New Year. Many Japanese families purchase a new Daruma doll yearly — it is hoped that this doll will bring good luck to their home. At the end of the year, the old doll is burned in a celebration and a new doll is purchased.

The self-righting quality of the doll is symbolic of man's ability to bounce back to normal after facing life's problems.

There are many different kinds of Daruma dolls from simple to elaborate. The original Daruma dolls were made of baked clay. One special type of "wishing" Daruma, without eyes, is given to children. When a child makes a wish he may paint on one eye. After the wish comes true, the second eye is given to the doll.

MATERIALS:

½ Tennis balls — to be used as molds		
2 Tbs.	(30ml.)	Plaster of Paris
2 Tbs.	(30ml.)	Water
Margarine tubs and coffee stirrers		
Empty toilet paper rolls		

Pattern, if desired, may be run as a ditto on red construction paper or the children may paint their own paper to fit toilet paper rolls

PROCEDURE:
1. Color pattern to resemble Daruma doll.
2. Mix in a margarine tub and stir to consistency of buttermilk: 2 Tbs. (30ml.) plaster of paris and 2 Tbs. (30ml.) water.
3. Pour mixture into mold of ½ tennis ball and allow to set for 2-5 minutes.
4. Tape or staple the Daruma doll pattern around a toilet paper roll. Press roll to botttom of mold. Allow to set several hours or overnight.
5. Forms may be easily removed from plaster of paris after drying.

PATTERN FOR DARUMA DOLL

 FAMILY CREST

BACKGROUND: In Japan the art of paper folding is called origami. When combined with paper cutting, a new art is created — Mon-Kiri. Family crests are often created using this paper craft. Historically family crests were placed on banners or lanterns and were sometimes used to identify friends and/or enemies when at battle. Each family name has its own design and special coloration. Today in Japan, these crests are most commonly worn on the back of formal kimono(s) during special ceremonies.

MATERIALS:

> 8" Square of white paper
> 6" Square of black paper
> Scissors
> Compass or circle pattern

PROCEDURE:

1. Cut a circle form from black paper.
2. Fold the circle in half and then in thirds to form a wedge. (Oval patterns are also widely used).
3. Sketch a design or cut freehand to form a pattern. For example, if shown design is chosen, shaded areas would be completely removed.
4. Open the black design and glue it to a piece of white paper.
5. Encourage the children to use this crest to represent their name as they would with Chinese Chops or a British coat of arms.

PATTERN FOR FAMILY CREST

 FANS

BACKGROUND: A bamboo-ribbed fan can be a comfort on a hot day in Japan. The first fans may have been palm leaves. It is believed that artists copied this leaf design with bamboo and silk or paper. Fans are often made for a specific person and may carry the emblems of that family. Fans may be carved from bone, sandalwood or ivory and painted by an artist with water colors.

MATERIALS:

        12" x 12" Square of poster board
        Tongue depressor
        Stapler
        Poster paints and brushes
        White glue and brushes
        Wax paper

PROCEDURE:

1. Fold poster board in half and cut two of any geometric shape.
2. Glue the two pieces of poster board together with one end of the tongue depressor placed between the poster board at one point.
3. Paint fan and handle any one solid color. Red is a favorite color in Japan.
4. When paint is dry, create your own design or transfer any of the felt-tip embroidery or family crest designs to your fan (use carbon paper as you trace over the design) and paint design.
5. Paint over entire fan and handle with white glue — allow to dry on wax paper — for a shiny finish.

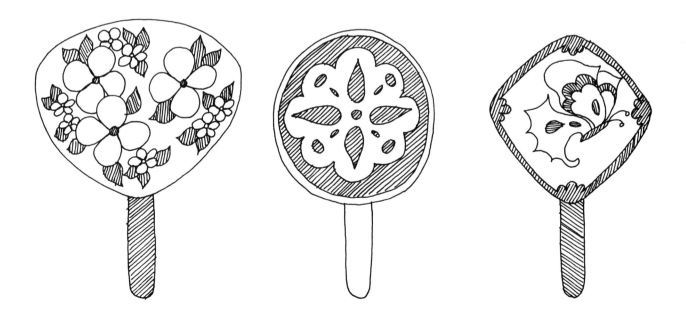

KITES

BACKGROUND: Kites have been made in Japan for hundreds of years. The Japanese hold fighting kite competitions in some communities. At these contests, kites cut each other down by crossing flying ropes, which have been covered with ground glass. Some kites are as large as 50 feet in diameter and weigh several thousand pounds. It can take up to two hundred men to fly one kite.

MATERIALS:

Bamboo teriyake sticks
Construction paper
String
White glue
Felt-tip markers
Scissors and hole punch

PROCEDURE:

1. Use carbon paper to transfer the kite pattern to construction paper.
2. Glue teriyake sticks in place as illustrated on the pattern.
3. Punch holes as illustrated on the pattern. A hole punch may be used by folding the paper near the glued stick area.
4. Attach strings as indicated by arrows and extend about twelve inches to meet single flying string. Allow four to five feet of kite string per child.
5. Hold a kite flying contest.

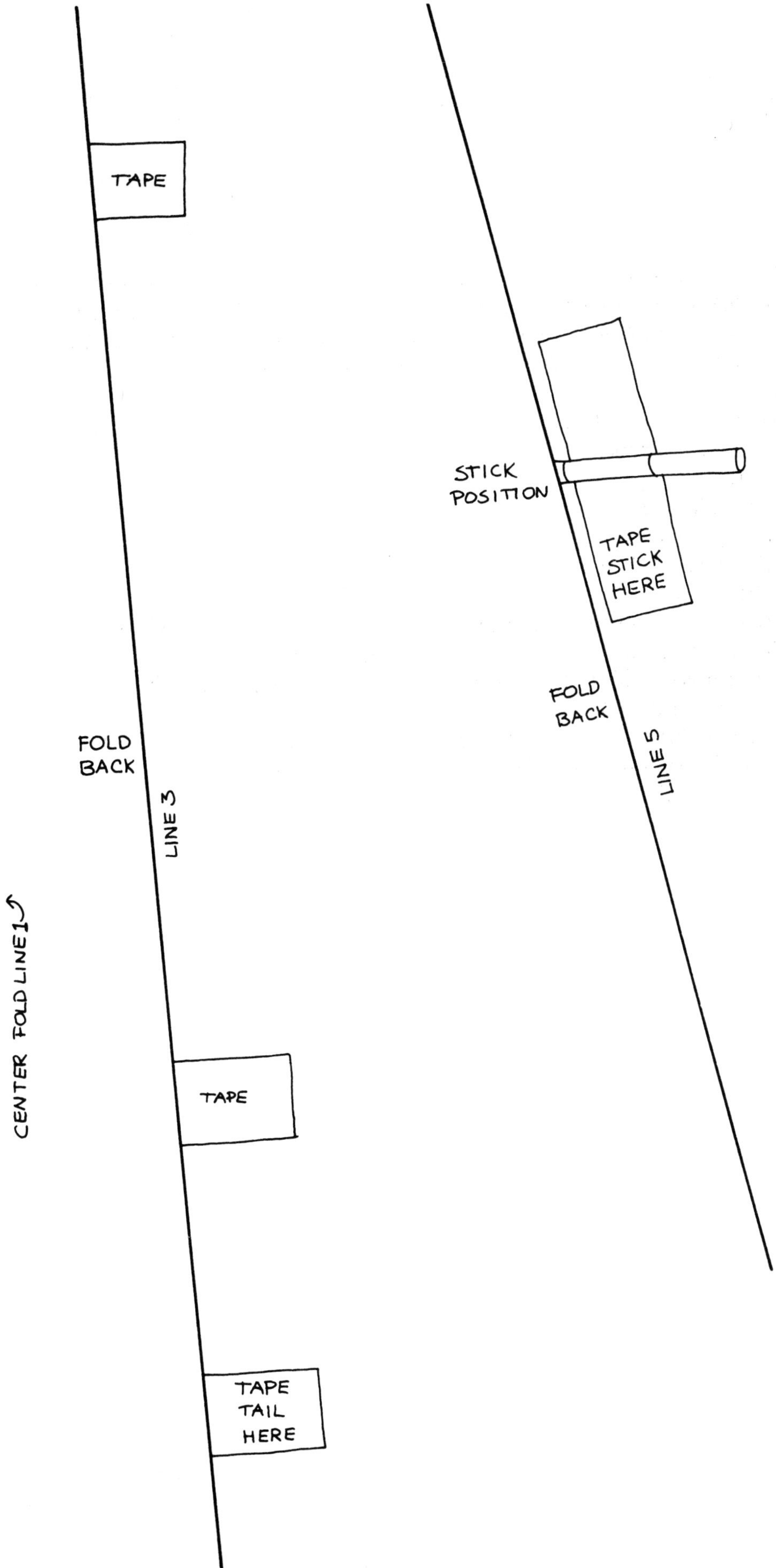

TAPE

STICK
POSITION

TAPE
STICK
HERE

FOLD
BACK

FOLD
BACK

LINE 3

LINE 5

CENTER FOLD LINE 1

TAPE

TAPE
TAIL
HERE

CUT OUT

CUT OUT

CUT OUT

CUT OUT

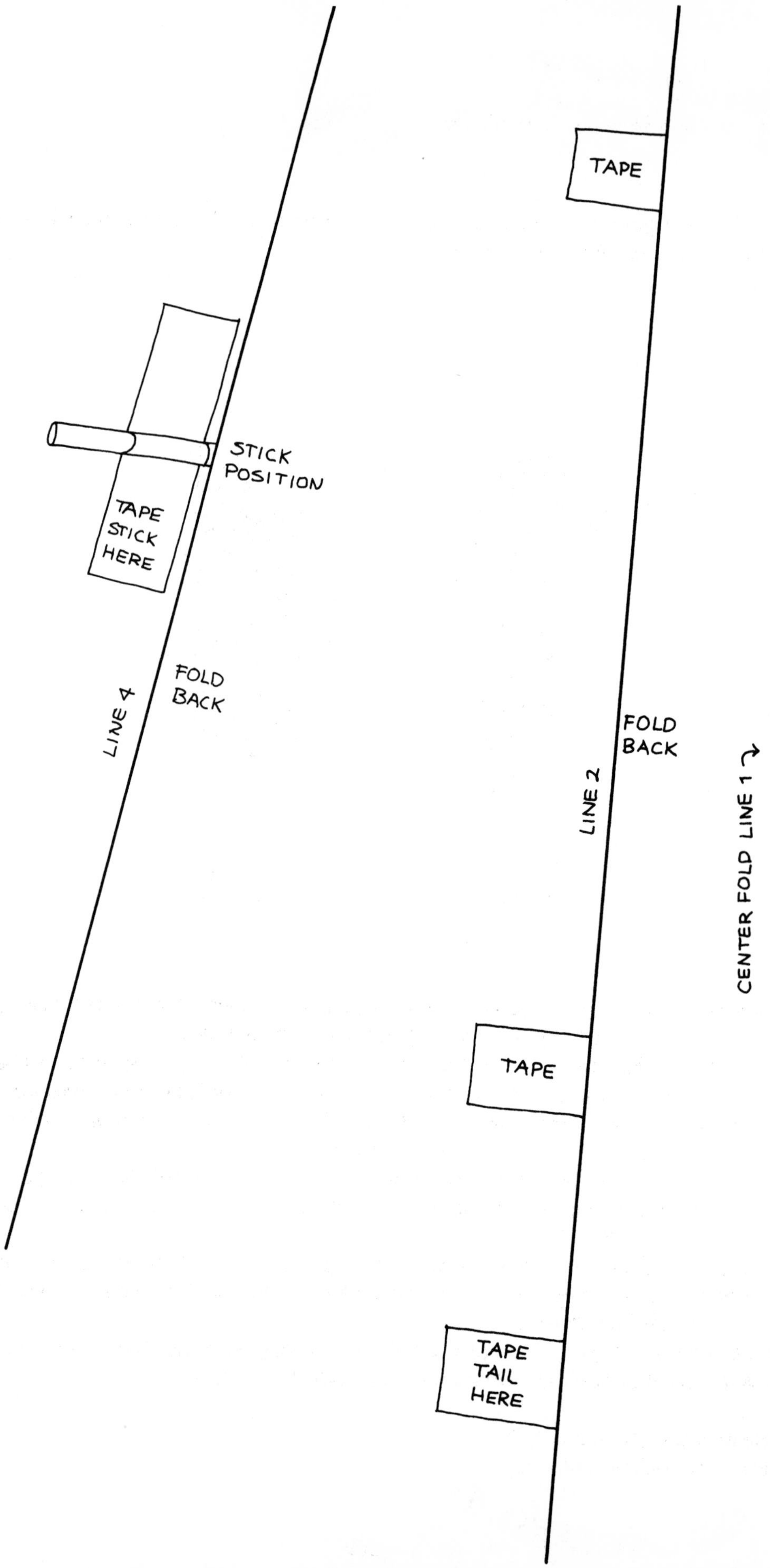

TAPE

STICK
POSITION

TAPE
STICK
HERE

FOLD
BACK

LINE 4

FOLD
BACK

LINE 2

CENTER FOLD LINE 1 ↰

TAPE

TAPE
TAIL
HERE

 MASKS FOR NŌ THEATER

BACKGROUND: Men have been wearing masks for a long time. Sometimes men wear masks for disguise, entertainment, ceremonies, or just for fun.

In early Japan (8th century), masks were used to frighten others. Twenty devil dancers, who wore frightening masks, were used to protect the royal palace from demons.

Today in Japan, masks are worn for many of the festivals. Masks are worn for Kabuki theater. To show appreciation to any actor, cries and laughter were all right while personal emotions should not be shown. For example, in real life, a man would be expected to smile while describing a death in his family. This smile would mask his true feeling of death.

Perhaps the most unique Japanese masks are used for Nō drama. Nō drama is performed by men only; however, they play the parts of both men and women. Generally the actors wear lacquered wood masks that are painted shiny white.

In Nō theater, the chorus chants the story in poetry while the actors portray in pantomime. Each Nō drama lasts about one hour. The actors generally present six Nō dramas in one day, with light entertainment between each drama.

A quick, simple way to produce Japanese Nō masks is suggested here. This is not the way that they are made in Japan; however, this method produces a good simulation.

MATERIALS:

       Heavy-duty aluminum foil

       Black permanent markers

PROCEDURE:
1. Tear foil off in sheets so that when it is folded in quarters, it produces a rectangle approximately 5" x 8"
2. Have the children work with a partner and mold the foil to each others facial features (model should keep eyes closed) The foil corners may be rounded as the face is molded. (Folding the foil under is better than cutting because sharp edges may be avoided.)
3. Use a black felt-tip marker to show a few feature lines. The Nō masks use a minimum of feature lines as illustrated.
4. These masks may be mounted on construction paper for display. If they are to be worn, small slits for eyes, nose and mouth may be cut with a linoleum knife by the volunteer.
5. A more complicated version of this mask would be to cover the foil base with a layer of white papier mâché. Allow to dry and then paint.

 ORIGAMI

BACKGROUND: The Japanese have found many decorative uses for papercrafts. They have developed a highly skilled art of paper sculpture called origami which utilizes many paper-folding techniques. Animals and flowers are popular motifs.

Books on origami are plentiful in libraries and bookstores throughout the United States. This text offers some techniques for papercrafts without any specific origami finished products. Three books which are easy for the children to understand and that we have enjoyed using are *Origami in the Classroom* by Chiyo Araki (Tokyo, Japan: Charles E. Tuttle Co., 1968), and two books by Sheri Lewis and Lillian Oppenheimer. They are *Folding Paper Puppets* (New York: Stein and Day, 1962), and *Folding Paper Toys* (New York: Stein and Day, 1963). Both books offer step-by-step construction ideas for numerous papercrafts.

MATERIALS:
    Construction or tissue paper
    Scissors and hole punch

PROCEDURE:
1. Paper Bending: Cut diagonal slashes from the corners of a square to within 1" of the center. Bend the corners to the center and glue or staple in place.
2. Paper Curling: Roll strips of paper tightly around a pencil. Carefully unroll the strips and they will remain loosely curled.
3. Paper Pleating: Fold strips of paper one on top of each other in alternating directions. Crease carefully and then allow the paper to expand on its own.
4. Paper Scoring: Working on a board, or non-marring surface, lightly use the inside edge of a scissor point to mark indentation of heavy paper. A straight edge may be used to guide the scoring.
5. Paper Spirals: Cut a circle and continue to cut spirals to the center.
6. Practice all these techniques and then combine them in your own special origami creation. Use any origami book for specific ideas and suggestions.

PAPER LANTERNS (CHOCHIN)

BACKGROUND: At one time the people of Japan used lanterns which bore their family crest. This identified them to their neighbors. Lanterns are used for practical reasons (light) and to enhance the beauty of festivals and decorations. The Japanese enjoy the beauty of the light reflecting as a lantern bobs down the street.

There are many kinds of paper lanterns. There are large ones for temple gardens, small round ones may be carried on the end of a long stick, long cylindrical ones may be folded and stored, and delicate oval lanterns are often painted with lovely designs.

In Japan, lanterns are used in exciting festival contests when competitors balance a large pole on their forehead with as many as fifty paper lanterns hanging on the pole.

MATERIALS:

    Colored construction paper (approximately 12" x 18")
    Yellow or red tissue paper
    Scissors and tape
    Felt-tip markers
    Ruler and pencil

PROCEDURE:

1. Cut a 1" strip off the end of the construction paper to form a lantern handle.
2. Fold the paper in half lengthwise.
3. Draw a heavy line 2" from the open end of your paper.
4. Use a ruler and pencil to mark cutting lines from the fold to the heavy line.
5. Cut slits across the fold and to the heavy line you have marked with your pencil.
6. Unfold the paper and form it into a cylinder. Staple the ends together.
7. Decorate the lantern with strips of foil or tissue. Draw Japanese characters on the lantern for decoration. Place a crushed piece of yellow or red tissue inside the lantern to simulate light.

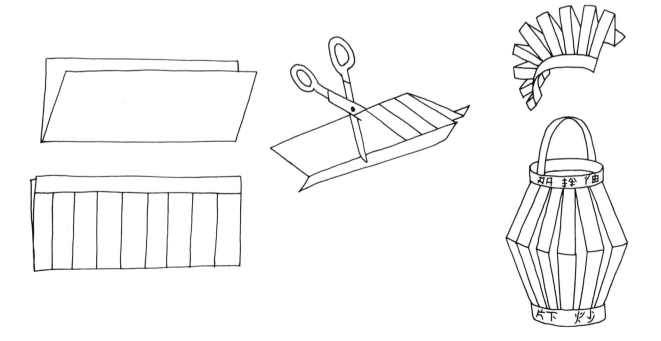

 TRAY GARDENS

BACKGROUND: Beautiful gardens are very important to most Japanese. The Japanese attempt to create a balance of natural beauty with the inclusion of a tree, rock, and pond to represent the forests, hills and waters of Japan. Garden arrangements are designed to suggest rest and meditation rather than to be a flowery place to play. Many Japanese enjoy spending money on their gardens and are proud to have them admired by friends and neighbors. A few items carefully arranged seem preferable to a crowded space. In very small Japanese homes where no garden is possible, the family may display a tray garden with a miniature tree. These dish gardens have peat, sand, soil, or even soaked paper as a base and include small plants, pebbles, a miniature bridge and sometimes a teahouse. Sand and stone arrangements are also made by some families.

MATERIALS:

> Cardboard gift box
> Aluminum foil and plastic wrap
> Dirt
> Small rocks
> Sand
> Small plants
> Peat moss

PROCEDURE:

1. Cover the cardboard box with plastic wrap and aluminum foil so it will be waterproof. Styrofoam or plastic meat trays may also be used for this activity, if they are available.
2. Arrange the soil and add peat moss wherever plants will be planted. Remember that simplicity is very important in the Japanese garden.

 WOODCUTS

BACKGROUND: Printing with the use of wood blocks reached Japan from China together with Buddhism. Woodcuts can produce numerous copies of the same print. This helped make art available even to the poor. Colored block prints are made by carving several different blocks and then combining them.

Since woodcut carving is too difficult for young children, you may want to substitute potato printing in this experience.

MATERIALS:

> Gouge or chisel
> Potato or balsa wood
> Metal spoons and knives (plastic serrated)
> Poster paints and brushes
> Construction paper

PROCEDURE:

1. Cut a potato open to produce two flat surfaces.
2. Use gouge and chisel (for balsa wood) or plastic knife (for potato). Scrape to form a design.
3. When the potato cut (or woodcut) is completed, paint the raised sections with any poster paint.
4. While the paint is wet, use the potato cut (or woodcut) as a stamp and transfer the design to a piece of construction paper.
5. Combine several stamps and colors to create an interesting composition.

 INTRODUCING THE COOKING OF JAPAN

To the Japanese, food is seen as an esthetic experience. One of the most important aspects of Japanese cooking is the manner in which the food is served. Great emphasis is placed on the table decor, arrangements and appearance of the food. For generations it has been the informal custom to eat and serve their food in a particular order: mountain products first, then sea products, next field products, and finally products of the towns. Busy people of the twentieth century have changed this practice but try to keep the spirit of it. For example, in sashimi, the ingredients are arranged in a design representing the landscape of a hill, field and water. Meals are also planned according to the season. For example, hot meals, particularly nabemono(s) (one-pot cooking) are served during winter; cold or room temperature meals such as sashimi, sushi or chilled sunomono are served during hot weather.

Limited access to foods, especially meat, has caused the Japanese cooks to develop many varied ways to prepare the same foods (pickling, steaming, deep frying, pan frying, etc.). Menus offer many variations according to the limitations of the geography or agricultural offerings; however, there are certain items that are served at almost every meal. There is nearly always at least one soup with each meal. Hot, plain, boiled rice is served at every meal, except when noodles or another rice dish is the main course. Tsukemono, or pickles, are served at most meals. The Japanese enjoy pickles so much that it is a typical dessert and it is often served at breakfast with hot rice.

The Japanese feel that the touch of a metal utensil to the mouth is unpleasant and therefore use chopsticks. Today in Japan, both Eastern and Western foods are enjoyed. When spaghetti, hamburgers, eggs and salads are eaten, they use knives and forks instead of chopsticks.

 CHICKEN BAKED IN SILVER FOIL (TORI NO GIN-GAMI YAKI)

BACKGROUND: In Japan today classic Nipponese cooking has blended with the styles of China, Europe and America, and a unique and varied style of cooking has developed. This recipe of chicken baked in foil is an adaptation of the Chinese paper chicken.

INGREDIENTS:

1" Piece of boned, skinned chicken		
1 Fresh mushroom, sliced		
1" Piece of sweet potato, cut into thickness of a pencil		
1 tsp.	(5ml.)	Grated cheese
Butter		
Cellophane or wax paper — 6" square		
Aluminum foil — 6" square		

PROCEDURE:

1. The chicken, vegetables and cheese can be prepared ahead of time by the volunteers or the children may participate in the preparation.
2. Lay out the sheet of aluminum foil; over this lay the sheet of cellophane (wax paper).
3. Lightly butter the surface of the cellophane (wax paper).
4. Arrange the chicken, mushroom, and sweet potato on the buttered cellophane (wax paper).
5. Sprinkle with the grated cheese.
6. Fold over the cellophane (wax paper) then fold up the aluminum foil, encasing the cellophane tightly.
7. Bake at 375°F, 190°C for fifteen minutes.

 EGG ROLL

BACKGROUND: These Japanese egg rolls are not at all like Chinese egg rolls. They are not covered with pancake-like skins, instead they are more like a pancake that is rolled. These could be compared to the latkes or patatokeftehes.

INGREDIENTS:

1 oz.	(30gms.)	Halibut or Sole (Precooked)
1½ tsp.	(7.5ml.)	Sugar
1		Egg
2 tsp.	(10ml.)	Clam juice
1 tsp.	(5ml.)	Soy sauce
1 tsp.	(5ml.)	Sherry
2 Tbs.	(30ml.)	Oil
Pinch		Salt

PROCEDURE:
1. Heat the oil in the skillet to 350°F, 176°C.
2. Flake the fish with a fork.
3. Beat the egg in a margarine tub and combine with the fish.
4. Add the sugar, clam juice, soy sauce, sherry and salt.
5. Pour the mixture into the pan and fry until lightly browned on both sides.
6. Remove from pan and roll like a jelly roll.
7. Let cool five minutes, then slice in one inch pieces.

 EGG SOUP

BACKGROUND: Soup is a part of almost every Japanese meal. There are two basic types, suimono (clear soup) and miso-shiru (soy bean paste soup).

INGREDIENTS:

1 Tbs.	(15ml.)	Cornstarch
1 C.	(240ml.)	Beef broth
1 C.	(240ml.)	Clam juice
1 tsp.	(5ml.)	Soy sauce
1		Egg
1 Tbs.	(15ml.)	Chopped scallions

PROCEDURE:
1. Mix the cornstarch with a small amount of the broth.
2. Add soy sauce and the rest of the broth and clam juice.
3. Boil gently.
4. Beat the egg and slowly pour it onto the surface of the boiling broth.
5. Cook until the eggs are set.
6. Sprinkle on the scallions when serving.

 JAPANESE SALAD

BACKGROUND: Most Japanese salads include as main ingredients cucumbers and seafood, because both items are abundant.

INGREDIENTS:

1¼ tsp.	(6.2ml.)	Vinegar
1/3 C.	(80ml.)	Soy sauce
¼ tsp.	(1.2ml.)	Grated fresh ginger or ½ tsp. (2.5ml.) cut up crystallized ginger.
1		Large cucumber, sliced
½ C.	(120ml.)	Cooked shrimp

PROCEDURE:
1. If you use crystallized ginger, wash the sugar off the slices, dry them, and cut them into small pieces.
2. In a cup, mix the vinegar, soy sauce and ginger.
3. In a cereal bowl, mix the cucumbers and shrimp.
4. Cover shrimp and cucumbers with soy sauce dressing.

 SUKIYAKI

BACKGROUND: In Japan sukiyaki is known as the "friendship dish". The ingredients are sliced uniformly and arranged beautifully on a platter. The cooking is done in an orderly ritualistic manner. This recipe cannot be made in individual portions but the children may chop one ingredient and then add it to the pan while the volunteer is cooking.

INGREDIENTS:

1 lb.	(.45kilo.)	Thinly sliced sirloin tip
1		Onion
1 Bunch		Green onions
6		Large fresh mushrooms
1 Can		Bamboo shoots (drained)
½ lb.	(.23kilo.)	Fresh spinach
6 ribs		Celery or Chinese cabbage
1 can		Shirataki (spaghetti-shaped yam shreds, drained) or 2 C. (480ml.) bean sprouts
½ C.	(120ml.)	Soy sauce
½ C.	(120ml.)	Stock
1 tsp.	(5ml.)	Sugar
½ tsp.	(2.5ml.)	MSG
3 Tbs.	(45ml.)	Cooking oil

PROCEDURE:
1. Put the suet or cooking oil in a skillet over medium heat.
2. Saute the beef slices in the oil, turn frequently and do not allow the meat to brown, approximately three minutes.
3. Push the meat to one side and saute the vegetables. Add them in sequence beginning with the vegetables that require longer cooking.
4. First saute the onions until they are golden.
5. As you add the green onions, mushrooms, bamboo shoots, spinach and celery pour in the soy sauce and stock mixture a little at a time.
6. Sprinkle the sugar and MSG over the vegetables while you are stir-frying them.
7. The sauteing of vegetables from onions through celery should take about seven minutes.
8. Push the meat into the center of the skillet, add the shiritaki or sprouts, and heat and stir for about four more minutes.
9. You may serve this mixture in a well-beaten raw egg. Boiled rice is often served to compliment this dish.

 SUSHI

BACKGROUND: Sushi is centuries old and one of the most authentic Japanese dishes you can experience. Of the Japanese culinary arts, sushi is probably the most refined in visual artistry and taste. There are several varieties of sushi. Nigiri is a small mound of rice flavored with vinegar and sugar. It may be topped with raw fish. Maki-zushi is made by wrapping the flavored rice with seaweed. Inari-zushi is the same type of rice wrapped in a deep-fried bean cake.

INGREDIENTS:

3 or 4 C.	(720ml. or 960ml.)	Cooked *short* grain rice
		Fresh dried seaweed

Vinegar Sauce:

½ C.	(120ml.)	Vinegar
1/3 C.	(80ml.)	Honey
1½ tsp.	(7.5ml.)	Salt

PROCEDURE:

1. Volunteer makes rice before the group enters.
2. The group measures and makes sauce together.
    a. Combine the vinegar, honey and salt in a stainless steel saucepan.
    b. Bring to boil and remove from heat.
3. Combine rice and sauce while both are hot.
4. You may serve these plain or you may add chopped cooked carrots, peas, mushrooms, celery or cucumber.
5. You may also serve them the authentic way by rolling the rice mixture on a sushi mat or waxed paper.
6. Place a sheet of dried seaweed on the mat or waxed paper.
7. Spread the rice on the seaweed to within ½" of the edges.
8. You may roll without filling or add fish, scrambled egg, pickled ginger, or vegetables sliced in thin strips.
9. Hold paper or mat and roll seaweed and rice into a tight roll. Keep as tightly rolled as possible.
10. Cut rolls into 1" thick sections. It helps to dip knife in hot water before each slice.
11. Serve with soy sauce.

 TEMPURA

BACKGROUND: Tempura is a delightful and special dish of Japan that was brought to their culture by the Portuguese. The Japanese adapted and perfected the technique to create a unique dish of their own.

To make it, vegetables are cut imaginatively so that when dipped in the batter and deep fried, each texture and subtle flavor can be appreciated. The secret to successful tempura lies with the batter and the oil. The batter must be fresh, made after the vegetables are cut and the oil heated. Cornstarch or mochi rice flour makes the batter lighter and crisper and more authentic, however, regular flour may be used. The water should be ice-cold for an authentic light batter.

INGREDIENTS:

Batter:

1 Tbs.	(15ml.)	Egg
3 Tbs.	(45ml.)	Flour
½ tsp.	(2.5ml.)	Salt
1 Tbs.	(15ml.)	Ice-cold water

Vegetables:

    Carrots
    Zucchini
    Parsley sprigs
    Others (Onions, snow peas, broccoli, etc.)

PROCEDURE:

1. Prepare the vegetables in small decorative pieces.
2. Preheat oil to 350°F, 176°C.
3. Prepare batter by:
   a. Beating the egg in a margarine tub.
   b. Adding the flour, salt and ice water, mixing well until smooth. (Do not overstir).
4. Dip vegetables in batter with slotted spoon, then slide them into deep hot oil.
5. Remove from oil when golden brown, drain on paper towels.
6. Serve with soy sauce.

 TSUKEMONO (JAPANESE PICKLES)

BACKGROUND: Japanese pickles are served at nearly every meal, even breakfast. They are beneficial in the aiding of digestion, especially after the eating of fried foods and rice. Many different vegetables are pickled under pressure in a special jar called a tsukemono-ki.

INGREDIENTS:

¼ C.	(60ml.)	Salt
½ C.	(120ml.)	Sugar
1 Tbs.	(15ml.)	White vinegar
3 C.	(720ml.)	Boiling water
2 lbs.	(900gms.)	Chinese celery or cabbage

PROCEDURE:

1. Mix the salt, sugar, vinegar and water together, stir until the salt and sugar have dissolved.
2. Cut the cabbage in half through the heart, and then in half again.
3. Soak the cabbage in the solution for one to one and a half days.
4. Remove from the solution, drain and refrigerate.
5. To serve, cut the cabbage into 1" sections. Serve with soy sauce.

 INTRODUCING THE RECREATION OF JAPAN

Fishing, golf, mountain climbing, skiing, and walking are favorite leisure pastimes of many Japanese. The hot communal baths are also a form of recreation and relaxation. Baseball, fencing, judo, and wrestling are favorite sports. Children enjoy the same sports as adults, as well as kite flying, battledore, shuttlecock, and Go (a complicated form of checkers).

BIG LAMP, LITTLE LAMP

This game requires three or more players. The players sit in a circle. "It" calls, "Big Lamp" but indicates small lamp with arms. The group must indicate a big lamp. They should always indicate what leader says, not what he does (the game is similar to "Simon Says").

 FIVE EYES

This game requires two players. It uses a checkerboard and checkers. The players take turns, one at a time, placing checkers on the squares of the board. The object is to get five checkers in a row up and down, across, or diagonally. Opponents must try to prevent this from happening.

 FLOWER BASKET

This game requires five to ten players. The players sit on chairs in a circle. "It" stands in the center. All the players are given a flower name (i.e., rose, snapdragon, pansy...). "It" calls out two flower names and those two flowers must change places before "It" can sit in their chairs. The unseated player becomes "It". If "It" calls, "Flower Basket", all players must change places.

 FUKU WARAI

Fuku Warai is a Japanese game played during the New Year's celebration. It is similar to our Pin the Tail on the Donkey game
MATERIALS:
    Give patterns out for Fuku Warai game (face and features)
PROCEDURE: Player is blindfolded and given cutouts of duplicate features to place on face during one-minute period, or while the other children count aloud to a given number. It's fun to laugh at the funny faces which result.

 HANA, HANA, HANA, KUCHI

This game requires two or more players, and is much like "Simon Says". The players sit in a circle. "It" says the name of the game, which means "Nose, nose, nose, mouth. On the first three words, he taps his nose. On the fourth word, he taps some other part of his body. The idea of the game is to follow what "It" commands rather than "It's" actions. In Japan, when a child errs in this game, he is daubed on the cheek with flour and water. The word for ear in Japanese is mimi, and for eye is me. The game may also be played in English.

221

 HANDBALL (YEMARI)

This game is like handball or bounce the ball. The children form a circle and bounce a tennis ball back and forth within the circle with open hands. If the players miss, they drop out until there is one champion remaining and bouncing ball to self.

 HUNTING THE TREASURE

This game requires three or more players. The players sit in a circle and pass a coin without "It" seeing who really has the coin. At a signal from "It", everyone puts their closed fists on their knees. "It" asks a player to open a fist, i.e., "Nancy, open your left fist." The idea is to leave the fist holding the coin until all other fists have been shown. When coin is found, all fists still closed are counted and scored against "It".

 JAN-KEN-PON (STONE, PAPER, SCISSORS)

Two players face each other with hands on the table and repeat, "Jan-ken-pon". On "pon" they stretch out their hand slightly and mime:
    Stone — Closed fist
    Paper — Palm flat on table
    Scissors — Two fingers (index and middle) extended to represent cutting with scissors.
The winner is determined by:
    Stone beats scissors because it can crush them
    Scissors beats paper because they can cut it
    Paper beats stone because it can cover it
This game may be used to determine who is first in a game or until a member has five wins.

 JAPANESE TAG

This game requires four or more players. "It" tries to tag other players while keeping his hand on the place on his body where he was tagged. He is relieved of his position after he has tagged someone else to be "It". For a large group, use several "Its".

 JUGGLING

Rice bags (similar to our beanbags) are tossed by player from one hand to another as if juggling. The player who juggles for the longest period wins the game.

 OCCUPATIONS

This game requires two equal teams. One team mimes an occupation, agreed on by the group, while the other team guesses it. When the home team guesses correctly, "It" runs to safety area behind a given line. All those captured must join the home team. At the end of the game (after agreed time period) the side with the most players wins.

 POEM CARDS

The Japanese play a traditional game with waka poetry. The first half of the poem is on one card and the second half is on another. The second half of the poems are dealt out evenly to all the players while the leader holds the first half of every poem. An adaptation of this game may be played by three players using nursery rhymes. The player who finds the second half gets to keep the pair of cards. The player with the most pairs wins.

 SLAP HANDS

Two players face each other. One has palms up and the other player has his palms down. The palms down player gently strokes the palms of the other player and then hits their palms. If the opponent withdraws in time, he gains a point. If striker hits, he gains a point. Opponents alternate turns. If striker hits down, it is considered an attempt even if he's just faking. Score the game to seven points.

JAPANESE POEM CARDS Winner is deter- mined by which player accumulates the most points	LITTLE MISS MUFFET SAT ON HER TUFFET	EATING HER CURDS AND WHEY
LITTLE JACK HORNER SAT IN A CORNER	EATING HIS CHRISTMAS PIE	I HAVE A LITTLE PUSSY ITS COAT IS SILVERY GRAY
IT LIVES IN THE BIG WIDE MEADOWS IT NEVER RUNS AWAY	JACK BE NIMBLE JACK BE QUICK	JACK JUMP OVER THE CANDLESTICK

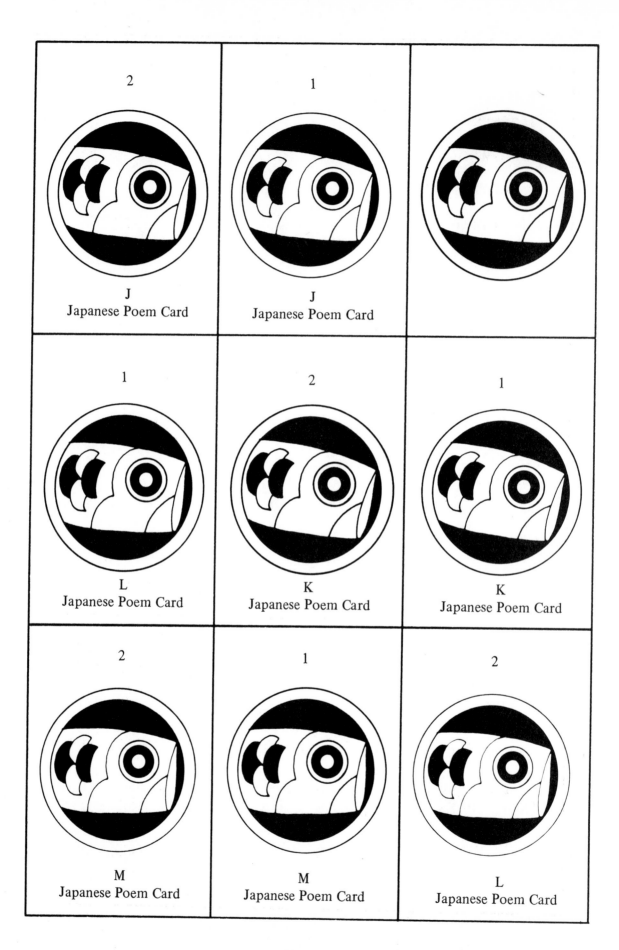

2	1	
J Japanese Poem Card	J Japanese Poem Card	

1	2	1
L Japanese Poem Card	K Japanese Poem Card	K Japanese Poem Card

2	1	2
M Japanese Poem Card	M Japanese Poem Card	L Japanese Poem Card

HOW DOES YOUR GARDEN GROW	MARY HAD A LITTLE LAMB	HIS FLEECE WAS WHITE AS SNOW
THREE LITTLE KITTENS LOST THEIR MITTENS	AND THEY BEGAN TO CRY	HICKORY, DICKORY, DOCK
THE MOUSE RAN UP THE CLOCK	LITTLE BOW PEEP LOST HER SHEEP	AND DIDN'T KNOW WHERE TO FIND THEM

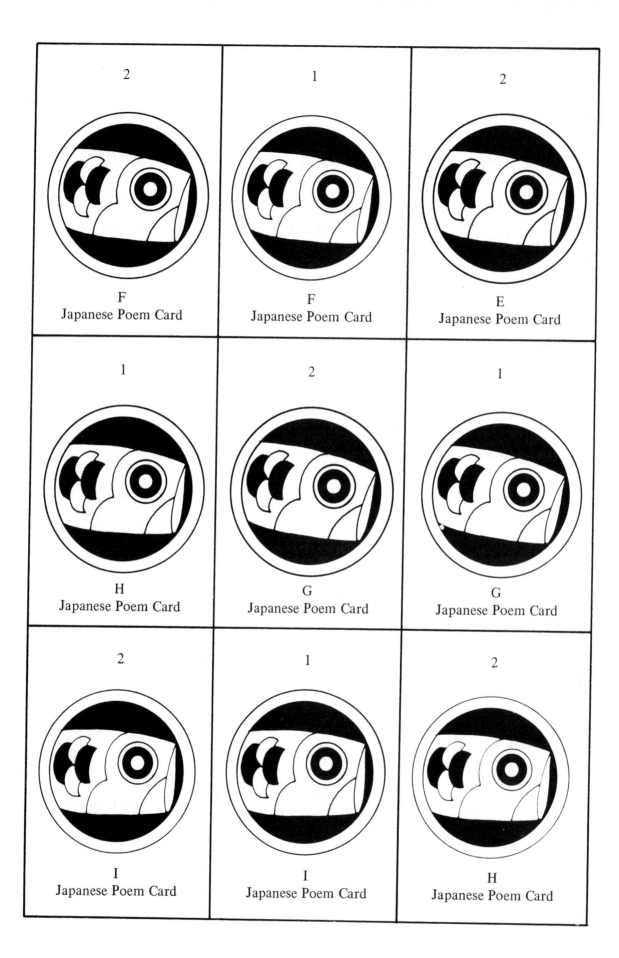

LITTLE BOY BLUE	COME BLOW YOUR HORN	OLD KING COLE
WAS A MERRY OLD SOUL	PETER, PETER PUMPKIN EATER	HAD A WIFE AND COULDN'T KEEP HER
HUMPTY DUMPTY SAT ON A WALL	HUMPTY DUMPTY HAD A GREAT FALL	MARY, MARY QUITE CONTRARY

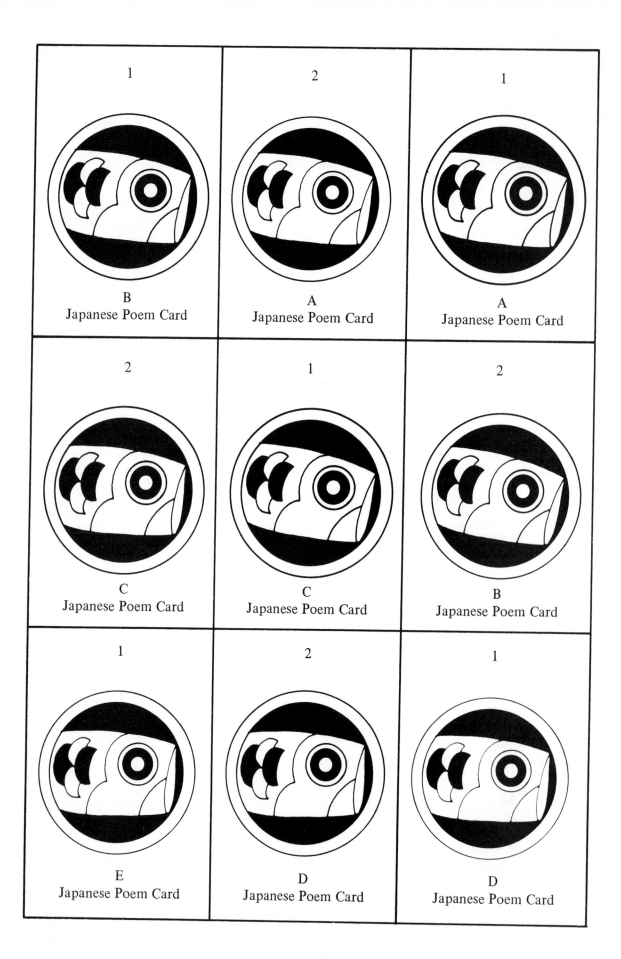

CHAPTER X
MEXICO

INDEX

ABOUT MEXICO

Mexico lies to the south of the United States and the two countries share a common border. Mexico prides itself in many bustling, modern cities. A relaxed colonial life is more common, however, in the small towns and villages.

Most Mexicans have ancestors of both Indian and Spanish blood; although, a small percentage of people are still of unmixed descent. Most of the people of Mexico speak Spanish. There are, however, still nearly fifty Indian dialects spoken.

The government of Mexico has been designed with a system of checks and balances similar to that of the government of the United States.

Mexico has a wealth of folklore. We have offered here a representative sampling.

INTRODUCING THE ARTS OF MEXICO

Mexican art has been influenced by North American Indians, the Spaniards, the Chinese, and many peoples of Europe and the United States. Geographic influences are especially important since Mexico is a country of mountains; therefore, many villages are remote and their crafts have a unique character of that region.

Mexican artists have developed bold and colorful murals to illustrate their way of life and legends of their country. These may be found as paintings or mosaics on sides of large buildings.

Mexican art does not limit itself to paintings, mosaics, and jewelry, but is extended into all items, even those used daily. Mexico is a country rich in brightly colored, handmade arts and crafts.

 AMATL WITCHCRAFT DOLLS

BACKGROUND: Amatl paper is made by pounding several layers of wet bark, which has been pressed flat and allowed to dry. The paper resembles brown shopping bag paper, although it is thicker and looks wrinkled.

Some of the Indian villages of Mexico make witchcraft dolls from this bark paper. Light colored amatl is used to make dolls which bring happiness and love. The use of darker paper is thought to bring evil on a person.

MATERIALS:

> Brown wrapping paper or grocery bags
> Brown poster paint and large brushes
> Scissors

PROCEDURE:

1. Paint a square of brown wrapping paper with heavy brown paint. Allow this to dry.
2. Crumple the paper into a small ball and then flatten it out. Press to smooth.
3. Fold the paper in half, lengthwise.
4. Lightly sketch the outline of one side of an amatl witchcraft doll along the open edge of the paper.
5. Cut along sketched line. Mount this paper craft on colored construction paper if desired.

233

 **BARK PAINTING**

BACKGROUND: Bark paintings are made on amatl (see background on amatl witchcraft dolls). These works of art are usually paintings of birds, animals, and flowers in interesting designs. Frequently fluorescent colored paints are utilized and accompanied by a black outline technique to produce a dramatic effect.

MATERIALS:

        Brown wrapping paper or grocery bags
        Brown poster paint and large brushes
        Scissors
        Fluorescent tempera and small brushes
        Black felt-tip marker (permanent)
        Patterns and carbon paper

PROCEDURE:

1. Paint a square of brown wrapping paper with heavy brown paint. Allow this to dry.
2. Crumple the paper into a small ball and then flatten it out. Press to smooth.
3. Use carbon paper to transfer the designs to your bark paper or create your own design.
4. Use fluorescent colors to add color to your design.
5. When paint is dry, outline your work with a black permanent marker.

 MARACAS

BACKGROUND: Early musical instruments of Mexico consisted of wooden drums and flutes made of wood, reeds, clay, shells, or bone. Clay, gourd, and bone were also fashioned into rattles. Some very ancient forms of maracas may be found in the museums of Mexico.

Most Mexican instruments are produced today in two forms — quality musical devices and scaled-down children's toys. Even the very smallest toy instruments are capable of producing sound.

MATERIALS:

> Newspapers, paper toweling, or any absorbent paper
> Scissors, or paper cutter
> Paste thinned to the consistency of cream
> Container for mixing paste
> Large burned-out electric light bulb
> Sandpaper
> Paints (tempera, enamel, oil paint, etc.) and brushes
> Clear plastic spray, shellac, or varnish for protecting finish if tempera paint is used

PROCEDURE:

1. Cut newspaper into strips, approximately ½" wide.
2. Mix the paste in a bowl or pan to the consistency of cream.
3. Place a strip of paper into the paste until it is saturated. Remove the strip from the bowl and wipe off the excess paste by pulling it between the fingers.
4. Apply the paste-saturated strip directly to the light bulb.
5. Continue to apply strips until the entire bulb is covered. Repeat until at least six layers of paper strips are applied. (The number of layers can be readily counted if a different kind or color of paper is used for each layer.) The strength of the finished maraca will be much greater if each strip is applied in a different direction. Also, make sure that all wrinkles and bubbles are removed after each strip is added.
6. Place the maraca on a crumpled piece of paper and allow to dry thoroughly. (Crumpled paper allows the air to circulate around the maraca.)
7. When the maraca is completely dry, rap the maraca against the floor, to break the bulb inside the paper covering. The broken pieces of glass provide the sound when shaken. If a hole is punctured it is easily repaired with the addition of more strips.
8. Sandpaper the surface until smooth. Decorate with colorful designs.
9. If tempera paint is used for decorating, the surface should be sprayed with clear plastic or painted with shellac or varnish for permanence.

 MASKS

BACKGROUND: Children of Mexico wear masks for almost any festival. Masks are made from wood, tin, papier mâché, or cardboard. The most enjoyable faces are usually grotesque and funny.

MATERIALS:

White paper plates	Felt-tip markers
Glue	Pencils
Scissors	Stapler

PROCEDURE:

1. Draw on the paper plate with felt-tip markers.
2. Pieces may be cut from other paper plates and may be glued or stapled to the central plate. These could represent a headdress, ears, beard, or a collar.
3. Carefully darken in the appropriate areas to give depth to the face.

 OJO DE DIOS (EYE OF GOD)

BACKGROUND: To the wise Mexican Indians, the God's Eye was a sacred decoration that brought good fortune, luck, health, and long life. The colorful weaving represented the "eye of God" and all His good powers. Even today, God's Eyes are believed to bring happiness and good luck — and everyone can use some of each.

God's Eyes can be made in many designs and shapes and can be hung on walls, in windows or as mobiles; worn as hair ornaments and other types of jewelry; or carried as "good luck" charms if sufficiently small.

The custom of making an Ojo de Dios is believed to have begun among the Indians of Jalisco and Nayarit. It was made by the father of an infant to bring a long and healthy life to the child. When the child is born, the father weaves the center God's eye. An additional God's eye is added on each birthday until the child's fifth birthday.

Ojo de Dios seems to be a universal symbol that is used as decorative art and as a good omen to bring luck to the home. They are found in homes in Egypt, Africa and Native North Americans as well as Mexico.

MATERIALS:

White glue
Scissors
Yarn
Ice cream sticks

PROCEDURE:

1. Cross two popsicle sticks in middle, tie with yarn to keep sticks spread apart.
2. Weave yarn over one leg, then under and around same leg.
3. Knot different colors together and continue weaving.
4. End yarn with a touch of white glue.
5. A similar ornament is available in the section of this text which covers Native Americans. More detailed instructions may also be found in that section.

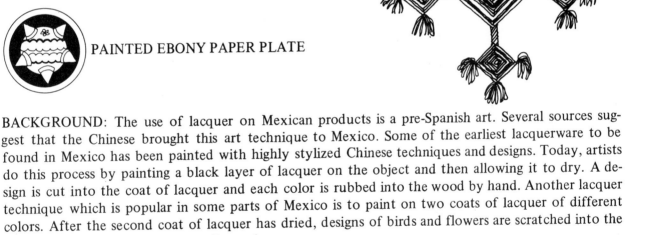

 PAINTED EBONY PAPER PLATE

BACKGROUND: The use of lacquer on Mexican products is a pre-Spanish art. Several sources suggest that the Chinese brought this art technique to Mexico. Some of the earliest lacquerware to be found in Mexico has been painted with highly stylized Chinese techniques and designs. Today, artists do this process by painting a black layer of lacquer on the object and then allowing it to dry. A design is cut into the coat of lacquer and each color is rubbed into the wood by hand. Another lacquer technique which is popular in some parts of Mexico is to paint on two coats of lacquer of different colors. After the second coat of lacquer has dried, designs of birds and flowers are scratched into the top layer of lacquer, exposing the first color.

MATERIALS:

Paper plate
Assorted poster or tempera paints and small brushes
Black tempera and large brushes

White glue and brushes
Carbon paper

PROCEDURE:

1. Paint the paper plate with two coats of black paint. Allow paint to dry after each coat.
2. Use carbon paper to transfer one of the Chinese designs to your plate or create your own design.
3. Paint the design and allow it to dry.
4. Paint the entire plate with at least two coats of white glue. Allow plate to dry between coats.

 PIÑATA

BACKGROUND: The piñata was first used in Italy during the time of the Renaissance. A piñata was considered as a source of delightful entertainment especially at masquerade parties. This custom spread from Italy to Spain, and then to Mexico. The piñatas which break the best are those which are made of terra-cotta and covered with crepe paper or colored paper combined with papier mâché. Many fun designs have produced pinatas which resemble globes, animals, stars, people, or cakes.

To play, the piñata is hung from a high place; children are blindfolded; each takes a turn to break the piñata with a stick. A leader holds a rope attached to the piñata. He pulls the rope up or down to increase the difficulty of the target.

When the piñata has been broken there is much fun and excitement as everyone struggles to claim the most rewards for himself.

Piñatas may be filled with toys, candies, fruits, money, vegetables, and various other surprises. The piñatas that are made of papier mâché and brightly colored paper over a clay pot are the most fun because the bursting of the pot produces a dramatic effect.

MATERIALS:

Paper bag (lunch size)
Newspaper
Crepe paper and tissue paper
Construction paper circles (12" diameter)

Stapler, scissors
White glue
Pattern, if desired
Poster paints and brushes

PROCEDURE:

1. Crumple pieces of newspaper and stuff them inside the paper bag. Secure the top with a rubber band, forming a sphere. The newspaper may be removed when you are ready to fill the finished piñata.

2. Paint the sack a solid color. It may help to hang the sack on a clothesline while the paint is drying.

3. To make satellite piñata, form several cones from wedges of circles that have been cut into quarters. Glue or staple the cones together and attach them to the sphere.

4. Fringe cut from crepe or tissue paper may be glued at the center of each cone's apex for added decoration.

5. Staple some string for hanging to the top of the piñata or use coat hanger wire which has been pushed through the sphere.

 **POTTERY**

BACKGROUND: Many Mexican terra-cotta (baked clay) pots seem very breakable. This is because the Indians of Mexico, at one time, believed that they should only use pots for a set number of years and then these pots should be thrown against rocks and destroyed. It was, at this time, considered a bad omen if a pot did not readily break and release its spirit. Although this is not part of the Mexican peoples' present day belief, the tradition of breakable pottery is still maintained in many villages.

There are several pottery designs that clearly depict particular regions of Mexico, for example, brightly glazed pottery is common in Oaxaca, whereas the people of Jalisco decorate their pottery with animal and floral designs of more subdued colors.

MATERIALS:

Newspapers, paper toweling or any absorbent paper

Scissors or paper cutter

Paste thinned to the consistency of cream (wheat paste, library paste, etc.). See Chapter V for recipes

Container for mixing paste

A smooth bowl or plastic margarine tub to be used as a mold. The bowl should also have a small base and a wide mouth with no undercuts.

Vaseline, grease or cream

Sandpaper

Paint (tempera, enamel, oil paint, etc.)

Brush

Clear plastic spray, shellac, or varnish for protective finish if tempera paint is used

Asphaltum to waterproof bowl

PROCEDURE:

1. Cover the outside surface of the bowl with a film of cream, vaseline, or grease. This will keep the papier mâché from sticking to the bowl.
2. Place the bowl upside down on newspaper or cardboard.
3. Cut newspaper or paper toweling into strips approximately ½" wide.
4. Mix the paste in a bowl or pan to the consistency of cream.
5. Place a strip of paper into the paste until it is saturated. Remove the strips from the bowl and wipe off the excess paste by pulling it between the fingers.
6. Apply the paste-saturated strips directly on the oiled surface of the bowl. One or two layers of strips of just-wet paper applied directly to the bowl before applying the paste-saturated strips will serve the same purpose as greasing the bowl.
7. Continue to apply strips until the entire bowl is covered. Repeat until at least six layers of paper strips are applied. The number of layers can be readily counted if a different kind or color of paper is used for each layer. The strength of the finished bowl will be much greater if each strip is applied in a different direction. Also, make sure that all wrinkles and bubbles are removed after each strip is attached.
8. Allow the papier mâché to dry thoroughly before removing the bowl.
9. Trim the edges of the bowl and apply additional strips to strengthen and smooth the edges. Other imperfections can also be repaired at this time.
10. When thoroughly dry, sandpaper the surface until smooth and decorate.
11. If tempera paint is used, a coat of white glue must be applied to seal the surface.
12. Asphaltum painted on the inside of the bowl will waterproof the container.

 TISSUE PAPER FLOWERS

BACKGROUND: Tissue paper flowers and cutouts are used in Mexico as decorations during festivals and church holidays. They may be seen in the streets of most Mexican towns during the holiday season.

MATERIALS:

       Tissue paper squares (five to 10 inches)

       Heavy wire (coat hanger is fine)

       Green tape

PROCEDURE:

1. Make a stack of eight tissue paper squares.
2. Keeping the stack together, fold the squares two times to yield a smaller square.
3. Cut a heart shape using the closed corner as the base of your heart.
4. Unfold the heart shape to look like the diagram, and place a staple in the middle of the flower.
5. Begin at the top of the tissue stack and lift and crimp to the center, one layer of tissue at a time.
6. Do step number five with each layer of tissue, squeeze near the staple.
7. To mount the flower, fasten the bottom layer of tissue around the piece of heavy wire and cover the tissue and wire with green tape. Tape or glue tightly.

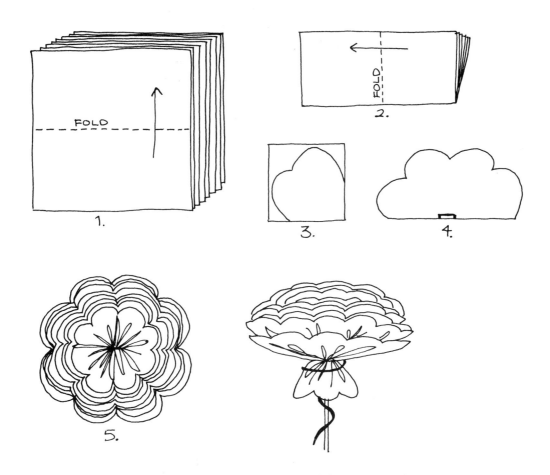

 YARN PAINTING

BACKGROUND: The yarn paintings of Mexico are called Ofrendas, or picture offerings to God. They are generally made on thin boards, about the size of this page (or smaller). The boards are coated with a thin layer of wax. The artist presses different colors of yarn (fitted tightly together on the board) to form abstract designs or animals.

MATERIALS:

        Cardboard — medium weight
        White glue
        Colorful yarn
        Patterns — if desired
        Scissors
        Carbon paper to transfer designs
        Wax paper

PROCEDURE:

1. Use carbon paper to transfer a design to your piece of cardboard or draw your own design.
2. Cut out the design. Place the design on a piece of wax paper.
3. If you want to hang your completed yarn painting, glue a loop of yarn, for hanging, in place at this time.
4. Complete one side by spreading a thin layer of white glue on one section at a time. Tightly coil the pieces of yarn into place. Do the small designs first and then the background.
5. When one side of the design is completed, turn the cardboard over and complete the other side.

INTRODUCING THE COOKING OF MEXICO

Mexican cooking today has been influenced by the Aztec, Spanish, and to a lesser extent, French cultures. When the conquistadores came to the Americas, they found foods previously unknown to them: chocolate, vanilla, corn, chilies, tomatoes, avocados, squash, beans, sweet potatoes, pineapple, and papaya. The conquistadores added the oil, wine, spices, rice, wheat, and cattle important to their cuisine and some culinary contributions from Europe, Asia and Arab countries (since Spain was just free from Arab domination). Later, during the reign of Maximilian, French dishes were introduced.

The typical Mexican day begins with desayuno (breakfast), usually a sweet bread with cafe con leche (milk coffee) or chocolate. Then almuerzo, a heartier second breakfast, is eaten about 9:00 a.m. (including fruit or juices, beans, and tortillas). In the city, Almuerzo (lunch) follows at approximately 11:30 a.m. The comida, main meal of the day, takes place anywhere from 2:00 to 5:30 p.m. At night there is the merienda, which is eaten by children at 6:00 to 7:00 p.m. or by adults as late as 9:00 p.m. and is a light meal. Cena is a dinner on a special occasion that is eaten at any time between 8:00 p.m. to midnight. This cena is a meal that closely follows the Spanish eating pattern.

 BROWN SUGAR CANDY

BROWN SUGAR CANDY (DULCE DE PILONCILLO)

BACKGROUND: Most Mexicans like their candy really sweet. In the market places and in the streets at fiestas, you will see vendors carrying trays high overhead, heaped with thick squares of colored creamy candy.

INGREDIENTS:

½ C.	(120ml.)	Brown sugar
2 Tbs.	(30ml.)	Water
¾ tsp.	(3.7ml.)	Vinegar
¾ tsp.	(3.7ml.)	Butter
¼ C.	(60ml.)	Broken pecans or walnuts

PROCEDURE:
1. Mix the brown sugar, water, vinegar and butter in a saucepan.
2. Stir and cook over low heat about fifteen minutes until mixture spins a thread when dropped from a spoon into cold water.
3. Add the nuts.
4. Remove the mixture from the heat and beat until creamy.
5. Drop from a spoon onto waxed paper and allow to cool. This recipe makes about 5 candies.

 BUTTERCAKES (MANTICADOS)

BACKGROUND: In ancient Mexico, cakes were not prepared because people did not have wheat flour, sugar or butter. A typical dessert was sweet tamales stuffed with fruit. These buttercakes are a sweet enjoyed by Mexican children today.

INGREDIENTS:

2½ Tbs.	(40ml.)	Butter or margarine
2½ Tbs.	(40ml.)	Sugar
1		Egg
1/3 C.	(80ml.)	Flour, sifted
1 tsp.	(5ml.)	Powdered sugar

PROCEDURE:
1. Cream together butter and sugar.
2. Add eggs and beat.
3. Add flour gradually.
4. Beat until smooth.
5. Pour into two dozen muffin tins lined with paper cups.
6. Sprinkle with powdered sugar.
7. Bake at 375°F, 190°C fifteen to twenty minutes.

 CHIMICHANGAS (DEEP FRIED FILLED TORTILLAS)

BACKGROUND: A common variation of the taco or quesadilla is a regional dish from the state of Sonora called Chimichangas.

INGREDIENTS:

6		Flour tortillas (7" diameter)
1 C.	(240ml.)	Meat filling (recipe follows)

Filling:

½ lb.	(225gm.)	Lean ground beef
1 Tbs.	(15ml.)	Oil or lard
¼ C.	(60ml.)	Onion, chopped
1 Tbs.	(15ml.)	Red chili sauce

Filling Procedure:
1. In frying pan, brown the beef, adding oil or lard if needed.
2. Add onion and cook until soft.
3. Moisten with red chili sauce.
4. Slowly simmer for ten minutes.

PROCEDURE:
1. If time permits, have children make the filling. If not, have it ready for them to use.
2. Spoon 3 Tbs. (45ml.) filling down center of tortilla.
3. Roll tortilla around filling and fasten with a toothpick.
4. Fry in 1" of hot oil over medium heat (about 350°F, 176°C) turning until golden.
5. Drain on paper towels.

 CHURROS

BACKGROUND: These fried batter cakes are named after the churro, a Spanish sheep with long, coarse hair. They are sold in market places from small portable cooking stalls called churrerias (churro shops) where they go straight from the fry pan to the customer. In Mexico, the churros have a distinctive flavor because cut-up lime is heated in the cooking oil.

INGREDIENTS:

Oil for frying
One lime or lemon, quartered
Pinch of salt

1/3 C.	(80ml.)	Water
1 tsp.	(5ml.)	Sugar
½ C.	(120ml.)	Flour
1 Tbs.	(15ml.)	Egg

PROCEDURE:
1. Preheat oil and lime or lemon pieces to 390°F, 200°C.
2. Combine the water, salt and sugar in a saucepan and heat just to boiling.
3. Add the flour and beat until smooth.
4. Add the egg and beat until mixture is smooth and satiny.
5. Remove lime or lemon pieces from oil.
6. Force the mixture through a pastry tube or large funnel.
7. Fry in long strips until golden.
8. Drain on paper towels.
9. Cut into 3" (7.5 cm.) pieces.
10. Roll in granulated sugar.

 FLAN (MEXICAN CUSTARD)

BACKGROUND: This dessert of Spanish origin is made in custard cups so that when it is unmolded it is covered with a caramel glaze.

INGREDIENTS:

2 Tbs.	(30ml.)	Sugar
1		Egg
3 Tbs.	(45ml.)	Sugar
½ C.	(120ml.)	Milk

245

PROCEDURE:

1. Heat and stir 2 Tbs. (30ml.) sugar in a saucepan over low heat until it becomes brown and syrupy (caramelized).
2. Pour into a custard cup, covering the bottom and sides.
3. In a bowl beat the egg, 3 Tbs. (45ml.) sugar and the milk. Make sure they are thoroughly mixed.
4. Pour into the baking dish over the caramel.
5. Bake in a 350°F, 176°C oven or electric skillet 35 to 40 minutes.
6. Test by inserting a knife. When the custard is done, the knife comes out clean.
7. Allow the custard to cool.
8. To serve, place a plate over the custard, quickly turn it out upside down on the plate. Custards may be baked in four individual cups.

 MEXICAN CHOCOLATE

BACKGROUND: Chocolate is a historical pre-Columbian drink that in the past was only enjoyed by the king, merchant nobility, and the upper ranks of the priesthood and military. Its name comes from two Nahuatl words, "Xoco", meaning bitter, and "atl", meaning water. It is served in many ways. Sometimes it is sweetened with honey and flavored with vanilla. It is always beaten with a "molinillo" (a small wooden beater that is twirled between the palms).

Mexican children today enjoy "chocolate" and when they use the "molinillo" to mix their chocolate they sometimes sing this song:

Uno – dos – tres cho
Uno – dos – tres co
Uno – dos – tres la
Uno – dos – tres te
Cho –co – la – te
Bate bate
Cho – co – la – te

INGREDIENTS:

1 oz.	(30ml.)	Unsweetened chocolate
1 C.	(240ml.)	Cold water
		Honey to taste
		Vanilla to taste

PROCEDURE:

1. Mix the ingredients to taste.
2. Stir with the molinillo (a wire whisk or electric blender may be used.)
3. Sing song while mixing.

NAQUIS (DOUGHNUTS)

BACKGROUND: Another kind of deep fried cake similar to churros.
INGREDIENTS:

(Note to volunteers: mix together well 1/3 C. (80ml.) buttermilk and one egg.

½ C.	(120ml.)	Flour, sifted
1/8 tsp.	(.6ml.)	Salt
Small pinch		Baking soda
2 Tbs.	(30ml.)	Sugar
1½ Tbs.	(22.5ml.)	Buttermilk-egg mixture
		Fat for deep frying
		Cinnamon and sugar for coating

PROCEDURE:
1. Mix all the ingredients together to form a soft dough.
2. Add more milk if necessary.
3. Roll and shape into tiny doughnuts, or into cigar shapes.
4. Fry in hot deep fat 350°F, 176°C.
5. Drain on paper towels.

 PASTELITOS DE BODA (WEDDING CAKES)

BACKGROUND: These easy-to-make, delicious cookies are also known as Bride's Cookies or Wedding Cakes.
INGREDIENTS:

¼ C.	(60ml.)	Flour, sifted
2 Tbs.	(30ml.)	Butter or margarine
1½ tsp.	(7.5ml.)	Sugar
		A few grains of salt
¼ tsp.	(1.2ml.)	Vanilla
¼ C.	(60ml.)	Finely-ground pecans or walnuts
		Powdered sugar

PROCEDURE:
1. Cream butter and sugar.
2. Add flour, salt, flavoring and nutmeats.
3. Mix well.
4. Form into small balls and place on a lightly greased cookie sheet.
5. Bake in a hot oven 400°F, 204°C for ten minutes or until very lightly browned.
6. Remove from oven and cool slightly, about three minutes.
7. Roll immediately in powdered sugar; repeat when cold.

 QUESADILLAS

BACKGROUND: Quesadillas are another kind of snack. The ingredients and cooking method of quesadillas vary widely depending on the local taste of the region. They get their name from the Spanish word for cheese which is queso. The boiled, white cheese of Oaxaca is the number-one queso of the country; therefore, we recommend Jack cheese for this recipe. Cheddar cheese and corn tortillas are also quite good prepared this way.

INGREDIENTS:

		One corn or flour tortilla
1 to 2 Tbs.	(15-30 ml.)	Jack cheese (grated) — or any mild, semi-dry white cheese

PROCEDURE:
1. Traditionally, the tortilla is folded in half and then fried; however, if your budget will not allow one tortilla per child, or you feel it is too much for one child to eat, cut the tortilla in half and have child fold over this portion.
2. Preheat greased skillet to 375°F, 190°C.
3. Fill tortilla with cheese.
4. Fold over tortilla.
5. Fry quesadilla on both sides until cheese melts.

 SALTED PEPITAS

BACKGROUND: Mexicans enjoy the crunchy nut-like pumpkin seeds, or pepitas. Roasted, they are a good salad garnish or protein-rich snack.

INGREDIENTS:

1¼ C.	(300ml.)	Water
2 Tbs.	(30ml.)	Salt
½ lb.	(225gm.)	Untreated hulled pumpkin seeds

PROCEDURE:
1. Boil water and salt for five minutes.
2. Pour water over seeds.
3. Let stand at room temperature overnight.
4. Drain.
5. Place on cookie sheet.
6. Bake at 325°F, 165°C for 40 minutes, stirring occasionally.
7. Cool. Store in an air-tight container.

 TACOS

BACKGROUND: The word "taco" actually means a "snack". In popular usage it has come to mean a particular dish. The word now means a sandwich type of snack with meat filling, garnish and spicy sauce. Sometimes the tortillas are folded in half, often they are rolled all the way around the filling, depending on the region.

INGREDIENTS:

One		Tortilla for each child
1 Tbs.	(15ml.)	Precooked, shredded or ground meat (beef, pork, or chicken)
		Shredded lettuce
		Chopped tomatoes
		Grated cheese
		Optional: cilantro (Mexican or Chinese parsley)
		Salsa (Mexican sauce used in many dishes, sometimes too spicy for children)

PROCEDURE:
1. Preheat oil in fry pan for cooking tortillas.
2. If the child chooses to have tortilla folded in half, have him place tortilla in oil, fry lightly on one side, turn over and fold in half with tongs.
3. Fry both sides of tortilla to desired crispness.
4. Drain on paper towel.
5. Fill with meat and desired condiments.
6. If rolled taco is preferred, have the child place the meat in the tortilla and roll before frying.

 TORTILLAS

BACKGROUND: In Mexico, corn is ground into flour and mixed with water to create a soft flat bread which is eaten plain or may be filled with some other food and rolled and eaten.

Every culture has its own type of bread. Each bread has some common and some different elements depending on the culture and the climate where the group of people live.

INGREDIENTS:

4 Tbs.	(60ml.)	Masa Harina (corn flour)
3 Tbs.	(45ml.)	Water

PROCEDURE:
1. Mix the Masa Harina and water. Knead to make dough more pliable.
2. Roll into two balls.
3. Flatten by hand or press on wax paper.
4. Brush skillet with oil and fry briefly on both sides.

INTRODUCING THE RECREATION OF MEXICO

Mexico has a wealth of folk music, games, and dances. Many of these recreational activities are from Mexico's ancient heritage. Prior to Spanish occupation, most folkways were chiefly forms of prayer. Today much of that same music is used both secularly and religiously.

Dance is a favorite diversion of many Mexican people. Many dances are passed down as ancestral customs. During ceremonies and festivals, ritual dances are performed. Sometimes the dancers dress to tell a story or wear colorful costumes of the region. The many different dances of Mexico represent different regions. A common dance of Mexico is La Raspa.

Many Mexican games are similar to those played in the United States. For example, La Gallina Ciega (The Blind Hen) is played like Blindman's Buff. A Mexican game called Sacos is a sack race just like any sack race in the United States. Another favorite game of Mexico is La Rueda de San Miguel (The Wheel of San Miguel). La Rueda is played like London Bridge but there is no tug-of-war at the end.

 COCKFIGHT

Only two children at a time may play this game; it is, however, a fun game for spectators.

MATERIALS:

Several strips of construction paper (of various colors)

Straight pins or masking tape

PROCEDURE:

1. The two players should be asked to face each other with their eyes closed.
2. The leader then pins a colored strip of paper to each player's back.
3. The players open their eyes and move about, without touching each other, in an attempt to see what color each is bearing.
4. The first player to call out the others' color correctly is the winner.
5. Two new players may then be chosen or the champion may meet a challenger.

 COLORES (COLORS)

PROCEDURE:
1. Choose one leader, one devil, and one angel, then secretly assign individual colors to the rest of the group.
2. Mark a safe area some distance from the group.
3. Dialogue:
    Leader: What do you want?
    Devil: A ribbon
    Leader: What color?
    Devil: Names a color
4. The child who has been assigned the color that is named by the devil runs from the leader to the safety area.
5. The devil tries to catch the runner before he reaches the safety area. If he is caught, the color joins the devil and becomes his helper.
6. Next, the angel repeats what the devil did (numbers three - five).
7. The game is over when all the colors have been captured. The devil or the angel win according to who has the largest number of captives.

 COYOTE AND SHEEP

This game requires eight to twelve players, two teams. The leaders are one shepherd and one coyote. The rest of the team members are sheep.

PROCEDURE:
1. The children of each team line up facing each other single file. With the leaders in front, the two lines approach each other.
2. As the coyote approaches, this dialogue occurs:
    Shepherd: What does the coyote want?
    Coyote: I want fat meat!
    Shepherd: Then go to the end of the line where the fattest sheep are.
3. When the Shepherd says this, the coyote breaks for the end of the line and tries to tag the last sheep.
4. The Shepherd defends his flock by extending his arms in all directions to prevent the coyote from getting his last sheep. The line may help by weaving.
5. Lines may not be broken. If they are, the Shepherd becomes the next coyote and the next man in line becomes the Shepherd.
6. The game change in number 5 occurs when the coyote tags the last player in line.

ENCANTADOS (ENCHANTED)

This game requires a group of children.
PROCEDURE:
1. A home base (tree or rock) should be chosen as a safe area.
2. One child is chosen to be "It".
3. This game is like any tag game. "It" chases all the children. The child who is touched by "It" becomes the next "It".
4. Runners are safe when they are touching home base.

 JUAN PIRULERO (JOHN THE PICCOLO)

This game requires one group and one leader.
PROCEDURE:
1. Children sit in a circle with the leader in the center.
2. All pretend to play instruments different from the leader (guitar, piano, tuba, flute, etc.).
3. At intervals the leader changes over to any other instrument being played in the group.
4. Those children playing instruments the same as the leader's must quickly switch to a new instrument.
5. Those forgetting to change quickly are out of the game.
6. This chant or any similar one may be used:
   Este es el juego
   This is the game
   De Juan Pirulero y cada
   Of John the Piccolo and everyone
   Quien atiende a su juego
   Pays attention to this game

 LA PELOTA (THE BALL)

This game requires two or more players.
PROCEDURE:
1. a 12" - 18" circle target should be placed on the floor, 5' to 10' from the group.
2. The players take turns rolling a ball within the circle.
3. Those who miss the target pay a forfeit. Some examples of forfeits may be:
   a. Bend your head to the floor.
   b. Laugh three different ways.
   c. Say: Bob's Big Black Bear Bit a Big Blue Bug — three times quickly.
   d. Pantomime a babysitter caring for a crying baby.
   e. Imitate a girl combing her hair at a mirror.

 LA RASPA

LA RASPA STEP (Theme A in the music)

Count 1 – Jump in place to stride position, right foot forward, toes pointing up

Count 2 – Again jump in place, this time placing left foot forward

Count 3 – Again jump in place, right foot forward

Count 4 – Hold position – don't move!

(Repeat these steps but begin with the left foot forward this time)

(Repeat again but beginning with the right foot)

(Repeat again beginning with the left foot)

(Repeat)

CHORUS (Theme B)

Partners link right elbows and do eight skip steps around each other.

Reverse elbows and directions and repeat.

Chorus goes for 4 sets of 8-counts.

THE MUSIC REPEATS THREE MORE TIMES AND YOU MAY SIMPLY USE THE SAME TWO STEPS FOR THE REMAINDER OF THE RECORD.

1. Raspa Step
   a. Ask one couple to stand and do what directions indicate as you read: count 1, 2, 3, 4 together. Counting without music, try doing this together with all couples.
   b. Sit down in place and listen just to that part of music.
   c. Stand. Do La Raspa to count.
   d. Do La Raspa to theme A and repeat.
2. Chorus: teach as in E but use 8-count. Walk through first.
3. Try putting themes A and B together counting without music. Say:
   Jumping, 2, 3, 4, 1, 2, 3, 4, 1, 2, 3, 4, 1, 2, 3, 4, Skip, 2, 3, 4, 5, 6, 7, 8, Other elbow, 2, 3, 4, 5, 6, 7, 8.
4. Try whole dance. Stop and have others sit at rug's edge when you need to help a couple over a problem area. Use more skilled dancers to demonstrate correct methods.
5. As much as possible, praise and make positive comments. The uncoordinated child will be able to have fun jumping along even if he can't really do steps.

 **CHAPTER XI**
NATIVE AMERICANS OF THE
SOUTHWESTERN UNITED STATES

INDEX

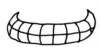

ABOUT NATIVE AMERICANS

Native Americans inhabited both North and South America before the arrival of Christopher Columbus. Each group of Native Americans had names for themselves and other groups who lived near them. These names could usually be interpreted to means people or group. Native Americans did not refer to themselves as tribes or as Indians. These terms were coined by Europeans who moved to the Americas.

There is no "typically" Native American way of life because every group of Native Americans is different from every other. Since the Southwestern United States is our present location, we have chosen to focus primarily upon those groups which might have been found in California, Arizona, or New Mexico.

It is believed that the Native Americans of California were primarily seed gatherers. They lived in moveable shelters because they would often move three to four times per year in their search for ripe foods and berries. Hunting provided some food but this was not their main source.

The folklore for each group of Native Americans varies greatly. The activities presented here represent common elements of several groups.

INTRODUCING THE ARTS OF NATIVE AMERICANS

Generally, each piece of Native American decorative art has a specific meaning. Circles within a design suggest goodness or everlasting life. Arrows are used both for direction and to indicate time, for example, an arrow pointing up suggests day, an arrow pointing down suggests night. Color, too, often has a special significance:

Black — growth cycle (from birth to death)
Blue — power or heavens
Grey — fatigue or gloom
Orange — peace or calm
Red — beginning or end of day or good health
White — day or clear water
Yellow — the moon or a sunny day

Specific explanations of Native American art precede each activity.

A GLOSSARY OF NATIVE AMERICAN PICTOGRAPHS

We are providing these pictographs for use in the various activities that require the use of Native American picture writing.

These pictographs are used with the permission of Aren Akweks, Six Nations Indian Museum, Onchiota, New York.

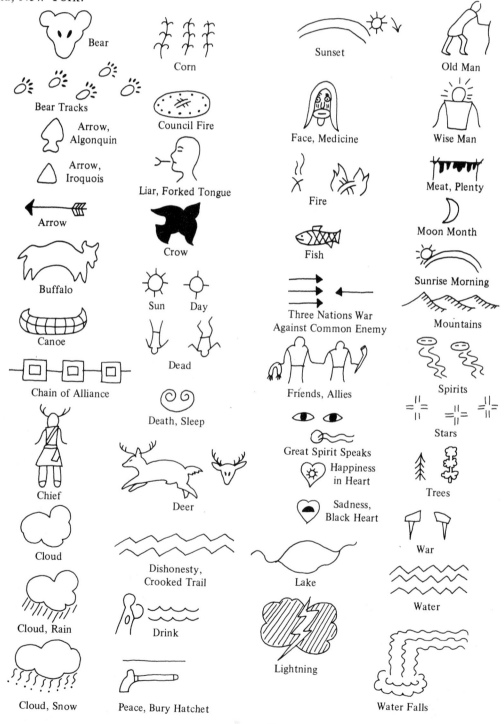

258

BURDEN BASKET AND TUMPLINE

BACKGROUND: Native Americans had a myriad of purposes for the beautiful baskets they wove. Different sizes and shapes denoted the use for the basket. The large, bowl-type baskets with flat bottoms held grain. Circular flat baskets were used for winnowing grain. They wove some baskets with just sides and no bottom; these baskets had a very ingenious purpose — when the acorn grinding stone was new, it would not have been worn down in the center, so with the flat top, the acorns would fall off the stone while they were being ground. Consequently, they wove a basket with the sides and hole in the bottom and attached it to the stone with tar or pitch. In this way, they would not lose any of the acorn meal while grinding on a new stone.

Burden baskets were made to carry anything that the women would gather, i.e., acorns, roots, berries, firewood. The baskets were attached to a strap called a tumpline. The tumpline fit over the head and the basket was carried on the back. Women would sometimes wear a hat to protect their head when carrying a heavy burden. The hat was a woven basket that looked like a small bowl.

MATERIALS:
>   2 paper bags of the same size
>   Scissors
>   1½" wide tape (masking or the type used for packages)
>   Paint
>   Paint brushes
>   Crayons
>   Wide strips of cloth
>   Glue or staples

PROCEDURE:
1. Place the two bags together one inside the other.
2. Fold down the top edge of the bags one inch and tape on the inside and on the outside.
3. Paint Native American pictographs on the basket.
4. Cut a 1 to 2 inch wide strip of cloth, long enough to go from the burden basket (which rests on the back) and over the forehead.
5. Draw a border design on the strap with crayons.
6. Connect the strap to the basket with glue or staples.

 CORN HUSK WREATH

BACKGROUND: Native Americans had many uses for the entire ear of corn. They prepared the kernels in a variety of ways for eating. The husks were used to make useful and decorative items. When the husks were braided, they made mats, baskets, and clotheslines from them. The corn husk wreath was made as a decorative item.

Native Americans made the form for the wreath from green branches that would bend easily.

MATERIALS:

        Wire hanger

        Corn husks (green husks must be dried in the sun for a few days)

        Pins

PROCEDURE:

1. Soak the dried husks until they are soft enough to bend easily.
2. Bend a wire hanger to form a circle.
3. Fold one husk and tie it over the wire.
4. Repeat step 3 (A, B, & C) until the wire is full.
5. Use the pin to shred the ends of the husks.
6. Allow the wreath to dry in some place where it may be hung.

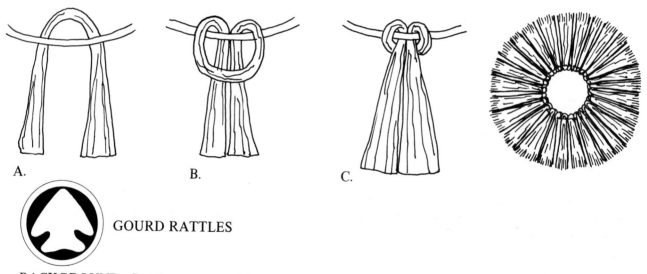

A.   B.   C.

GOURD RATTLES

BACKGROUND: Rattles were used by most Native American groups to embellish the beat of the drum. Ceremonial rattles were made in various shapes and designs; a variety of materials were used. Some rattles were made of carved wood, gourds, hide, or shells. A special rattle, known as the moon rattle, was spherical and had a face carved into each side. Other rattles had trinkets hanging from them that would produce further pleasant sounds when shaken. Some rattles were attactive works of wood sculpture.

MATERIALS:

        Gourd

        Small pebbles

        6" stick of ½" diameter

        ½" drill bit and drill

        Leather pieces, felt, and feathers

PROCEDURE:
1. Clean gourd.
2. Drill out hole for stick.
3. Place several small pebbles inside gourd.
4. Place 2" square of felt over gourd opening and force felt and stick into gourd until secure.
5. Decorate stick with feathers and leather.

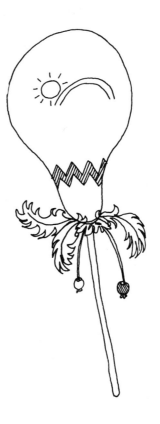

 HEADBANDS

BACKGROUND: Native American braiding was generally done from the center to each end. Several interesting designs were created by braiding — working several wefts (clumps of yarn strands) at a time and bringing them all together.

MATERIALS:
Yarn cut in 36" lengths
Feathers and beads (optional)

PROCEDURE:
1. Work with a partner
2. Use 12 pieces of yarn (36" lengths)
3. Arrange the yarn neatly together, matching each end.
4. Have the partner hold the middle of the yarn. (You may find the center by matching the opposite ends of one piece of yarn.)
5. While your partner holds the center of the yarn, begin your braiding.
6. Divide the 12 strands of yarn into three equal segments of four strands each.
7. Begin to braid each weft as illustrated and continue until all yarn is used.
8. Tie each end with a short piece of yarn.
9. Fit the two ends of the finished piece of weaving together to fit your head. Tie to secure.

 KACHINA MASKS

BACKGROUND: The Hopi and Zuni groups once believed that gods brought the rain. When these gods left man's land, they left their Kachina masks behind so that they could easily return to help man. The tribesmen believed that, when they did certain dances while wearing a Kachina mask, they would become a Kachina god. Many of these dances and the ways to make Kachina masks are still well-kept secrets from all but those who have inherited this knowledge from their fathers.

Since we do not know the Kachina secrets, we can only try to make masks that seem similar to Kachina masks.

MATERIALS:

Manila tagboard	Macaroni
Scissors	Egg cartons
Stapler	Wire
White glue	Feathers
Construction paper	Any scrap art materials (i.e.: excelsior, styrofoam, packing
Yarn	materials, beads, cornhusks)
Buttons	

PROCEDURE:

1. Staple a piece of manila tagboard together at each end to form a cylinder.
2. Cover the tagboard with colored paper of different shapes. A combination of triangles and straight lines can look like face painting. Glue all of the trim securely.
3. Allow the glue to dry and then fit cylinder over head and cut eye holes at any point, as desired. The eye holes may be easily disguised at chin level of the mask.

262

 MOCCASINS

BACKGROUND: Native Americans wore soft shoes made from animal hides. The moccasins were often decorated with beads or feathers. These soft shoes helped the Native Americans to walk quietly so that they would not scare away the animals while hunting.

MATERIALS:

        A pair of socks
        Scissors
        Needle
        Yarn
    Optional:
        Beads
        Thread
        Glue

PROCEDURE:

1. With the sock on the child's foot, draw around the sock to form a moccasin shape, allowing ¼-½ inch to turn down.
2. Cut off the top part of the sock.
3. Fold the hem down ¼-½ inch.
4. Starting almost at the center of the front, sew the hem using a running stitch with yarn and a needle.
5. Put the moccasin on and pull the draw-string to make it fit snugly. Tie the yarn in a bow.
6. The tops of the moccasins may be decorated with beads.

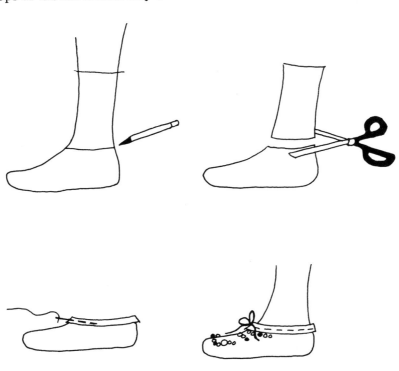

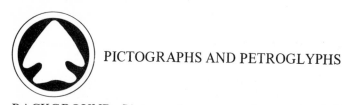 PICTOGRAPHS AND PETROGLYPHS

BACKGROUND: Pictographs were made on animal skins or tree bark. The petroglyphs were carved in stone on cave or mountain canyon walls. Most of the Native Americans drew scenes of daily life and seemed to prefer drawings of the hunt or of themselves at war. They made their paints from minerals and plants. By boiling the tails of beavers, they produced a glue additive to make their colors adhere. Their early paint brushes were made from sticks and animal horns or hair. It is difficult to draw fine details on bark or hide, so Native American art appeared blocked and more primitive for this reason. In later years, as Indians began trading with settlers for paper, pencils, etc., their art became more detailed.

We can only speculate as to the meaning of many of the pictures. They may be people, animals, ideas, stars, nature objects, or just designs. They may be something special for the people who made them, tell a story or be symbols for special ceremonies.

MATERIALS:

> Rectangles cut from brown shopping bags and prepainted with a medium brown wash of brown paint
> Water colors mixed in earth shades (these should not be too vivid)
> Newspapers
> Brushes
> Scissors

PREPARTION BY VOLUNTEERS:

1. To mix new earth shades of paint when necessary (1 part each: color powder, starch, and two parts water).
2. To complete this activity in one session, have the volunteers cut out grocery bags and paint one side with brown poster paint, allow to dry.

PROCEDURE:

1. Place your name and room number on back of paper.
2. Wad paper tightly. Squeeze again.
3. If you wish, you may use scissors to curve the edges.
4. Use some of the suggested designs for pictographs (see Glossary of Native American Pictographs, page 258) or design your own. (Try to make them look like Native American designs.) Allow to dry and then display.

 ROLLED CLAY BOWL

BACKGROUND: Native Americans used clay pots for containers and for cooking and eating. After the clay was dry, they would often paint these containers with various designs before using.

MATERIALS:

> Air-dry molding clay or a salt-clay mixture
> Waxed paper
> Shortening
> Bowl-shaped margarine tubs (one per child)
> Small bowl of water by each child — fingers should be wet while working the clay

PROCEDURE:

1. Turn the margarine tub upside down. Cover the outside completely with shortening. This will insure the easy removal of your bowl from the form.

2. Working on your wax paper, roll several "snake-type" ropes of clay as close to the same diameter as possible.

3. Place one end of the clay rope in the center top of the upside-down bowl. Continue to spiral the clay around itself and work it down the sides of the bowl. Press the coils firmly together. Use water to secure the coils and be certain that no open spaces remain.

4. Add coils until the bowl shape is completed.

5. Allow the bowl to dry for several days (depending on the weather) until it is very hard.

6. When dry, turn the bowl right side up and carefully remove the margarine tub from the clay bowl.

7. The bowl may be used as it is now or be painted with tempera in natural colors with border designs (see Glossary of Native American Pictographs, page 258).

8. This bowl will not hold water. Use it as a catchall or decorative piece.

 SAND PAINTING

BACKGROUND: Sand painting is used by Navajo medicine men to drive away evil spirits. The medicine man chants while sifting different colors of sand through his fingers. A sick person is carefully laid on the sand painting to be near his gods. After the ceremony, the sand painting is destroyed and the sand thrown in four directions. This confuses the evil spirits. Many medicine men successfully cure mental illness for their people using sand paintings.

Sand paintings are sacred. It is believed that they must be destroyed by sunset of the day they are begun. Any copies of the more than 400 traditional sand painting desings must be imperfect copies in order not to offend the Holy People of the Native American tribes.

MATERIALS:
Fine sand or salt of various colors (see recipe below)
Jars or bowls for mixing and stirring the sand
Heavy cardboard or sandpaper
Paper cone or spoon
Varnish, shellac, glue or paste
Watercolor paint
Carbon paper (to transfer design)
Brushes or Q-tips for glueing, toothpicks
Tempera and paint brushes

PROCEDURE:
1. Sketch or trace a design on the cardboard sheet.
2. Use tempera paint to brush in the background colors where sand is not desired.
3. Choose the areas to be done in a particular color sand and paint a thin coat of shellac, varnish, glue or paste on these parts (paint a small area at a time).
4. Trickle or sprinkle the colored sand from a paper cone or spoon onto the areas that have been covered with paste, varnish or white shellac.
5. Allow the work to dry for a few minutes, then lift the work and tap it lightly so excess sand is removed.
6. Repeat this process for all additional colors until the picture is completed.

Note: Native Americans poured sand from the hand along the second joint of the index finger. The thumb was used to stop the flow of sand.

Recipe for colored sand and colored salt:
1. Place sand (use white sand for best results) or salt on a piece of wrapping paper or several thicknesses of newspaper.
2. Combine with powdered chalk or tempera until a color of sufficient depth is obtained.

THE SUN SYMBOL

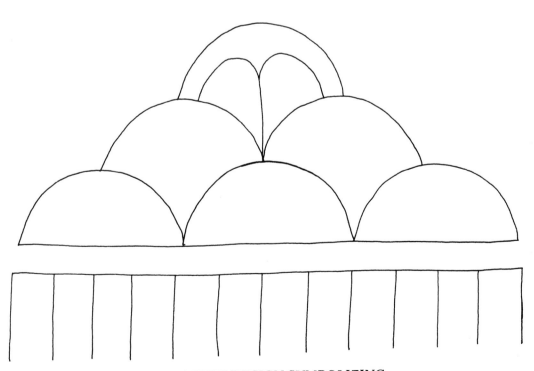

A HOPI DESIGN SYMBOLIZING
CLOUDS AND FALLING RAIN.

267

 TEPEE

BACKGROUND: The types and sizes of the housing used by Native Americans have varied a great deal over the years from group to group. Some popular construction materials have included logs, earth, bark, and sticks. There have been different purposes for the many kinds of homes that were built by Native Americans. The tepee was used by some groups during periods of travel. The tepee provided a mobile home of poles and animal skins. Children will enjoy making simple reproductions of this one form of shelter used occasionally by a variety of Native Americans.

MATERIALS:

       Brown paper grocery bag
       Brown tempera and brushes
       Pattern
       Tape
       Teriyake sticks or toothpicks

PROCEDURE:

1. Paint the brown paper with brown tempera. Allow it to dry.
2. Crush the paper.
3. Flatten and trace the tepee outline onto the brown paper.
4. Add some Native American designs, see the Glossary of Native American Pictographs.
5. Cut and construct the tepee using tabs to join. Cut on the solid lines. Fold on the broken lines.
6. Use toothpicks or teriyake sticks at the top of the tepee to resemble poles.

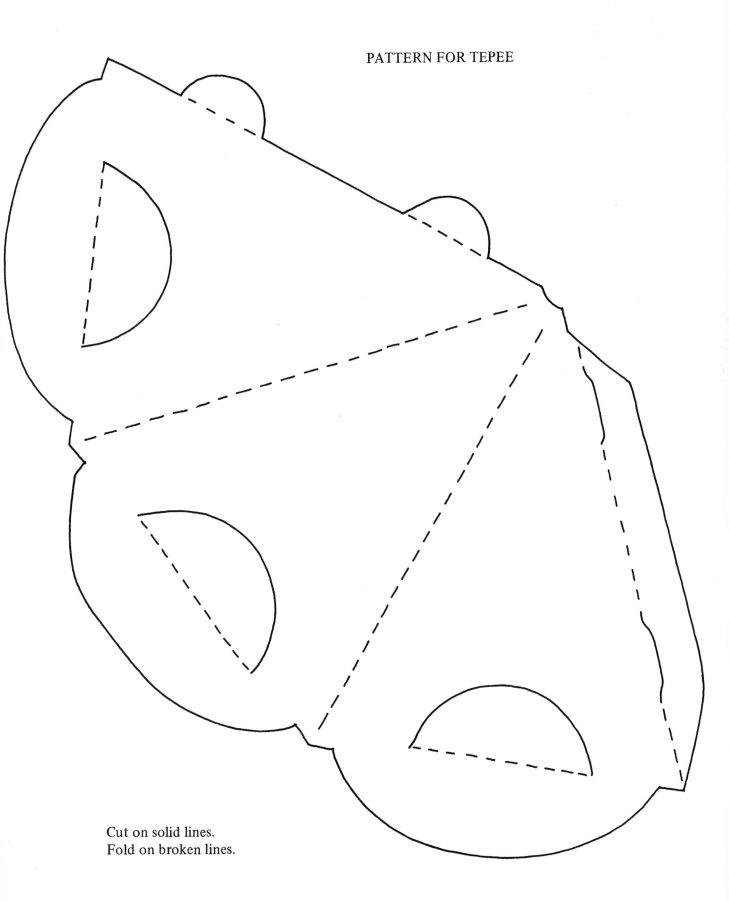

PATTERN FOR TEPEE

Cut on solid lines.
Fold on broken lines.

 **TRAVOIS AND DOG**

BACKGROUND: Travel was difficult for Native Americans. Until the white men came, there were no horses. Carts and other vehicles did not exist because Native Americans had no knowledge of the wheel. The travois was used to carry burdens. Generally dogs were the only animals tamed by the Native Americans so they were used to pull the travois. A dog could pull a forty pound load.

MATERIALS FOR DOG:

> Tongue depressor or popsicle stick
> Six peanuts
> Needle and thread
> Pipe cleaner and paper scraps
> Felt-tip pens, stapler

PROCEDURE:

1. Choose one large and five small peanuts.
2. Use thread and needle to correctly attach the five peanuts together as a dog. Knot securely.
3. Cut ears and tail from scraps of paper and glue in place. Use felt-tip pens to paint the dog with spots, eyes, nose....
4. Attach string through dog's shoulder area, as shown, and attach to puppet stick.

MATERIALS FOR TRAVOIS:

> 2 BBQ teriyake sticks
> String or yarn
> Scrap paper
> Stapler or glue

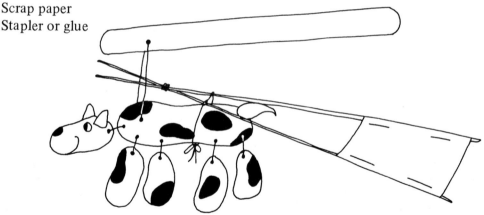

PROCEDURE:

1. Tie the two sticks together at one end, as shown.
2. Secure a piece of construction paper to four points of the travois.
3. Cut a piece of string to attach the travois to the dog. Tie it securely to the two legs of the travois.

4. Attach string through dog's shoulder area, as shown, and attach to puppet stick.

5. Place the travois on the dog's back so that the top is just behind the dog's ears. Tie the string under the dog's body.

 TURKEY LEG WHISTLE

BACKGROUND: The Native Americans made many toys and musical instruments from items found in nature. A favorite was whistles made from bird legs — especially pelican and turkey legs.

MATERIALS:

> Clean turkey leg bone (thigh bone may also be used — chicken legs do not work well)
> Coat hanger segment
> Half round file and hacksaw
> Drill and small bit (1/8")

PROCEDURE:

1. Saw off each end of the turkey leg bone.
2. Clean marrow from inside of bone using coat hanger and by blowing. Wash.
3. Using a half round file, file a small opening 1½" down from the narrow end.
4. Chew ½ stick of gum well. Stuff gum in small end of bone, to block opening. Gum should fill entire blow end.
5. Using coat hanger, place small hole at top of gum close to file hole.
6. Blow whistle. If whistle makes squeak, hole is too small. If whistle sounds like airy sound, hole is too big.
7. Gum may be pushed around to adjust for correct sound. Native Americans used tar or pitch instead of gum.
8. Drill three small holes, as illustrated, with a small drill bit.

 WARRIOR'S EYE OF GOD AMULET

BACKGROUND: An amulet is an ornament worn as a charm against evils. Small eye-of-god amulets were worn by the southwestern Native Americans. Large eyes of god were hung in their homes to protect them from evil. If a person was sick, the medicine man made an amulet to ward off evil spirits.

The eye-of-god amulets were made from sticks, yarn, beads, shells, and feathers. A similar ornament is available in the section of this text which covers Mexico.

MATERIALS:

        2 sticks (popsicle or shoe stretchers work well)
        Yarn
        Scissors
        String or fishing line
        Glue
     Optional:
        Beads
        Shells
        Feathers

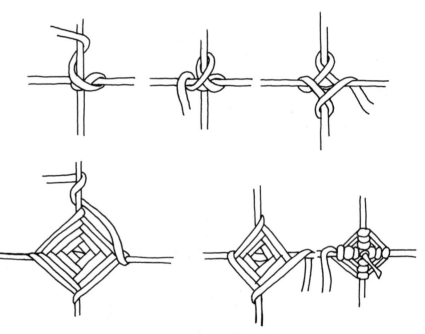

FRONT   BACK

PROCEDURE:

1. Cross the two sticks in the middle.
2. Tie with yarn to secure the sticks and keep the sticks perpendicular.
3. Weave yarn over one leg, then under and around the same leg.
4. Go to the next leg and weave the same way.
5. Continue until you reach the ends of the sticks. You may use several different colors of yarn; simply tie the new color to the end of the previous color used.
6. Tie the end of the yarn to the closest stick.
7. String the beads on thin string or fishing line and tie to two adjacent stick ends. You may incorporate skills with beads by glueing them on.
8. String a longer length of string or fishing line with beads and tie to the opposite adjacent sticks. This is the string from which you hang the amulet.
9. Decorate with feathers or more shells.

INTRODUCING THE COOKING OF NATIVE AMERICANS

California's Native Americans cooked and ate what was readily accessible near their home. Their diets included berries, nuts, corn, meat (especially small game), shellfish, locusts, grasshoppers, acorns, and seeds.

On the plains, there were farmers and they used corn as their staple food. In California, they didn't have to farm because all their natural resources were plentiful. Acorns were used in the same manner that the Native Americans of the plains used corn. After they ground the acorns and leached the tannic acid from the meal, they used the acorn to make mush and bread.

The natives of the plains were very innovative farmers and developed many methods used today for fertilizing and crop rotation. We can also thank them for the hybrid corn that we eat today. The early corn was very primitive and through selective planting they developed the corn we enjoy today.

In California, Native Americans cooked in a simplified manner. For example, to boil water they would simply drop red-hot stones into the water. After the water started to boil they would drop in food and more hot rocks.

It is difficult to cook exactly as the Native Americans did because many of their food items are not easily available today and many of them we would not enjoy eating.

 ATOLE

BACKGROUND: Seven kinds of oak trees grow wild in the California area. These produce seven distinctly different tastes of acorns with varying degrees of bitterness. To leach out the bitterness (tannic acid) Native Americans would crack the acorns between two rocks and grind the acorns to a powder. They would then pour boiling water through the acorn meal and a fibrous material in order to leach out the tannic acid.

INGREDIENTS

2 Tbs.	(30ml.)	Masa
½ C.	(120ml.)	Water — add a little at a time
1 pinch		Salt

PROCEDURE:

1. Mix the masa, a little warm water and salt.
2. Form a smooth paste and thin with remaining water.
3. Boil 10 minutes over low heat. Stir constantly. Serve.

 BEEF JERKY

BACKGROUND: Native Americans utilized this slow-drying process to preserve some of their meat. Beef jerky is most easily done as a group activity. Marination and drying are difficult for individual portions.

INGREDIENTS:

1½ lbs.	(680gms.)	Flank steak
½ C.	(120ml.)	Soy sauce
1 tsp.	(5ml.)	Liquid smoke (optional)
1 tsp.	(5 ml.)	Seasoned salt
1 C.	(240ml.)	Water
½ tsp.	(2.5ml.)	Garlic salt
½ tsp.	(2.5ml.)	Celery salt
¼ tsp.	(1.2ml.)	Pepper

PROCEDURE:

1. Freeze the flank steak for about one hour. Cut into thin strips.
2. Marinate in sauce overnight. To make sauce, mix the last seven ingredients above.
3. Cover oven rack with foil and make little troughs between rungs for excess juice to drain. Lay strips on rack.
4. Bake at 140°F, 60°C for six to eight hours.
5. To store: do not use airtight container.

 CORN

BACKGROUND: Corn was an important part of the diet for many Native Americans. Originally corn was much smaller and was shaped somewhat like a pine cone. Each of the kernels was completely enclosed in a tough, pointed husk. The Native Americans used ingenuity and selective planting to produce better crops.

Native Americans did not grind their entire corn crop. The ripe ears were eaten as a vegetable, being boiled with the husks on. They also ate the tassels which are rich in protein. Popcorn was also cultivated and it was used both for eating and decoration. Husks were used to make floor mats and woven decorative items.

Only in the New World does the word "corn" refer specifically to maize. Throughout most of the world, corn has been used as a descriptive term to describe the grain common to the area. Columbus and his crew reported to the Santa Mariz that the Native Americans had a sort of grain called mahiz. The scientific name for maize is Zea Mays. (Zea is the Greek word for grain; mays is derived from makiy. Makiy is the word for corn in the language of Tainos — an extinct tribe of Native Americans.)

CORNMEAL BREAD

INGREDIENTS:

¼ C.	(60ml.)	Cornmeal
1 pinch		Salt
Stir while adding:		
1 Tbs.	(15ml.)	Bacon grease
2 Tbs.	(30ml.)	Boiling water

PROCEDURE:
1. Mix the cornmeal and salt.
2. Stir while adding the grease and boiling water.
3. Use hands to shape dough into small rolls the shape of hot dogs.
4. Wrap rolls in fresh cornhusks. Dampened parchment paper or well-greased wrapping paper may be substituted for cornhusks.
5. Bake at 350°F, 176°C for six minutes.

CORNMEAL CRISPS

INGREDIENTS:

¼ C.	(60ml.)	Cornmeal
2 Tbs.	(30ml.)	Flour
1 pinch		Salt
1 Tbs.	(15ml.)	Melted butter
2 Tbs.	(30ml.)	Milk

PROCEDURE:
1. Sift together the cornmeal, flour and salt.
2. Add the melted butter and milk.
3. Stir. Knead. Divide into 4 balls.
4. Flatten balls and place on ungreased cookie sheet.
5. Bake at 350°F, 176°C for 12-15 minutes. When done, crisps should be lightly browned around edges.

 FRUIT LEATHER

BACKGROUND: Native Americans ground berries on a stone, allowed it to dry, and then removed the dried sheet of sweet-tasting fruit. This substance would not easily spoil; therefore, they could enjoy this delicacy for a longer period of time.

PROCEDURE:

1. Fruit should be at room temperature.
2. Wrap top of cardboard square (approximately 6x6") in plastic wrap.
3. Wash fruit and remove blemishes, skins, and pits. Fruit may be overripe if unspoiled.
4. Puree fruit with sieve or masher. A blender may also be used. Add sweetener, if desired, according to fruit type as listed under "Special Directions for Specific Fruits".
5. Spread puree over plastic wrap, leaving margin at edges.
6. Dry in hot sun until fruit leather feels dry, yet tacky. A thin curtain or screen may be used to keep bugs away. To speed drying, you may cover the leather with more plastic wrap and flip it to dry other side. Another quick way to dry fruit leather is in a closed car sitting in direct sunlight.
7. When dry and tacky roll up in plastic wrap.
8. Store in airtight container.

SPECIAL DIRECTIONS FOR SPECIFIC FRUITS:

Apple: Use early summer apples rather than crisp, hard apples. Add ¼ tsp. cinnamon and ½ C. shredded coconut to 2 C. puree.

Apricots: Do not peel. Add 1 Tbs. honey to each cup puree. Do not chill fruit.

Berry: Wash and hull. Sweeten to taste.

Peach: Peel. Sweetening is optional. Cinnamon may be added.

Pear: Peel. Do not add sweetener.

Plum: Add 1 Tbs. honey to 1 C. puree.

 NAVAJO FRY BREAD

BACKGROUND: This bread was often cooked on a flat black stone, called a soapstone, that can withstand heat and was used much like we use frying pans today.

INGREDIENTS:

Sift:

¼ C.	(60ml.)	Flour
1 pinch		Baking powder/salt mix (combined 2:1)

Add:

2 Tbs.	(30ml.)	Lukewarm water

PROCEDURE:
1. Sift the flour, baking powder and salt mixtures.
2. Add the lukewarm water.
3. Combine and knead.
4. Roll out and cut into four 2''squares (about ¼''thick).
5. Brown by turning in hot shortening in electric skillet.
6. Drain on paper towel.
7. Serve hot with jam or honey.

 PEKEE BREAD

BACKGROUND: The Native Americans of several different groups were known to make a form of Pekee or paper bread. They cooked it on flat stones, which they laid over their fire. For daily eating, the bread was sometimes mixed with ashes and looked grey. On special occasions they would color the bread red by adding small amounts of red dirt. Pekee bread was often rolled to use as an eating utensil to scoop up their stew, similar to the way Mexicans use tortillas.

VOLUNTEER PREPARATION:
Mix: 5 Tbs. (75ml.) powdered milk to make one cup of milk. Place margarine tub of milk and one of salad oil on the table. Children will go to cooking supply table for dry ingredients. Shake or stir 4:1 baking powder and salt mixture.

INGREDIENTS:
Mix:

1 Tbs.	(15ml.)	Rye flour
1 Tbs.	(15ml.)	Corn flour
Pinch		Salt and baking powder mixture

Add:

2 tsp.	(10ml.)	Milk
1 tsp.	(5ml.)	Corn oil

PROCEDURE:
1. Stir well. This should form a thin paste that may be poured onto the griddle.
2. Cook in lightly greased electric skillet 350°F, 176°C, for five to ten minutes.
3. Turn with spatula. Serve with berry jam.

 PEMMICAN

BACKGROUND: Pemmican is a tasty variation on a combination of dried foods.

INGREDIENTS:

1 C.	(240ml.)	Ground beef jerky
1 C.	(240ml.)	Beef suet
3 oz.	(50ml.)	Dried raisins or berries
3 oz.	(50ml.)	Dried shelled sunflower seeds

PROCEDURE:
1. Melt suet over low heat.
2. Pour suet over ground jerky and mix with dried fruit and seeds.
3. Cool. Pack in sausage casing or a plastic bag.

 TSE ASTE (BREAD COOKED ON A STONE)

BACKGROUND: This bread was often cooked on a flat black stone called a soapstone that can withstand heat and was used much like we use frying pans today.

INGREDIENTS:

3 Tbs.	(45ml.)	Cornmeal
1 pinch		Salt
½ C.	(120ml.)	Boiling water

PROCEDURE:
1. Combine cornmeal and salt.
2. Add the boiling water.
3. Grease soapstone griddle or electric skillet at 350°F, 176°C with small piece of mutton tallow or bacon fat.
4. Preheat griddle until a drop of water sizzles when placed upon it.
5. Stir batter frequently. Measure by tablespoons onto griddle.
6. Cook until bread is crisp and loosened at the edges.
7. Turn with spatula to crisp other side.

 INTRODUCING THE RECREATION OF NATIVE AMERICANS

Native American children did not attend any formal school so they had many free moments. Most Native Americans were game lovers and enjoyed many sports, gambling, and ceremonial games. Athletes were honored as highly as warriors. Native Americans are credited with the invention of the game, Lacrosse.

Indians played games both for enjoyment and to build skills, strength, and stamina of the players. The Cherokee Native Americans called their games "the little brother of war" because they believed that games made their boys into better warriors. Some games were rough and dangerous, i.e., spear fighting and mud throwing.

Native Americans enjoyed games of chance as well as games of dexterity. The children often played games with the adults but there were special children's games too. Generally boys and girls played separately and sometimes they would play the same game with different rules. Some games taught animal stalking or egg hunting. Some common games were similar to: Blindman's Buff, Follow the Leader, Hide and Seek, Ring-Around-a-Rosy, Tug of War, top spinning, pop gun play, stickball, and make-believe games.

Native Americans kept score on games by using sticks. Generally two players would try for the best of seven games. Seven sticks would be placed in front of them and as a game was won, the winner took one stick. This continued until all seven sticks were awarded. (This works well for guessing games.)

 ARROW GAME

2 Players

An arrow is stuck in the ground as a target. The players take turns throwing their arrows at it.

 ARROW THROUGH HOOP GAME

2 Players

Native American children played a game where they would throw sticks at, or through, a rolling hoop. Sometimes their hoop was laced or had a solid woven center. The object of the game was to embed a spear into the center of the hoop as the hoop rolled by. We suggest a variation of that game below.

 BALL AND RING GAME

2 Players

Equipment — tire and tennis ball.

Two players face each other 6 to 10 feet apart. Player number one rolls tire toward player number two. Player number two throws ball through tire. Players alternate positions. The player who hits the ring or shoots through it most wins.

 BALL RACE

2 Players

Equipment — ball.

Native Americans used a 5-6 inch wooden or stone ball which they covered with mesquite gum. The players compete in a foot race where they kick the balls ahead of them without using their hands. Each player has his own ball.

 BUCKSKIN BALL

Teams

Use a large playground ball and hit at it with four-foot branches which have a bend at one end. Set up goal points for each team.

 CAT'S CRADLE

Make a large loop with string. Players weave with fingers and pass string back and forth. Place hands as shown.

Pull loops to opposite middle fingers. Player who ruins weave forfeits one of the seven score-keeping sticks to his opponent. Some complicated designs require use of another set of hands to maintain a weave.

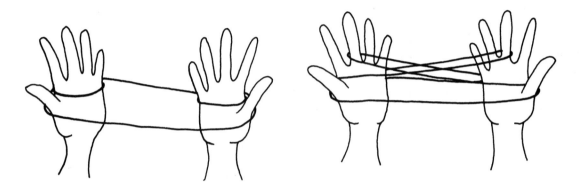

 CHERRY STONES

Two to four players may play this game.

MATERIALS:

Flat basket or box

Six cherry pits (the pits of any fruit may be adapted). Paint one side of each pit black or mark with a permanent marker.

PROCEDURE:

1. Shake the box of cherry stones in alternate turns in order to accumulate points.
2. 5 points= all 6 stones the same (all black or all plain)

   1 point= 5 stones of same color

   0 points= any other combination
3. The first player to accumulate 20 points is the winner.

 CUP-ON-A-STICK

Native Americans played several varieties of games where an object was tossed up and caught. The top section was connected by string to a pointed stick. The object of these games was to swing the stick, thereby tossing the object up and catching it on the pointed stick. This game is similar to the Mexican game of Balero.

MATERIALS:

    12 inch stick
    Needle or pin
    Paper cup
    15 inch length of string

PREPARATION BY VOLUNTEER:

1.   Use pin to make hole in bottom of paper cup.
2.   Insert thread through hole and knot on inside of cup.
3.   Wrap opposite end of string around stick and knot.

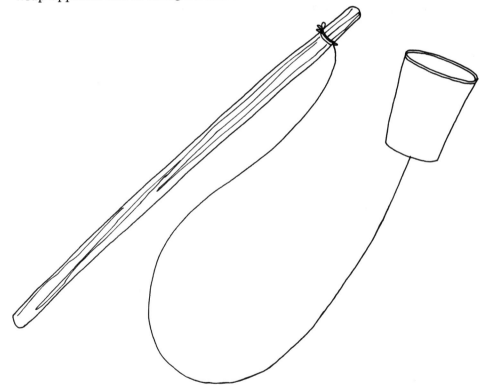

PROCEDURE:

Take turns swinging the cup in the air while trying to catch it on the top of the stick.
    Note: Each child could make this game as a craft if desired.

FERN LEAF GAME

Native American children played a game using fern leaves. The child who was able to collect the most fern leaves one-by-one, while holding his breath, was the winner. We invented a derivative of this game: the children were given a blue counting man and ten clothespins. Holding their breath, they will clip all the clothespins one-by-one to the counting man and down again to the holding tray. Each player has a possible 20 point score.

FRUIT AND NUT TOSS

2-4 Players

MATERIALS:

> 3-lb coffee can or shoe box for goal
> 5 different fruit pits or nuts. Assign a point value to each different seed, i.e.:
>> Walnut   = 1 point
>> Acorn   = 2 points
>> Peach seed   = 3 points
>> Almond   = 4 points
>> Cherry seed   = 5 points

PROCEDURE:
1.   Each player takes his turn standing at the line (about five feet from the goal) and throws his seeds at the goal, one seed after the other. He receives a point total of all seeds which remain in the goal.
2.   The winner is the first person who accumulates 20 points.

GAME OF THE MOCCASIN

Any number of players form a circle and each child holds one of his shoes in his hand. The object of the game is to pass the shoes with the beat of the music. A drum, chant or record may be used. With each shoe, the child taps lightly on the floor two times and then continues the shoe clockwise around the circle (tap, tap, pass to left, tap, tap, pass to left). Any child with more or less than one shoe when the music stops is out of the game.

 HUMMING TOY

MATERIALS:

Button
30 inches of string
2 small wedges of cardboard

PROCEDURE:
1. Cut two "V" shapes of tagboard and glue them on a large round button as shown.
2. Thread a 30 inch piece of string through the holes and tie.
3. Swing the disc until the cord is tightly wound, holding the string at the two looped ends.
4. As you quickly pull hands apart, the toy will rapidly unwind, making a humming sound.

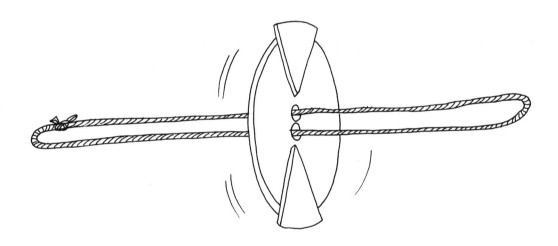

 MOCCASIN HIDE AND SEEK

MATERIALS:
Four moccasins
Four pebbles (one pebble should look different than the other three)

PROCEDURE:
1. One player hides a pebble in each moccasin.
2. His opponent tries to guess which moccasin contains the special pebble. (Two players take turns for best of seven games.)

 PAPAGO

2 or more Players

MATERIALS:
> 4 cups, 1 small rock, sand

PROCEDURE:

Player number one takes the four cups and conceals a rock in one cup and fills all the cups with sand. He gives the filled cups to player number two. Player number two returns these to player number one one at a time.

If rock is in first cup, player number one scores 10 points; second, 6 points; third, 4 points; fourth, 0 points.

Players alternate turns. The winner is the first player to accumulate 50 points.

 RING STICK GAME

2-4 Players

MATERIALS:
> 5 sticks, hula hoop or a circle which has been marked on the floor, marker line, four feet from target.

PROCEDURE:
1. Lay the hoop on the floor and stand 4 feet away with player's back to hoop.
2. Each player should take his turn to toss the five sticks over his shoulder, one at a time, and hit the circle target.
3. Each player scores one point for each stick.
4. The winner is the first player to accumulate 20 points.

 SILENCE

Children may return to their classrooms playing the Native American game of Silence: the last person to make any sound wins; therefore, the children must return to their classrooms on tiptoes and without making any sounds. Tell them that there may be more than one winner and that the winners will know who they are when they arrive at their room and are sitting in their desks.

 STICK GUESSING

Native Americans used bones or small sticks for this game.

MATERIALS: Two sticks or bones of similar size and shape. Use a permanent marker to mark on one end of one of the sticks.

PROCEDURE:
1. The two players hold the sticks so the mark is covered by their hand. Player number one holds the two sticks behind his back and shuffles the sticks.
2. Player number two chooses one stick when they are both presented to him.
3. If player number two chooses the stick with the mark, he may be the one to present the sticks. If he chooses the unmarked stick, he must take another turn to guess.

 STICK PASSING GAME

Any number of players form a circle.

MATERIALS:
Set of sticks, one stick for each player with one stick having a special marking.

PROCEDURE:
1. The sticks are passed to the beat of music. Using this pattern, tap, tap, pass to right, take stick from left with left hand and quickly pass it to your own right hand.
2. When music stops, player with marked stick is out of circle. As children are eliminated they may become the musicians and clap or play instruments to the rhythm.

 STONE PASSING GAME

The group chants or leader plays music while stone is passed. "It" closes his eyes and opens them when music stops. He then tries to guess which player in the circle is concealing the stone.

CHAPTER XII
WESTERN AFRICA

INDEX

ABOUT WESTERN AFRICA

Many of the Black Peoples of the United States have traced their ancestors to what were then countries in the area of Western Africa. Despite its many lovely cities, Africa still has several unexplored areas and their transportation systems are not fully developed.

The continent of Africa faces special problems because there are so many diverse tribes, languages, and countries. The land of Western Africa is conducive to farming. Those tribes which live on farms seem to have a more traceable history. Farming tribes, as a general rule, have made more objects to supplement their lifestyle and promote more tradition and rituals than the nomadic or wandering tribes.

The activities presented here generally reflect the lifestyle of those groups living outside the cities of Western Africa. An increased awareness of one's heritage has helped to encourage the world-wide availability of African folklore.

INTRODUCING THE ARTS OF WESTERN AFRICA

African art has been the forerunner of modern art. The qualities and techniques used go beyond representation of natural forms. The simple beauty of African art expresses the power of nature. Students of modern art have studied these art forms to develop new directions in art such as cubism and surrealism.

As in most countries, available materials in African countries seem to control the direction of the artist. For example, Ghana has some of the richest gold mines in the world. The Ashanti cast their gold weights into different shapes, such as bugs, fish, or birds. Bug castings often have real bugs inside the gold casting.

Much of the available African art is made for religious ceremonies. Art forms are frequently connected with the daily life of the artist and may portray the planting, harvesting, hunting or even the experience of birth or death. African crafts are an extremely important method of tracing history in areas where there is no written language.

 AKUABA DOLLS

BACKGROUND: Ashanti women and girls wear wooden dolls tucked into their waistcloths. Dolls are flat and have long necks. They are worn as good luck charms and insure the wearer that she will have handsome babies.

Woodcarvers make three styles of Akuaba dolls: to insure that the wearer will have a daughter, an oval head is shaped; a rectangular head produces a son. For a wise child, a round head is carved.

These dolls are shaped somewhat like the Egyptian Ankh (cross of life). Many believe they have common origin. Young Akan children make theirs out of mud or clay. Older boys carve them from wood.

Sometimes older girls dress them and carry them on their backs the way their mothers carry real babies.

When forming your own Akuba dolls, it is important to remember that the head and neck make up almost half of the doll's height. The body is long and the legs are short. The doll's arms should extend straight from the shoulder.

MATERIALS:

        Playdough or clay that will harden in air (see Chapter V for recipes)
        Ice cream sticks for shaping clay
        Wax paper
        String

PROCEDURE:

1.   Use the background information and illustration to help you shape an Akuaba doll of clay. Allow it to dry on wax paper.
2.   Attach a long string to the doll's neck so that the doll may be tied to the child's waist.

 BASKET MAKING

BACKGROUND: African basket designs vary from village to village. Slaves from Africa brought this craft to America where it is still practiced by some Black Americans.

Pairing weaving is common along the Gold Coast of Africa. In pairing weaving, the warp, or foundation, consists of an even number of spokes. Two woof are used, producing a cross between each warp.

MATERIALS:

        Plastic-coated paper cup
        Raffia, yarn or twine
        Glue

PROCEDURE:

1. Prepare for this craft by having an adult cut the plastic-coated paper cup into strips of ½" wide; cut to within 1" of the bottom of the cup. Since the pairing weave may be too difficult for some children, the cup should be cut to yield an uneven number of spokes for those children who must do the standard weave.
2. Allow the children to weave their basket with their choice of colors. Use whichever weave they can best complete.
3. Use glue along the top edge of weave to keep top strands from slipping.
4. Glue wrappings of raffia along the bottom of cup to complete basket effect.

 BATIK

BACKGROUND: It is believed that the art of adinkra cloth began over 300 years ago. There are many different adinkra symbols. These symbols tell about the people and their lifestyles.

In Africa, the adinkra symbols are cut from dried gourds or calabash. These carvings are used as stamps to transfer the design to the fabric. The ink for stamping is made from the bade tree.

The cloth is usually white or brown and woven on narrow-width looms. This cloth is the size of a king-size sheet and is the traditional dress of the Ashanti tribe of Ghana.

"Adinkra" means, "Saying goodbye to one another when parting". When the cloth is worn during mourning, it is covered with symbols to express the feelings about the dead person.

Stamps are carved from broken calabashes and the printer uses six to eight different symbols for each piece of cloth. He gets the adinkra effect by alternating the rows of symbols with geometric patterns. A woman's cloth has a colored background, and a man's has a white background.

MATERIALS:

>Rectangles of sandpaper
>Brown, black and blue crayons
>Iron and board
>Cloth and wax paper to protect iron when ironing on crayon

PROCEDURE:

1. Study chart of Adinkra symbols.
2. Using only black, brown, and blue crayons, place a design on the rough side of the sandpaper.
3. Crayon must be very heavy or it will not transfer with ironing.
4. When design is complete, go to ironing center and transfer the adinkra design to cloth using a medium iron.
5. See section on Lapa, Gele, and Danshiki for uses of Adinkra cloth.

GOD

 ALTAR TO THE SKY GOD

 RAM'S HORN

 WOODEN COMB

 MOON

WIND HOUSE

CROCODILE

 THE HEART

ADINKA RING

 WAR HORN

 BLANKET

SEAL OF THE LAW

LINK OR CHAIN

 SEED OF THE WAWA TREE

 KNIFE

 GOOD FORTUNE

 CIRCULAR HOUSE

HANDCUFFS

 DO NOT BOAST

FORGIVENESS

 KINGS EYE

SOUL

 PRINTING

 JEALOUSY

SEAL OF LAW AND ORDER

 DRUM

 THE KING'S GUN

 UNITY

 SYMBOL OF DEFIANCE

 STATE CEREMONIAL SWORD

 MOON AND STAR

 WISDOM AND KNOWLEDGE

CHILDREN'S CLOTHING (GIRL'S LAPA AND GELE)

A Lapa is a rectangular piece of fabric with dimensions long enough to wrap one and a half to one and three quarter times around a girl's hips. The lapa should extend to the floor.

A girl's Gele is generally two yards long and ten to fifteen inches wide. It is draped around the head.

Adinkra cloth or any cloth may be used by the girls so that they may try to dress like some tribeswomen do in Africa.

(BOY'S DANSHIKI)

In West Africa a danshiki is made by a tailor while you wait. You simply pick out the fabric. If you want to wait another day, special embroidery is added.

To make a danshiki, hold arms out and measure from mid-arm to mid-arm and then from shoulder down to the length you usually wear jackets. Cut a rectangle twice this size, to cover front and back, then fold it in half and cut an oval for the neckline. Cut out the side to form sleeves and stitch the sides.

 FANS

BACKGROUND: Fans were carried and waved by special fan bearers as a part of traditional ceremonial regalia.

African boys and girls have a special use for their fans. If their family cooks over wood fires, it is the child's responsibility to keep the fire going by adding wood and fanning the fire. Kitchen fans are usually long-handled and round.

MATERIALS:

    Raffia

    Some straw (you can get it from a broom)

    A stick

PROCEDURE:

1. Fasten the straws together in the center with raffia, add half a straw so that you have an odd number of straws coming from the center. An uneven number of warp must be used to produce alternate weaving on the woof.
2. Weave the raffia over and under the straws to form a round shape.
3. You can bind the outer end of the fan using a strand of raffia to whipstitch.
4. Use a piece of raffia to attach the sticks for the handle.

293

 FLY WHISKS

BACKGROUND: Traditionally the rulers and important men of the villages carried fly whisks as a part of their dress to symbolize authority. The whisks are made from different kinds of animal tails. Very special whisks are made from elephant tails. The common whisks and those that are still used today are made from horse and cow tails.

The handles of the ceremonial whisks were sometimes silver or gold plated. The common whisk's handle is sheathed in leather and a short strap is attached to the end so that it can be slipped over the wrist.

MATERIALS:

> Hair (from a discarded wig or hair switch) or yarn (makes a good substitute)
> A 4-5 inch stick
> Mystic tape or masking tape
> Aluminum foil (optional)

PROCEDURE:

1. Tie the hair or yarn to one end of the stick.

2. Tie a 7-8" loop of braid or cord to the other end of the stick. Bind the handle from end to end with the tape.

3. Heavy aluminum foil will make your whisk very special.

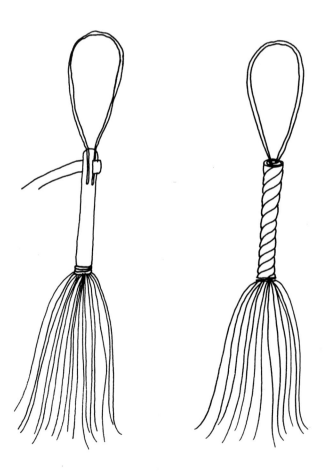

 MASKS

BACKGROUND: Even today, some West African tribesmen wear masks for fun and disguise. In some African ceremonies, children wear masks as they celebrate their entrance into adulthood. As parents watch the ceremony, they know their children are there, but they can't tell which child is theirs.

African masks may be made to look like a certain animal, fish, or bird. Masks are important to tribal ceremonies and are worn by secret societies. It is believed that man stops being himself and is more open to spirits when wearing masks. Male masks usually are black while white indicates death.

Headdresses and masks are worn with costumes made of tree fibers and leaves. The wearer dances to chanting and tribal drums.

MATERIALS:

Large brown grocery bags
Scissors
Crayons
Pencils
Stapler
Brass paper fasteners
White glue
Tempera paints
Construction paper
Aluminum foil
Grass
Toothpicks
Straws
Any scrap-art materials
Cardboard or tagboard scraps
    (for ears or other ornaments)

PROCEDURE:
1. Try bag on over your head and allow it to rest on your shoulders. Cut out a semi-circle from each side portion of the bag to allow it to fit securely down over your head.
2. Have a partner feel your face and mark the position of your eyes, nose, and mouth with chalk on the outside of the bag. Cut some holes in these places so you will be able to see and breathe while wearing the mask.
3. Decide on the type of face you want before cutting holes in the bag. Here are some ideas to show expression:
    Surprise: large, round eyes
    Sadness: eyes slant down
    Evil: eyes slant up
    Remember that the mask eyes may be anywhere on the mask and that you may easily look out of the mouth of the mask or any other convenient hole.
4. Attach ears or other ornaments using glue, stapler, or brass paper fasteners. Yarn may be attached as hair.
5. Allow all glue to dry before wearing.

 MONEY BAG

BACKGROUND: The money bag of Ghana is used as often by men as by women. It is generally constructed to be worn outside the clothing. However, in a busy market place, the cautious shopper may slip his money bag inside his clothing to discourage theft. A money bag is often made of leather and personalized with beads or feathers.

MATERIALS:

> Two pieces of heavy construction paper or tagboard (6x8" and 6x7")
> String or yarn (24" lengths)
> White glue
> Felt-tip markers
> Beads or feathers for decoration

PROCEDURE:

1. Place the two sheets of paper horizontally in front of you. Fold each paper left over right into a halfsheet.
2. Punch holes in the two top corners of the smaller folded paper; tie the yarn through the holes.
3. Glue this part of the money bag together at the side and bottom.
4. Slip the loop of yarn inside the other rectangle, as shown. Glue the top and side of this section allowing for a yarn opening at each corner.
5. When the glue is dry, the top section of the money bag should slip freely up and down the yarn or over the lower section of the money bag.
6. Decorate the money bag with beads and feathers. Add color with felt-tip markers.

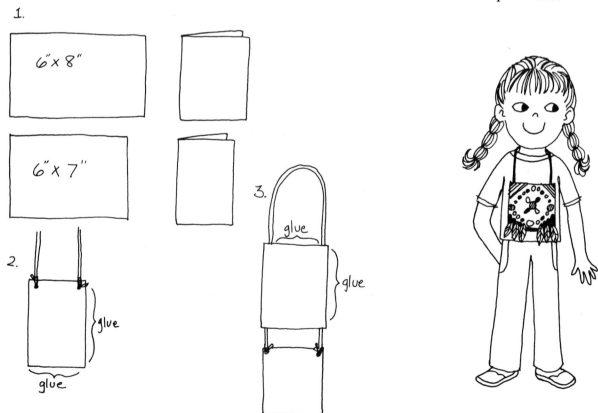

 PAPIER MÂCHÉ BOWL

BACKGROUND: Traditionally, each West African bowl or piece of pottery had either a strictly utilitarian purpose or it was used solely in religious ceremonies. In recent times, the decorative aspects of ritual pieces have crept into everyday usage.

MATERIALS:

Newspapers, paper toweling or any absorbent paper

Scissors or paper cutter

Paste thinned to the consistency of cream (wheat paste, library, etc. See Chapter V for recipes)

Container for mixing paste

A smooth bowl or plastic margarine tub to be used as a mold. The bowl should also have a small base and a wide mouth with no undercuts

Vaseline, grease or cream

Sandpaper

Paint (tempera, enamel, oil paint, etc.)

Brush

Clear plastic spray, shellac, or varnish for protective finish if tempera paint is used

Asphaltum to waterproof bowl

PROCEDURE:

1. Cover the outside surface of the bowl with a film of cream, vaseline, or grease. This will keep the papier mâché from sticking to the bowl.
2. Place the bowl upside down on newspaper or cardboard.
3. Cut newspaper or toweling into strips, approximately ½" wide.
4. Mix the paste in a bowl or pan to the consistency of cream.
5. Place a strip of paper into the paste until it is saturated. Remove the strips from the bowl and wipe off the excess paste by pulling it between the fingers.
6. Apply the paste-saturated strips directly on the oiled surface of the bowl. One or two layers of strips of just wet paper applied directly to the bowl before applying the paste-saturated strips will serve the same purpose as greasing the bowl.
7. Continue to apply strips until the entire bowl is covered. Repeat until at least six layers of paper strips are applied. The number of layers can readily be counted if a different kind or color of paper is used for each layer. The strength of the finished bowl will be much greater if each strip is applied in a different direction. Also, make sure that all wrinkles and bubbles are removed after each strip is attached.
8. Allow the papier mâché to dry thoroughly before removing the bowl.
9. Trim the edges of the bowl and apply additional strips to strengthen and smooth the edges. Other imperfections can also be repaired at this time.
10. When thoroughly dry, sandpaper the surface until smooth and decorate.
11. If tempera paint is used, a coat of varnish or shellac will protect the bowl.
12. Asphaltum painted on the inside of the bowl will waterproof the container.

 INTRODUCING THE COOKING OF WESTERN AFRICA

Just as foods vary from region to region in the United States, they also vary in Africa. Foods depend largely upon the climate and what foods are available in that region. Peanuts and peanut butter are major foods throughout much of Africa. There are 49 countries in Africa and many cultures have influenced African cooking.

The African mother cooks for her entire family including friends and in-laws. According to African custom, one must invite all visitors to join in a meal. Frequently, the African meal is served to as many as twenty persons.

In our research we came across this African proverb, "Come into my home. Sit at my table; then you will know me."

 AKARA (BLACK-EYED PEA FRITTERS)

BACKGROUND: In Africa these fritters are often passed with a tomato-base hot sauce.
INGREDIENTS:

½ lb. or 1¼ C.	(300ml.)	Dried black-eyed peas
¼ C.	(60ml.)	Chopped onion
1 Tbs.	(15ml.)	Ginger root, scraped
½ to 3/4 C.	(120-180ml.)	Water (½ C. then more by Tbs.)
¼ tsp.	(1.2ml.)	Red pepper
1 tsp.	(5ml.)	Salt
		Vegetable oil for frying

PROCEDURE:
1. Soak the peas in hot water.
2. Loosen and remove the skins with your hands.
3. Drain and repeat.
4. In a blender, combine the remaining ingredients and the cleaned peas and blend for 30 seconds at high speed.
5. Transfer the puree to a bowl and beat three to four minutes until light and fluffy.
6. At this point, each child can take a small handful of the mixture and make his own fritter to be fried.
7. Deep fat fry in vegetable oil at 375°F, 190°C for five minutes or until golden brown.

 BANANA FRITTERS

BACKGROUND: Another recipe that can be compared to potato pancakes, Japanese egg rolls, or any fritter.

INGREDIENTS:

½ C.	(120ml.)	All-purpose flour
2 Tbs.	(30ml.)	Sugar
1		Egg
1/3 C.	(80ml.)	Milk
One half		Very ripe banana, peeled and mashed

PROCEDURE:
1. Combine flour and sugar.
2. Add egg and milk.
3. Add the peeled and mashed bananas.
4. Form the fritters.
5. Deep fat fry at 375°F, 190°C for three minutes to a rich golden brown.
6. Drain on paper towel.
7. Sprinkle with confectioners sugar.

 CASSAVA CHIPS

BACKGROUND: These chips are much like Greek drachma fried potatoes or potato chips.
INGREDIENTS:

| One large cassava or yam | | |
| 1 C. | (240ml.) | Oil |

PROCEDURE:
1. Each child can take turns peeling the cassava.
2. Each child can take turns cutting paper-thin slices of the cassava with a potato peeler.
3. Fry in deep fat until golden brown.
4. Drain on paper towel and sprinkle with salt.

FRIED PLANTAIN (BANANA FINGERS)

BACKGROUND: Cooks on the Ivory Coast use the plentiful plantain in their everyday cooking. There are many ways to use the plantain. It can be prepared as an accompaniment to meat or fish or as a dessert.

INGREDIENTS:

> Two plantains or four bananas
> Lemon juice
> Peanut oil (about 1/3 C., 80ml.)
> Crushed corn flakes or bread crumbs
> Pepper or powdered sugar

PROCEDURE:

1. Cut bananas into quarters lengthwise and then into halves crosswise.
2. Cover with lemon juice for ten minutes.
3. Roll in the crumbs.
4. Fry quickly in ½ inch of peanut oil until crispy brown.
5. Sprinkle with pepper or powdered sugar.

 FUFU (CASSAVA BALLS)

BACKGROUND. The cassava is the staple food of many western African countries. It is prepared in a variety of ways. One possibility is the following.

INGREDIENTS:

1		Large cassava or yam
1		Egg
5 Tbs.	(75ml.)	Evaporated milk
1		Onion, grated
Pinch		Garlic salt
3 Tbs.	(45ml.)	Butter or margarine

PROCEDURE:

1. Children can take turns peeling and cutting the cassava or yam into small pieces.
2. Boil pieces until tender in ½ C. (120ml.) water approximately twenty minutes.
3. Drain off the water and mash until smooth.
4. Add the egg, milk, onion and garlic salt.
5. Beat and roll into 2" balls. If the mixture is too wet add a little flour.
6. Fry in butter until brown.

 GHANA CAKES

BACKGROUND: In Ghana, these delicious cakes are served at receptions and parties. Another name for them is twisted cakes. They are really more like doughnuts than like cakes.

INGREDIENTS:

(The volunteer can beat well 1 egg and 1 C. (240ml.) milk together for the egg-milk mixture below.)

1 Tbs.	(15ml.)	Shortening
2 Tbs.	(30ml.)	Sugar
¼ C.	(60ml.)	Flour
2 tsp.	(10ml.)	Milk and egg mixture
		Fat for deep frying

PROCEDURE:
1. Cream together the shortening and the sugar.
2. Add the flour and mix well.
3. Add the 2 tsp. (10ml.) milk and egg mixture and mix well.
4. Form the dough into approximately ten balls.
5. Fry in deep fat until golden brown.
6. Drain on paper towels.

 GROUNDNUT SOUP (GHANA PEANUT SOUP)

BACKGROUND: Ghana is an exporter of peanuts and also uses them frequently in their cooking. A typical example of their use of peanuts is groundnut soup.

INGREDIENTS:

1		Chicken, cut up
1		Onion, chopped
1 can	(480ml.)	Tomatoes
1 C.	(240ml.)	Peanut butter
		Water
		Ground red pepper to taste, if desired

PROCEDURE:
1. Brown the chicken and onions in a large saucepan until golden.
2. Add just enough cold water to cover the chicken and add tomatoes and salt to taste.
3. Bring to boil, lower heat and simmer for fifteen minutes.
4. Mix the peanut butter into a smooth cream with some of the hot stock.
5. Pour this creamed paste into the saucepan.
6. Cook slowly until the oil rises to the top of the soup.
   This recipe serves six.

 LIBERIAN RICE BREAD

BACKGROUND: Liberia was founded in 1821 for the resettling of freed Black people. Since then they have cultivated their own rice, sugar cane and cassava. Rice is their staple food and is eaten at least twice a day.

INGREDIENTS:

2 C.	(480ml.)	Cream of rice
3 Tbs.	(45ml.)	Sugar
4 tsp.	(20ml.)	Baking powder
½ tsp.	(2.5ml.)	Salt
One and one half		Mashed plantains or bananas
2		Eggs
1½ C.	(360ml.)	Milk
1 C.	(240ml.)	Oil

PROCEDURE:

1. Grease a 8x12" pan.
2. Preheat oven to 375°F, 190°C.
3. Mix dry ingredients.
4. Gradually add bananas, eggs and milk.
5. Add oil and blend thoroughly.
6. Pour into the well-greased pan.
7. Bake at 375°F, 190°C for 45 minutes.

 INTRODUCING THE RECREATION OF WESTERN AFRICA

Both music and games provide interesting recreation for the people of West Africa. Most African music is religious in nature and designed for dancing at religious ceremonies. Powerful African rhythms can be heard in American jazz negro spirituals and many Latin American songs. African dances represent birth, death, hunting, love, mourning, war and worship. The music is usually furnished by such traditional African instruments as drums, clappers, flutes, horns, and xylophones.

The ancient games and recreation of Western Africa were centered around the many learning skills necessary in hunting (in the interior) and fishing (in the coastal regions). African youth played games that would help them to one day obtain food and protect their families and tribal groups.

Today's Western African youth participate in many games that are adaptations of the games of ancient Africa. Within the metropolitan areas, European type games such as soccer, are common.

 AFRICAN BLINDMAN'S BUFF

This game requires five or more players. The players form a circle, with two blindfolded players inside. One has two sticks (he holds low) and hits frequently together. The other waves a piece of cloth to tag the stick player. When "It" tags the stickman, the stickman becomes "It" and a new stickman is chosen.

 CAT AND RAT

This game is played with a large group. One player is chosen to be the cat and one is chosen to be the rat. With the exception of the cat and the rat, all other players form three to four parallel lines. The number of lines will depend on the total number of players and the lines should then be adjusted to produce a fairly squared arrangement of children. These lines should be spaced just so far apart that the players can grasp each other's hands in either direction.

As the game begins, the players, all facing the same direction, join hands and form single lines. The rat runs down one lane and up another with the cat close behind. At any time, the rat may call out, "Mpuki, ekali" which means "Let the rat stop". The players immediately drop hands, make one quarter turns to the right and then join hands with the new players standing beside them. At this time, the former rat becomes the cat and the former cat becomes the rat. This role reversal may occur many times. When the rat has been caught or when play has continued for a lengthy period, a new rat and cat may be chosen by the two runners in order to replace themselves.

 GAME TRAP

Any number of players may play this game. Two make a bridge-like trap. This game is like London Bridge. The children chant and clap hands to:

> Lions and leopards
> Lions and leopards hunting at night
> Lions and leopards
> Lions and leopards catch the game!

On the word "game", the trap falls. The players caught form additional traps. The game continues until all have been caught. The players may not sneak through but continue to move in a rhythm.

 HANDBALL

This game requires six or more players. Divide the players into two equal teams. Every time a ball is caught, all members of that team (except the catcher) must clap their hands and stamp their feet.

 HEN AND WILDCAT

This game requires five or more players. One player is the hen and one player is the wildcat. The rest of the players are chickens. The wildcat hides and jumps out to tag the chickens. The hen yells the warning to stoop before wildcat can get you.

 JARABADACH

This game requires two players. It is much like tic-tac-toe. One player has three white stones and the other has three black ones. The plays are made on the nine points of this diagram. The players place markers, on turn, one at a time on any of the nine points of the square. The purpose of the game is to get three in a row first. After six pieces are played, players take turns moving along lines, one space at a time, until one player wins.

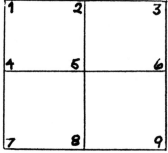

304

 JUMPING

Two players face each other and simultaneously jump up and down five times. On the sixth jump they extend one of their legs. Points are given in a predetermined manner; i.e., player number one gets a point if both players extend the same leg (both rights or both lefts). Player number two gets a point if both players extend opposite legs (right-left). The game may be played until one player accumulates ten points.

 MULAMBILWA

This game requires two teams of two to nine players each. Each player has a pin and a ball. Empty plastic bottles or two to three inch corncobs on ends are used as pins. The teams kneel in lines facing each other. At a signal, all balls are thrown at opposite pins. When all pins are down for a team, that team runs to its goal without being caught. If caught, they pay a forfeit or give points to the other team.

 NSIKWI

This game requires two or more players. Two players or two teams sit ten feet apart on the ground facing each other. Empty plastic bottles or two to three inch corncobs on ends are used as pins. Each player has a ball or top to throw at his opponent's pin on signal. The first to hit gets a point.

 OWARE

BACKGROUND: Oware or Star Play is a favorite game throughout most of Africa. It is one version of similar games played in several cultures throughout the world where tokens are accumulated by clever transfer. All games of this type are referred to as mancala games. It is said that mancala or kalah originated over 3,500 years ago in Africa. It has been played throughout the Near and Far East for centuries. Ancient carvings of the game have been found in Syria and on columns of temples in Greece and Egypt. In the Philippines a similar game is called sungka. Kalah, as the game is called in Hebrew, means "a study group".

In Mali, West Africa, this game is known as Game of Universe, or Star Play. (The beans or seeds represent stars being transferred from East to West from one end cup to the other.) Oware is generally played at noon. It is sometimes believed that only the lazy play Oware in the morning and that it brings bad luck if played at night. The rules of this game vary from village to village.

MATERIALS:

        One egg carton
        Masking tape
        48 seeds, beans, or marbles

PROCEDURE:
1. Cut lid off egg carton and then cut lid in half.
2. Use tape to attach the two lid halves to the ends of the egg carton bottom, forming a cup at each end.

HOW TO PLAY OWARE:
1. Two players sit with the Oware game between them. Each player owns the six egg cups on his side of the board and the end container on his right (his "pot").
2. Put four seeds in each of the twelve egg cups.
3. Player number one takes all the seeds from one of his cups and moving counterclockwise drops off one seed in each adjacent cup until he runs out of seeds. Any time his last seed is dropped into a cup belonging to player number two, player number one wins all the seeds in that cup and may place them in his "pot".
4. Play continues as players alternate turns. Each player always takes all the seeds from the cup he has chosen. The number of seeds in each cup is always changing.
5. When all twelve egg cups are empty, the game is over. The player with the most seeds in his "pot" wins.

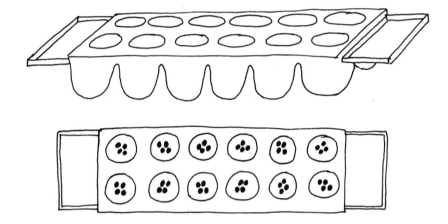

 SIMON SAYS

This game requires four or more players. The leader faces a straight line of other players and the players follow what the leader does. The player who errs takes the leader's place and the leader joins the group. If several err, the leader chooses one to take his place. On an agreed number of wins, the leader becomes a Chief and retires from the game.

BIBLIOGRAPHY

A. MULTICULTURAL MATERIALS

Alkema, Chester. *Masks.* New York: Sterling Publishing Company, 1971.

Association for Supervision and Curriculum Development. "Encouraging Multicultural Education", ASCD Multicultural Education Commission, *Educational Leadership* 34: 288-91, January, 1977.

Bank, James. "Evaluating the Multiethnic Components of the Social Studies," *Social Education,* November, 1976, pp 538-547.

Bank, James (bibliography Peabody). "Pluralistic and Educational Concepts: A Clarification", *Journal of Education* 54: 73-8, January, 1977.

Boyer, James. *Administrator's Checklist for Enhancing Multicultural Curriculum.* College of Education, Kansas State University. Available at California State University at Long Beach, Long Beach, California, Ed. 135-895.

Bronaugh, Juanita and Ayers, George. *Multiethnic Materials A Selected Bibliography.* ERIC Vol. 12, 2/77 No. 2.

Caney, Steven. *Toy Book.* New York: Workman Publishing Company, 1972.

Croft, Karen. *The Good for Me Cookbook.* San Francisco: R & E Research Associates, 1971.

Dodson, Fitzhugh. *How to Father.* Los Angeles: Nash Publishing, 1974.

Fiarotta, Phyllis and Fiarotta, Noel. *The You and Me Heritage Tree.* New York: Workman Publishing Company, 1976.

Field Enterprises Educational Corporation, *The World Book Encyclopedia,* Chicago: Field Enterprises Educational Corporation, 1967.

Freedman, Phillip. "Multi-ethnic Studies: Proceed With Caution," *Phi Delta Kappan* 58:401-3, January, 1977.

Fruehling, Royal. "Multicultural Education as Social Exchange; A Study By E. Aronson and Colleagues," *Phi Delta Kappan* 58: 398-400, January, 1977.

Gaer, Joseph. *Holidays Around the World.* Boston: Little, Brown, and Company, 1953.

Griffin, Louise (comp.). *Multi-ethnic Books for Young Children.* ERIC National Association for Education of Young Children, 1970. NAEYC, 1839 Connecticut Avenue, N.W., Wn. D.C. 20009.

Harbin, Elvin. *Games of Many Lands.* New York: Abingdon. 1954.*

Hunt, Kari and Carlson, Bernice. *Masks and Mask Makers.* New York: Abingdon, 1961.

Hymovitz, Leon. "Multicultural Education in the Bicentennial: Melting Pot, Atonement, or At-onement", *Journal of Ethnic Studies,* V3N4 pp 49-57, Winter, 1976.

Ilg, Frances and Ames, Louise. *Child Behavior.* New York: Harper and Row, 1955.

Joseph, Joan. *Folk Toys Around the World and How to Make Them.* New York: Parent's Magazine Press, 1972.

Laskin, Joyce. *Arts and Craft Activities Desk Book.* West Nyack, New York: Parker Publishing Company, Inc., 1971.*

Lovano-Kerr, and Zimmerman, E. Arts in a Multicultural Society Project: Development and Evaluation, Viewpoint 52: 1-14, May, 1976.

Marquevich, Pat and Spiegel, Shelly. *Multiethnic Studies in the Elementary School Classroom.* Pico Rivera, California: Education in Motion, 1976.

McLeish, Minnie and Moody, Ella. *Teaching Art to Children.* New York: The Studio Publication, 1953.*

McNeill, Earldene and Allen, Judy and Schmidt, Velma. *Cultural Awareness for Young Children at the Learning Tree.* Dallas, Texas: The Learning Tree, 1975*.

Millen, Nina. *Children's Festivals from Many Lands.* New York: Friendship Press, 1964.*

Multiethnic Literature. Boston: Houghton Mifflin, 1972.

National Council for the Social Studies. "Curriculum Guidelines for Multiethnic Education," *Social*

Education 40: 387-434, October, 1976.

Nelson, Esther. *Dancing Games for Children of All Ages.* New York: Sterling Publishing Company, Inc., 1974.

Newsome, Arden. *Crafts and Toys from around the World,* New York: Julian Messner, 1972.

Nichols, Margaret S. *Multicultural Bibliography for Preschool Through Second Grade.* Minneapolis: Lerner, 1972.

Osborn, D. Keith and Haupt, Dorothy. *Creative Activities for Young Children.* Detroit, Michigan: The Merrill-Palmer Institute, 1966.*

Pearson, Craig and Marfuggi, Joseph. *Creating and Using Learning Games.* Palo Alto, California: Learning Handbooks, 1975.

Reed, Robert D. and Kathy S. *We Care Cookbook.* San Francisco: R & E Research Assoc., 1972.

Reis, Mary. *Batik.* Minneapolis: Lerner Publishing Company, 1973.

Rojas-Lombardi, Felipe. *The A to Z No-Cook Cookbook.* New York: R-L Creations, 1972.

Roy, Mary. Action: *A Handbook for Teachers of Elementary Physical Activities.* Stevensville, Michigan: Educational Service, Inc., 1967.*

Shapiro, Rebecca. *A Whole World of Cooking.* Boston: Little, Brown and Company, 1972.*

Shaver, James (President of the National Council for the Social Studies). "Administrator's Checklist for Enhancing Multicultural Curriculum", *Social Education:* October, 1976.

Temko, Florence. *Folk Crafts for World Friendship.* Garden City, New York: Doubleday, 1976.

Temko, Florence. *Paper Cutting.* Garden City, New York: Doubleday, 1973.

Veitch, Bev and Harms, Thelma. *A Child's Cook Book.* Walnut Creek, California: Acme Press, 1976.*

Wagner, Guy and Gillvley, Laura. *Social Studies Games and Activities.* New York: Teachers Publishing Division Macmillan Publishing Company, 1975.*

Waldo, Myra. *The Complete Round-the-World Cookbook.* Garden City, New York: Doubleday and Company Inc., 1954.

Wankelman, Willard, Wigg, Philip, and Wigg, Marietta. *A Handbook of Arts and Crafts for Elementary and Junior High School Teachers.* Dubuque, Iowa: William C. Brown, 1968.

B.   PARAPROFESSIONAL MATERIALS

Hendricks, Meg and Enk, Jean. *Lighten Your Load with Volunteers.* Long Beach: Hendricks and Enk, 1976.

Hunter, Madeline and Breit, Sally. *Aide-ing in Education.* El Segundo, California: TIP Publications, 1976.

Todd, Vivian and Hunter, Georgennie. *The Aide in Early Childhood Education.* New York: Macmillan Company, 1973.

Ornstein, Allan and Talmage, Harriet and Juhasz, Anne. *The Paraprofessional's Handbook.* Belmont, California: Fearon Publishers, Inc., 1975.

C.   CHINA

Abisch, Roz. *Mai-Ling and the Mirror.* Englewood Cliffs, New Jersey: Prentice-Hall, 1969.*

Batterberry, Michael. *Chinese and Oriental Art.* New York: McGraw-Hill, 1968.

Carter, Michael. *Crafts of China.* New York: Doubleday and Company, 1977.

Chen, Joyce. *Joyce Chen Cook Book.* Cambridge: Nimrod Press, 1962.

Fessler, Loren. *China.* New York: Time Inc., 1963.*

Glubok, Shirley. *The Art of China.* New York: Macmillan, 1973.

Hahn, Emily. *The Cooking of China.* New York: Time-Life Books, 1968.

Harrington, Lyn. *How People Live in China.* Westchester, Illinois: Benefic Press, 1968.*

Huang, Paul. *The Illustrated Step by Step Chinese Cookbook.* New York: Simon and Schuster, 1975.

Jennings, Jerry and Hertel, Margaret. *China.* Grand Rapids, Michigan: The Fideler Company, 1977.

Lo, Kenneth. *Chinese Food.* New York: Hippocrene Books, 1973.

Lo, Kenneth. *Peking Cooking.* New York: Pantheon Books, 1973.

Manning-Sanders, Ruth. *Festivals.* New York: Dutton, 1972.

Purdy, Susan. *Festivals for You to Celebrate.* Philadelphia: Lippencott, 1969.

Sunset Book Editors. *Oriental Cook Book.* Menlo Park, California: Lane Books, 1970.

Wu, Sylvia. *Madame Wu's Art of Chinese Cooking.* Los Angeles: Charles Publishing, 1973.

D. GREECE

Gidal, Sonia and Tim. *My Village in Greece.* New York: Pantheon Books - Random House, 1960.

Glubok, Shirley. *The Art of Ancient Greece.* New York: Atheneum, 1966.*

Masters, Robert. *Greece in Pictures.* New York: Sterling, 1973.*

Nickles, Harry and the Editors of Time-Life Books. *Middle Eastern Cooking.* New York: Time Life Books, 1971.

Pappas, Lou. *Crossroads of Cooking.* Los Angeles, W. Ritchie Press, 1973.

Tor, Regina. *Getting to Know Greece.* New York: Coward-McCann, 1959.*

Warren, Ruth. *The First Book of Modern Greece.* New York: Watts, 1972.

Wason, Betty. *Greek Cookbook.* London: Macmillan, 1969.*

Yianilos, Theresa. *The Complete Greek Cookbook.* New York: Funk and Wagnalls, 1970.*

E. ISRAEL

Comay, Joan and Pearlman, Moske. *Israel.* New York: Macmillan, 1964.

Fine, Helen. *Behold the Land.* New York: Union of American Hebrew Congregations, 1968.

Gidal, Sonia. *My Village in Israel.* New York: Pantheon Books, 1959.

Golann, Cecil. *Our World: The Taming of Israel's Negev.* New York: J. Messner, 1970.

Kubie, Nora. *Israel, Israel, Israel, Israel.* United States of America: Franklin Watts, Inc., 1968.

Masson, Madeleine. *International Wine and Food Society's Guide to Jewish Cookery.* New York: Drake Publishers Inc., 1971.*

Nahoum, Aldo. *The Art of Israeli Cooking.* New York: Holt, Rinehart and Winston, 1971.*

Nickles, Harry and the Editors of Time-Life Books. *Middle-Eastern Cooking.* New York: Time-Life Books, 1971.

Papas, William. *A Letter from Israel.* New York: Franklin Watts, 1968.*

Purdy, Susan. *Jewish Holidays: Facts, Activities and Crafts.* Philadelphia: Lippincott, 1969.

F. JAPAN

Ashby, Gwynneth. *Looking at Japan.* Philadelphia: Lippencott, 1969.*

Boehm, David. *Japan in Pictures.* New York: Sterling Publishing Company, 1973.*

Buck, Pearl. *Oriental Cookbook.* New York: Simon and Schuster, 1972.

Caldwell, John. *Let's Visit Japan.* New York: J. Day Company, 1959.

Friskey, Margaret. *Welcome to Japan.* Chicago: Children's Press, 1975.

Glubok, Shirley. *The Art of Japan.* New York: Macmillan, 1970.

Pitts, Forrest. *Japan.* Grand Rapids, Michigan: The Fideler Company, 1974.

Sandler, Sandra. *The American Book of Japanese Cooking.* Harrisburg, Pennsylvania: Stockpot Books, 1974.

Uyeda, Frances and Sasaki, Jeannie. *Fold, Cut, and Say the Japanese Way.* Available at Childrens' Book and Music Center, Los Angeles, California.

Vaughan, Josephine. *The Land and People of Japan.* New York: J. B. Lippincott, 1972.

Waldo, Myra. *Complete Book of Oriental Cooking.* New York: David McKay Company, 1960.

Yaukey, Grace. *Made in Japan.* New York: Knopf, 1963.*

G. MEXICO

Comins, Jeremy. *Latin American Crafts,* New York: Lothrop, Lee, & Shepard Co., 1974.

Editors of Sunset Books and Sunset Magazine. *Cooking With a Foreign Accent.* Menlo Park, California: Lane Publishing Company, 1959.

Jones, Edward and Margaret. *Arts and Crafts of the Mexican People.* Los Angeles: Ward Ritchie Press, 1971.*

Martinez, Jimmie and Watters, Arlene. *Us, A Cultural Mosaic.* San Diego, California: San Diego City Schools, 1977.

Prieto, Mariana. *Play It In Spanish.* New York: The John Day Company, 1973.

Ross, Patricia. *Made in Mexico.* New York: Knopf, 1952.*

Sazer, Chloë: *Crafts of Mexico.* New York: Doubleday, 1977.

Toor, Frances. *A Treasury of Mexican Folkways,* New York: Crown Publishers, 1947.*

H. NATIVE AMERICANS

Albrectsen, Lis. *Tepee and Moccasin: Indian Crafts for Young People.* New York: Van Nostrand Reinhold, 1972.

Bauer, Helen. *California Indian Days.* New York: Doubleday, 1968.*

Bavlor, Byrd. *Before You Came This Way.* New York: Dutton, 1969.

Brandenberg, Aliki. *Corn Is Maize.* New York: Crowell, 1976.

Burnett, Millie. *Dance Down the Rain, Sing Up the Corn.* San Francisco: R & E Research Associates, 1975.

Cavin, Ruth. *1 Pinch of Sunshine, ½ Cup of Rain.* New York: Atheneum, 1973.

D'Amato, Janet. *Indian Crafts.* New York: Lion Press, 1968.

Glubok, Shirley. *The Art of the Southwest Indians.* New York: Macmillan, 1971.

Glubok, Shirley. *The Art of the North American Indian.* New York: Harper and Row, 1964.

Heuser, Iva. *Indians of California.* Camino, California: Sierra Media Systems, 1977.

Hunt, Walter. *The Complete Book of Indian Crafts.* New York: Golden Press, 1954.*

Lavine, Sigmund. *The Games the Indians Played.* New York: Dodd, Mead, and Company, 1974.

Leavitt, Jerome. *America and Its Indians.* Chicago: Children's Press, 1963.*

Long Beach East Stake Latter Day Saints. *Yankee Doodle and You Can Do.* Long Beach: LDS, 1975.*

Robinson, Maudie. *Children of the Sun.* New York: J. Messner, 1973.

Smiling Eagle. *Making Children's Moccasins.* Rescue, California: Smiling Eagle, 1976.*

Squires, John L. and McLean, Robert E. *American Indian Dances.* New York: The Ronald Press Company, 1963.

Turner, Alta. *Finger Weaving: Indian Braiding.* New York: Sterling Publishing Company, 1973.

Ziebold, Edna. *Indians of Early Southern California.* Los Angeles, Sapsis, 1969.*

I. WESTERN AFRICA

African Arts Study Kit, African Studies Center, Los Angeles, California, U.C.L.A., 1977. Grant from The National Endowment.

Carpenter, Allan and Hughes, James. *Enchantment of Africa: Ghana.* Chicago: Children's Press, 1977.

D'Amato, Janet and Alex. *African Crafts for You to Make,* New York: Julian Messner, 1969.

Davidson, Basil and Editors of Time-Life Books. *African Kingdoms.* New York: Time Inc., 1966.

Glubok, Shirley. *The Art of Africa.* New York: Harper, 1965.

Greig, Mary. *How People Live in Africa.* Chicago: Benefic, 1963.*

Joseph, Joan. *Black African Empires.* New York: Franklin Watts, 1974.

Kerina, Jane. *African Crafts.* New York: The Lion Press, 1970.

*Available in Public Libraries